Remaking the Rural South

Remaking the Rural South

INTERRACIALISM, CHRISTIAN SOCIALISM,
AND COOPERATIVE FARMING IN
JIM CROW MISSISSIPPI

Robert Hunt Ferguson

The University of Georgia Press

ATHENS

Most University of Georgia Press titles are
available from popular e-book vendors.

Printed digitally

Library of Congress Cataloging-in-Publication Data

Names: Ferguson, Robert Hunt. author.
Title: Remaking the rural South : interracialism, Christian socialism, and
   cooperative farming in Jim Crow Mississippi / Robert Hunt Ferguson.
Other titles: Politics and culture in the twentieth-century South.
Description: Athens : The University of Georgia Press, [2018] |
   Series: Politics and culture in the twentieth-century South |
   Includes bibliographical references and index.
Identifiers: LCCN 2017019750| ISBN 9780820351797 (hardback : alk. paper) |
   ISBN 9780820351780 (ebook)
Subjects: LSCH: Agriculture, Cooperative—Mississippi. | Collective farms—Mississippi. |
   Delta Cooperative Farm (Miss.) | Providence Plantation (Miss.) | Sharecropping—
   Mississippi. | Rural development—Mississippi. | Christian socialism—Mississippi. |
   Mississippi—Race relations. | Mississippi—Economic conditions—20th century.
Classification: LCC HD1491.U62 M74 2018 | DDC 334/.6830976209041—dc23
   LC record available at https://lccn.loc.gov/2017019750

For A.J., Izzy, Hunter, Addy, Grace, Graham, and Greta
May they be the architects of the Beloved Community
And to the memory of Charlie

CONTENTS

Acknowledgments   ix

Introduction   1

CHAPTER 1. The Problems of Collective Man   16

CHAPTER 2. From the Frying Pan into the Fire   44

CHAPTER 3. The Limits of Interracialism and the
Failure of Delta Cooperative Farm   79

CHAPTER 4. The Concrete Needs of the
Thousands among Us   106

CHAPTER 5. Preventing Another Emmett Till   137

Epilogue   165

Notes   177

Index   205

ACKNOWLEDGMENTS

Throughout the long process of crafting this book, I have been keenly aware of what E. P. Thompson famously called "the enormous condescension of posterity." Many of the characters in this strange but hopeful story left few documents for the historian to piece together in order to begin to understand the complicated, remarkable lives of sharecroppers. Luckily, the founders and managers of Delta Cooperative Farm and Providence Farm left boxes full of primary sources and had most of them deposited at the University of North Carolina at Chapel Hill and Mississippi State University. I must first thank the archivists who meticulously organized these papers and librarians who made my tasks much easier. Of exceptional help were Laura Clark Brown, Matt Turi, and the staff at the Southern Historical Collection at the University of North Carolina; Mattie Sink, Jennifer McGillan, and Jessica Perkins Smith in Special Collections at Mississippi State University; John Wall in Special Collections at the University of Mississippi; Eleanor Green and Emily Weaver at the University Archives at Delta State University; Henry Fulmer in the South Caroliniana Library at the University of South Carolina; Ed Frank and Chris Ratliff in Special Collections at the University of Memphis; Julia Young at the Mississippi Department of Archives and History; Michael Lange and Nathan Kerr at the Oakland Museum of California; and Heidi Buchanan at Western Carolina University.

I began thinking about the themes that shape this book long before I stepped foot in the archives. Three courses—taught by three exceptional historians— laid the intellectual basis for this project. As an undergraduate, I enrolled in Richard Starnes's seminar on the "History of the American South." Richard's captivating lectures and carefully chosen readings taught our filled-to-capacity class a history of the South most of us had never heard, but all of us needed. I fell in love with the history of my home region in that class, for all its beauty and tragedy. Since then, Richard has been an important mentor and friend. As an MA student, I took Elizabeth McRae's readings course in "African American History." There, I first understood C. Vann Woodward and read Charles Payne's *I've Got the Light of Freedom*. Woodward's ideas and Payne's book, more than any others, made me want to write the history of people engaged in the human rights struggle. Our heady class discussions made me feel, for the first time, like a serious scholar. Several years later, Libby and I would colead our own "Civil Rights History" travel course throughout the South. Libby's steadfast belief in my abilities as an educator and historian—and the lessons I learned on that bus—set me on a path that led to Chapel Hill and eventually back to Cullowhee. Finally, as a PhD candidate, I found myself among a serious and collegial group of graduate students in W. Fitzhugh Brundage's "Readings in the American South" course. Fitz's questions and my peers' discussions challenged me in ways I found arduous but exhilarating. The first reading list I used to prepare for this research grew from that course. Inspired by Fitz's ideas on southern history, an informal discussion group formed outside of class. With Catherine Conner, Brad Proctor, and other graduate students, the Southern History Drinking Group was born. Due to our excessive focus on the latter, however, the group survived only a few meetings. Fitz's influence has remained constant as he has guided my work with precision and pragmatism. His encyclopedic knowledge of history and culture, eloquent prose, and captivating teaching have influenced me well beyond this project.

I am grateful to a long list of scholars who read or heard portions of the manuscript and offered suggestions—and sometimes their own research—in formal and informal ways. This book began in earnest as a dissertation at the University of North Carolina. I benefitted from the careful criticism of my committee, Fitz Brundage, William Ferris, Jacquelyn Hall, James Leloudis, and Adriane Lentz-Smith. Having these tremendous scholars in one room, discussing my work, was a thrilling honor. Beyond my committee, I am particularly indebted to Lauren Acker, Randy Browne, Andrew Canaday, David Cline, Catherine Conner, Emilye Crosby, John Giggie, David Goldfield, Alison Greene, Valerie Grim, John Hayes, Mark Huddle, Jerma Jackson, Tracy K'Meyer, Anna Krome-Lukens, Rachel Martin, Elizabeth McRae, Cecelia Moore, David Palmer, Elizabeth Payne, Adrienne Petty, Brad Proctor, Jennifer Ritterhouse, Mark Schultz, Bryant Simon, Fred Smith, Richard Starnes, Kerry Taylor, Jason Ward, Jeannie Whayne, and the late Jason Manthorne for their insights. Invited talks for the Center for the Study of the American South, the Triangle African American History Colloquium, Georgia College and State University, and Western Carolina University helped me clarify major points of emphasis.

My colleagues at Western Carolina University have been supportive of this project since I joined the faculty in 2012. I could not ask for a better dean and department chair than Richard Starnes and Mary Ella Engel. Saheed Aderinto, Lily Balloffet, Rob Clines, Andy Denson, David Dorondo, Ben Francis-Fallon, Gael Graham, Alex Macaulay, Elizabeth McRae, Scott Philyaw, Honor Sachs, Jessie Swigger, and Vicki Szabo have made working in WCU's Department of History a true pleasure. I am proud to be among such serious scholars, hardworking educators, and witty coworkers.

While I was on lengthy research trips, Jason Ward and Alison Greene in Starkville, Mississippi, and Steve, Elise, and Katy Smith in Jackson, Mississippi, opened their homes to me so often that they could have made a small fortune if they had charged rent. As academics, they understood the importance of archival research and having a space of one's own to work, but they also understood the need to unwind from the archives. Jason and Alison discovered that I, too, was a native North Carolinian, and it wasn't long before we had figured out the friends we have in common. They offered meals, beer, a comfortable room, and occasional television access to an ACC basketball game, all while juggling deadlines for their exceptional books. In fact, Jason and Alison leave profound marks on this project. Jason's own work on politics and civil rights in Mississippi and his incisive comments on the entire manuscript have made this a better book. Alison's award-winning work on religion in the Delta and her eagerness to share pertinent research with me shaped my book in vital ways. If I have fallen short of their scholarly suggestions, it is my own fault. While I was in Jackson, the Smith family plied me with some of my favorite pastimes: home-cooked meals, conversation, music, and minor league baseball games. I met Steve and Elise through their daughter, Katy Simpson Smith, when she and I entered the PhD program in Chapel Hill the same semester. Katy was the first friend I made at UNC. I believe Katy would have rather kept to herself while she completed her work, but she has benevolently endured my company over the years. For that, my life has been immeasurably enriched. Katy's own work and friendship remain important sources of inspiration.

Susan, Sue, and William Minter—former residents at Delta and Providence—fleshed out questions that could not be answered in the archives. Sam Cohen prepared Freedom of Information Act requests that helped fill gaps in the narrative.

Fellowships and funding allowed me the time and resources with which to work on early drafts of this project. The Center for the Study of the American South (McColl Dissertation Year Fellowship in Southern Studies), the Department of History at UNC–Chapel Hill (Doris G. Quinn Dissertation Fellowship), the Folklore Curriculum at UNC (Archie Green Occupational Folklife Fellowship), the UNC Graduate School (Smith Graduate Research Grant), the Communal Studies Association, and the Department of History at Western Carolina University provided timely and generous support.

Staff at the University of Georgia Press have remained steadfast supporters of this project since its infancy. Jon Davies, Bethany Sneed, and Walter Biggins were always prompt, helpful, and exceedingly patient.

I have spent more of the past ten years thinking and writing about intentional communities than I care to admit or my family can bear to endure any longer. Yet they have steadfastly supported me during the process. My in-laws, Steve and Beth Stahlman, could not have been more encouraging, even proofreading an early draft. Vacations spent in Wisconsin and Colorado fishing with Steve and playing cards with Beth couldn't come often enough. My siblings-in-law, Jennifer, Jessie, Mary, and Mike, have been our recent vacation companions and provided welcome distractions from this project.

I have had so many adventures with my brothers, Al and Marty, that our stories could fill several books. I have the good fortune of not only enjoying my older brothers' company, but looking up to them as well. They are models as men, husbands, and fathers. As I have learned through experience, my brothers are always there to celebrate triumph or fight through tragedy. My grandmother, Delle Martin, who turned 101 years old as this book drew to a close, has supported me in many ways for longer than I can remember. Her stories about her own exciting history captivate me as much as any book. My parents, George and Liz Ferguson, have given freely of their modest resources to ensure that I followed my dreams. Their sacrifices, many of which will forever go unknown but to themselves, allowed me the guidance and space to figure out what I wanted to do with my life. They allowed their young, restless son to "drive all over creation" in his early twenties. The ability to take those solitary road trips, where I met extraordinary people and saw breathtaking landscapes, solidified my desire to become a historian of the American experience. Just as important, it was they who first instilled a love of history and teaching in me and have seen my education and career to fruition. They truly embody our family motto: *Dulcius Ex Asperis*.

My partner, Sara Stahlman, has been in my life since the month I decided to write a dissertation on Delta and Providence farms. Recognizing how important this work has been to me and understanding the sacrifices that families make when a parent works long hours, Sara often affectionately refers to this project as "our book." Her sense of social justice, compassion, patience, and strength has taught me more about how to build a loving, trusting community than an entire career writing about intentional communities ever could. For all of those qualities and many more, I admire her. Our journeys, first as partners, and then as parents to our children, Charlie, A.J., and Izzy, have been the greatest honors of my life. *Ici je suis.*

Our son, Charlie, is my hero. His twin sister, A.J., was born less than two weeks before I defended this project in its dissertation form. I read drafts aloud to her while she slept in the NICU at UNC Hospitals. One evening, five years later, she unexpectedly asked me to read aloud from my manuscript as I proofread the final draft. She, I, and this book have come a long way since the NICU. Two and half years after A.J.'s birth, Izzy joined us and now they both fill our lives with laughter and song. Many of our days have been spent together, exploring western North Carolina trails, rivers, waterfalls, lakes, and mountains. On those days, Delta and Providence farms seem unimportant or even burdensome. Yet when I think about the future I want to leave for my children, I hope it will include blueprints for building the beloved community so that they may succeed where we have failed. This book is dedicated to the next generation: my daughters and their cousins.

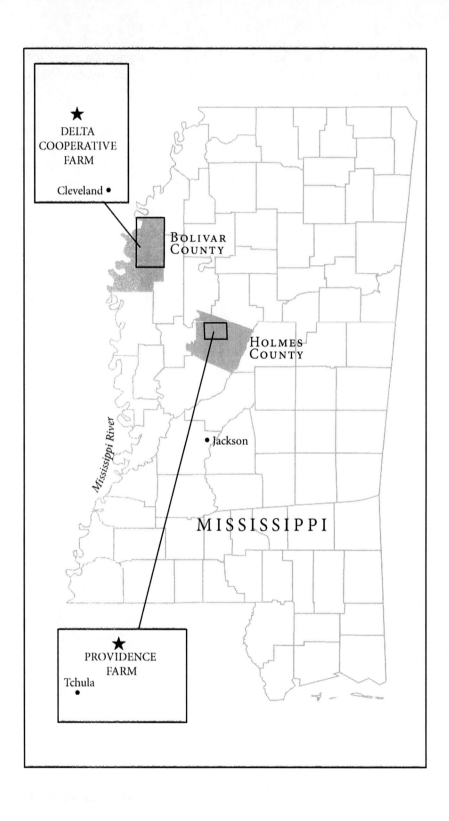

Remaking the Rural South

Introduction

In 1936 and again in 1938, hundreds of poor white and black sharecroppers, scores of educated Christian missionaries, dozens of stanch socialists, and a handful of labor union organizers built two interracial, socialist, cooperative farming communities smack-dab in the center of Mississippi's plantation economy and Jim Crow society. For twenty years, the residents lived cheek by jowl, built modern homes, praised the Lord's mercy, put sweat equity into their community, fell in love, and sometimes fought. During that time, they also founded a medical clinic and a federal credit union. The prosaic lives of the residents were not much different from those in many rural American communities. To call their lives mundane, however, is not to lessen the impact of what they did collectively. Their very existence defied Dixie's racial, economic, labor, and religious norms. Plantation owners fumed while "their negroes" banded together with the "crackers." Law enforcement intimidated community residents. Churches excommunicated parishioners. Neighbors threatened lynching. Politicians conducted witch hunts, hoping to ferret out "communists" and "miscegenators." That the farms existed at all is an extraordinary contingency of history. Even today, this history of two communities in segregation-era Mississippi sounds implausible.

Yet these communities are much more than nearly forgotten curiosities. They reveal a portion of a much larger history of the long twentieth-century struggle for human rights. The labor, economic, religious, and civic activism found on the farms sprang from—and existed alongside—a concurrent transnational struggle for human dignity that emerged in beleaguered communities during the Progressive movement and, in the Deep South, found traction during the New Deal. For twenty years during the age of segregation, a collective effort endured to build the "beloved community" through interracial cooperation and African American self-help.[1]

In the winter of 1936, two dozen black and white ex-sharecropping families settled on 2,138 acres in the Mississippi Delta. Thus began a twenty-year experiment—across two communities—in interracialism, Christian Socialism, cooperative farming, and human rights activism. Delta Cooperative Farm (1936–1942) and its descendent, Providence Farm (1938–1956), were intentional communities in rural Mississippi that drew on internationalist practices of cooperative communalism and made pragmatic challenges to Jim Crow segregation and plantation labor. When the New Deal's Agricultural Adjustment Administration allowed plantation owners to evict tenants and sharecroppers, a group of religious leaders, labor unionists, and socialists hatched the idea to emulate cooperative farms already established in Japan, Soviet Russia, and Great Britain. Philanthropic Christian Socialist, and YMCA national secretary, Sherwood Eddy purchased the land, while influential intellectuals such as sociologist Charles Spurgeon Johnson and theologian Reinhold Niebuhr served on the Board of Trustees. The staff, volunteers, and residents were a hodgepodge of sharecroppers, Christian Socialists, political leftists, and union organizers. When many white residents joined the war effort during World War II, Delta Cooperative Farm closed and a second farm, Providence, became the new hope for an increasingly African American–centered community less concerned with labor rights and more focused on local movements in education, religion, and civil rights. For twenty years, they lived close to the bone at Delta and Providence and attempted to enact an alternate version of the rural South antithetical to the oppression endemic to the region.[2]

A close examination of the political economy in which Delta and Providence farms existed reveals that the farms represented a moment of imagined possibility when heady ideas rooted in interracial cooperation, socialism, and Christian Realism were put into practice. The political and social climate of the Depression, New Deal, and World War II fostered opportunities for the rural poor to attain some economic and social autonomy. In the thirties, forties, and fifties, the rural poor were engaged in struggles that began as Jeffersonian dreams of agrarian subsistence and economic stability but evolved into a battle for civil rights and full participation in the democratic process. These struggles took many forms, communitarian cooperative farms among them.

Delta and Providence farms implicate rural America as a site of major transformations in human rights activism. Dynamic labor activism that had coalesced in the 1930s rural South abated during the war years when agriculture further mechanized and many dirt farmers moved off the land and into factories. Early civil rights activism, intimately entwined with rural and urban labor unionism in the 1930s, was grounded in interracialism, but World War II also changed this dynamic as whites left the rural South to join the war effort. After World War II, African Americans still living in the rural South deliberately engaged in black self-help that included such activities as voting initiatives and pushes for education, often using collective, autonomous spaces like Providence Farm to realize their visions for a democratic society. Yet just as the civil rights movement coalesced in the South, massive resistance—the concerted and myriad efforts by southern whites to resist racial equality and federal intervention—struck a blow for white supremacy, put enormous economic pressure on self-help initiatives like Providence, and helped advance Mississippi as a battleground in the long war over human rights.

Delta Cooperative Farm and Providence Farm sprouted in the most unlikely of landscapes—the Mississippi Delta, a place that is as much myth as reality. Eulogized in song, prose, and poetry, made romantic or grotesque by film and fiction, the alluvial plain running south from Memphis, Tennessee, to Vicksburg, Mississippi, has often been imagined as the cultural heart of Dixie. Yet the human struggles that took place in the Mississippi Delta from the Civil War to the civil rights movement were inseparable from national conflicts and anxieties. America's contests over race, labor, and religion played out in dramatic events in the Delta in ways that often revealed as much about the rest of the nation as they did about Mississippi. Human rights activists used Mississippi as a litmus test for the whole country. As Joseph Crespino has pointed out, during the civil rights movement, Mississippi often acted as a metaphor for the region and the nation. The same was true of the heady days of rural labor activism in the Delta. Activists believed that if they ameliorated race relations and rendered labor less exploitative in Mississippi, the same changes could be accomplished anywhere in the country.[3]

The hopeful nature of the endeavors at Delta and Providence farms seemed a world away from the region's violent past. As farm residents faced the anxiety of the Great Depression, the initial panic and subsequent mobilization of World War II, and the turmoil of the civil rights movement, they forged a path that often paralleled and occasionally took the vanguard in post–World War II struggles of minority and working-class Americans to attain the rights of full citizenship. Their foremost aim, however, was to destroy sharecropping—a form of labor organization that kept white planters atop an oppressive and exploitative economic hierarchy.

Sharecropping replaced slavery as the main mode of labor in the rural South after the Civil War. It solidified a working-poor underclass, provided white plantation owners with a labor force, and laid the groundwork for its wretched sibling, Jim Crow. Under the sharecropping arrangement, landowners rented small farms to poor white and black families and advanced them loans in the form of seeds, tools, and other supplies they needed to get through the year. Sharecropping families, in turn, secured those loans by giving the landowners a lien on their crops. When harvest time came, landowners had first claim on production. When the crops sold at market, sharecroppers had to pay off the landowners. Sharecropping families pocketed whatever profit was left—which often amounted to very little. Until sharecroppers settled all their debts, landowners owned everything. Additionally, planters devised a credit system based on the sharecroppers' need to mortgage future earnings in order to gain all the items needed to plant, cultivate, and harvest a crop. All too often, the sharecroppers were left with nothing come the end of the fiscal year. As a result, sharecroppers rarely saved enough money to purchase their own land. Because of plantation agriculture, the postslavery dream of freedom and hopes of subsistence farming turned into a nightmarish cycle of poverty.[4]

Delta and Providence allowed whites and blacks the liberty to imagine and, to an important extent, realize changes in southern society. Negotiated, collective spaces are essential to furthering ideas of democracy, political action, empowerment, and citizenship. Through voter drives, health initiatives, and educational institutes, African Americans at Providence used the physical and collective space of the cooperative for empowerment.[5]

In addition to being collective, interracial spaces, Delta and Providence were also spaces of leftist reform for the rural South's poor in the often bleak Jim Crow era. The farms signified a threshold between the old and the unexplored—the possible, where boundaries dissolved and historical actors departed into new territory. These thresholds were both psychological and physical for the ex-sharecroppers who lived there.

In the psychological sense, the farms helped former sharecroppers realize changes in social and economic structures that facilitated fuller expressions of their humanity. Additionally, the cooperative residents were "betwixt and between all fixed points of classification." On the farms, they were no longer sharecroppers nor tenants, neither "niggers" nor "crackers." They were something new. They were now "cooperators" or "members" of something ambiguous—an ill-defined relationship that would plague the endeavor from the outset. Divested of previous titles, the cooperators' new positions and classifications were uncertain, yet initially auspicious.[6]

The physical spaces at Delta and Providence were opportune thresholds to the unknown because the community store, church, medical clinic, dairy co-op, and fields were all locations on the farms where members challenged Mississippi's social or economic hierarchies. The cooperative farms were communities on the fringe, separated from the mainstream, which sought to change southern, and ultimately American, society from the margins. By incorporating the farms' four tenets in daily interactions, ex-sharecroppers sought to (1) cooperate equally in labor and production, (2) socialize the economy, (3) enact egalitarian race relations, and (4) practice Christian Socialism. Despite many limitations, Delta and Providence provided opportunities for southerners, particularly black southerners, to access avenues for racial and economic equality through collective space. Jim Crow–era Mississippi is not often thought of as a region of opportunity or possibility for poor agrarians. The history of Delta and Providence cooperative farms, however, allows a reconsideration of the emergence of the modern South, forged on the fringes of American society.[7]

The location of Delta and Providence played important roles in the endeavors' activist history. The farms were in the rural South, not the relative safety of college towns or urban areas. As Mark Schultz has pointed out, race operated differently in the Jim Crow–era rural South. Racial relationships were more fluid and malleable in the rural South where strict Jim Crow laws were not as enforceable or necessary for the maintenance of white supremacy as they were in New South cities. Cooperation across racial lines occurred by virtue of the fact that rural Americans had to rely on their neighbors to make it through illnesses and difficult harvesting seasons, or simply to borrow tools—what Schultz calls "personalism" between black and white neighbors. Racial hierarchies remained, but it was a far different system than that in the town and urban South. The relative fluidity of race in the rural South operated in similar ways at Delta and Providence.[8]

Even in the "closed society" of Mississippi, the rural poor and their leftist allies could challenge hegemonic social and economic structures by going about their daily routines. As the late University of Mississippi historian James W. Silver pointed out in the 1960s, Mississippi essentially operated as a police state where misinformation and intimidation were part of the daily lives of its citizens. Yet in his book, *Mississippi: The Closed Society*, Silver also documented the articulate and passionate "voices of dissent" who openly challenged Mississippi's intransigence in a variety of ways.[9]

Far from living in a closed, insular society, activists at Delta and Providence engaged in a local movement with national and international roots and consequences; namely, the cooperative communalism movement. This story provides new perspective on the intersections of race, class, labor, and religion that reveal multifaceted strategies to attain broader human rights in the rural South. The residents at Delta and Providence farms did not have succinct definitions or sometimes even concrete concepts for how they approached human rights. Living the quotidian struggle for human rights was often boring and devoid of strict orthodoxy. Their activism was variously—and sometimes vaguely—informed by socialist ideology, a commitment to interracialism, and an early form of Liberation Theology rooted in Christian Socialism—a kind of "practical Christianity" pioneered most notably by Reinhold Niebuhr and meant to put the teachings of Jesus into practice building a more socially just world. In practice, their activism took various forms that included labor unionism, health care reform, education initiatives, and economic parity. In the midst of Jim Crow Mississippi, the farms were a beacon of hope and safe haven for the South's most destitute class.

While the cooperative movement had international reach, it also had American colonial-era roots. Yet the first concerted cooperative movement to resemble what coalesced in the early twentieth century began in the 1830s, led by workers hoping to collectivize in order to improve working conditions and pay. Throughout the 1800s and up to the present day, various cooperative movements have existed on American soil. American cooperative movements, however, were inseparable from international movements. Even in relative recent history, the various approaches of Rochdale in England, Mondragon in Spain, and Soviet communes have had an influence in the United States. The most common forms of cooperatives are consumer and producer types. Both existed at Delta Cooperative Farm and, for a short time, at Providence Farm. Yet what made Delta and Providence unique from most American cooperative endeavors—and more akin to international iterations—was their approach based in cooperative communalism. As John Curl has noted, both communalist and cooperative movements are "for social justice and personal liberation. While cooperatives are limited to particular functions, however, communalism invites members to join in more intensive and inclusive ways." While many cooperative communalist endeavors in the nineteenth and early twentieth centuries were inspired by socialist ideology and religious conviction, few tried to meld socialism, Christianity, and communalism with interracialism. Delta and Providence proved distinctive in that regard.[10]

Yet rural black and white workers had banded together to fight agrarian exploitation through various means before the 1930s. Southerners participated in various interracial political movements in the years between Reconstruction and the solidification of Jim Crow at the turn of the century. The Readjuster Movement in Virginia, the national Populist movement, and the Fusionist alliance among white Populists and black Republicans in North Carolina were, for a time, viable movements aimed at creating cross-racial approaches to government. Interracial labor activism also gained support in various locales. As labor historians have noted, lumbermen and dock workers took part in pragmatic alliances across the color line before the turn of the twentieth century.[11]

The 1930s created another moment suited for interracial cooperation and labor unionism, even in the Jim Crow and antilabor South. As Anthony Badger attests, politicians and New Deal bureaucrats from the South often shaped programs to fit the segregated culture of the region. Yet Badger saw moments of opportunities for new social and labor orders arise from the New Deal, too. The National Industrial Recovery Act (NIRA) explicitly stated in Section 7(a) that the bargaining rights of labor unions would be protected by law. The federal government's explicit support of unions was initially an unmitigated victory for labor. Shortly, however, sharecroppers came to the hard realization that Section 7(a) did not apply to agricultural workers. The Southern Tenant Farmers' Union—a driving catalyst for the formation of the farms—would form as a direct challenge to the NIRA's exclusion of agricultural workers and a renewed faith in interracial organizing.[12]

Throughout the history of the rural South, blacks and whites have lived side by side. As master and slave, landlord and sharecropper, or often as members of the exploited working-class, black and white southerners had daily, personal interaction with one another. "Yet even when human sympathy and friendship drew people together," wrote Edward Ayers, "the rituals of Southern race relations constrained and distorted the feelings." Historians of the South have depicted rural race relations in a variety of ways. Some, like Leon Litwack, chose to underscore the absolute brutality of white supremacy and its physical and psychological effects on African Americans. Others, like Mark Schultz, found that interpersonal relationships between blacks and whites led to more malleable—although no less complex—forms of race relations than the ones Litwack presented. Both are true accounts of the southern past. Stephen Berrey has recently offered the most nuanced and intimate portrait of race relations in the late Jim Crow era. By focusing on the "performative nature of the everyday realm," Berrey demonstrates how the routine of Jim Crow permeated every interaction between whites and blacks, from the mundane to the volatile. Within that routine, however, there existed room for spontaneity and even militancy. While adequate accounts of race relations can be vexing and difficult to parse out, portrayals of interracial cooperation have become almost anathema to the southern past. Interracialism, however, existed alongside efforts to keep whites and blacks apart. Interracial cooperation was as southern as its warped adversary Jim Crow.[13]

I define interracialism as the act of seeking out, creating, or promoting spaces where blacks and whites could cooperate to accomplish mundane daily activities as well as pursue goals that had implications for equality writ large. It is, by necessity, an intentional act or series of events with the goal of cooperation and eventual equality in mind. Interracialism is different from integration.

Integration merely implies cross-racial space-sharing and does not always promote cooperation.

Two early twentieth-century organizations that promoted interracialism were the Young Women's Christian Association (YWCA) and the Commission on Interracial Cooperation (CIC). These organizations achieved some success and broadened the imagination of what was possible within the rigid rule of white supremacy. In the 1910s, the YWCA, called by a strong adherence to the Social Gospel, led efforts to promote interracial cooperation and understanding, especially by organizing interracial conferences at places such as the Blue Ridge Assembly in Black Mountain, North Carolina. The CIC began in 1919 as an answer to the upswing of racial violence across the South. While the commission was intentionally interracial, virtually all members were united by economic class. The CIC membership believed that change would come from the intellectual class, who could influence policy and model healthy, equitable cross-racial relationships for working-class Americans. But the CIC also addressed tangible problems by sending volunteers into local black communities to try to solve their most pressing needs. Although the CIC was successful in exposing the deleterious consequences of racial hatred and made positive changes in some communities, many of its members—and subsequent historians—criticized the organization for tepidity and tokenism during its early phases, for not involving the working classes in decision making, and for working within segregation rather than dismantling it. Yet they were an organization swimming against the tide. Few groups were working toward such lofty goals as the CIC.[14]

The interracialism pursued by the YWCA and the CIC was bold for the time, but by the mid-1930s, communists, socialists, and labor organizers had paved the way for more radical forms of interracialism. In many ways, what took place at Delta and Providence in the 1930s was the next phase in interracial cooperation: living interracialism. On the farms, interracialism was rooted in socialism and the radical teachings of Jesus, promoted by intellectuals but modified and enacted by the poor. Working side by side in the fields, breaking bread together, sitting in the same waiting room, and generally depending on each other for their livelihood was a radical sort of intentional interracialism. Yet this genus of interracialism was difficult. Interracialism—and socialism— at Delta and Providence took up too many evenings, to paraphrase a truism oft attributed to Oscar Wilde. Decisions were tedious, implementation was difficult, and living this variety of communal interracialism was onerous and nearly inescapable. Despite the challenges that living interracialism posed to farm residents, it represented a bigger challenge to white supremacists who grew suspicious of what the farm meant to southern customs.

Religion also played important roles in turning rural southern society on its head. Christianity took on a particularly activist tone in the 1930s as labor unionists modeled their rallies after spiritual revivals. As Alison Greene has pointed out, the Great Depression created new and convenient religious alliances. Most of the initial socialist union organizers or promoters of cooperative communalism were not experienced in rural prophetic Christianity. Many realized, however, that to reach the working poor in the Arkansas and Mississippi deltas, they had to at least speak the sharecroppers' spiritual language of ecstatic worship, or employ people who did.[15]

At Delta and Providence, residents approached their day-to-day interactions through a mixture of socialist ideology and what Reinhold Niebuhr called "Christian Realism." This mixture produced a type of religious activism that proved to be a precursor to Liberation Theology later put into practice during the civil rights movement and other movements around the world. The various ways farm residents approached interracial cooperation and religious activism were two of the main ways that they modified their philosophies and goals to fit the lived experience of human rights activism.[16]

Remaking the Rural South elucidates a twenty-year endeavor for human rights in rural America, details the eventual unromantic breakdown of cooperation between black and white, and demonstrates how moments of modification defined the trajectory of the movement. Similar to Francoise N. Hamlin's call to see the civil rights movement as "a mass of movements," this work examines the near-constant demands of the South's rural poor to be fully included in the promise of American citizenship and concludes that a long movement contained "multiple spheres of activity" and critical moments of modification. Residents at Delta and Providence had to modify their demands as they won concessions, suffered setbacks, and lived through two decades of economic, political, and social change. *Remaking the Rural South* defines "movements" more broadly by including a myriad of human rights reforms—such as religious, economic, and labor—addressed by black and white rural southerners. Indeed, one major moment of modification in how the rural poor approached their activism came when interracial cooperation, predicated on rural labor unionism, eventually transformed into a nearly exclusive African American struggle for freedom. While the nature of labor and religious activism changed over the twenty-year existence of the farms, the principal moments of modification occurred around interracial cooperation. The local story of Delta and Providence farms explains how and why that transformation took place.[17]

The modifications made on the farms were often the outgrowths of the simultaneous introductions of interracial and communal space. At Delta Cooperative Farm, private assumptions about race by ex-sharecroppers, for instance, were now necessarily opinions that were aired in public forums, like cooperative council meetings or collective work groups. The collective space of sharing church services with blacks or taking instructions from them in the fields now confronted whites who before had been privately racist. As W. Fitzhugh Brundage points out in his work on southern historical memory, controlling physical space is essential to shaping identity. The physical space of the cooperatives was collective and interracial and designed to delegitimize white supremacy. Within this collective space, negotiations were necessary to reconcile the private, individual space with public interactions. Public space and private space were often at odds on the cooperative farms, particularly when racial and class lines were at stake. Black and white sharecroppers and paternalistic employees had to share the public space, but many staff privately held onto their ideas of cultural inferiority. Put another way, collective space at the farms was often where the public and private converged—sometimes with toxic results.[18]

Additionally, many black cooperators now felt empowered by their new surroundings to publicly express their views on race and oppression that before had been private. In his work on Norfolk, Virginia, Earl Lewis argues that carving out public and psychic spaces for African Americans translated into tangible political power. When operations moved from Delta to Providence and residents transitioned from a cooperative model to a model of black self-help, African Americans used the new farm as a base for challenging Jim Crow—holding black minister retreats, college preparatory programs, and health initiatives.[19]

Conversely, residents at Providence had to negotiate the spaces carved out for interracial cooperation or black self-help with those neighbors who opposed them. The white racists who swelled the ranks of the Citizens' Councils and the Ku Klux Klan were at loggerheads with the men and women at Delta and Providence farms. By the mid-1950s, the opposition had consolidated power to such an extent that it became impossible for Providence Farm to function as a viable activist community.

In addition, plantation agriculture experienced its greatest transformation since Reconstruction. Almost as soon as Delta Cooperative was established, large-scale cooperative farming became obsolete in the face of changing agricultural production. As a result, the farm had to change with the times or face failure. The most tangible change occurred in the stock and equipment used for plowing, tilling, and harvesting. Both mule and man hours were reduced in the cotton South beginning in the 1930s. Although much of the American South did not tractorize as rapidly as the rest of the nation, the Mississippi Delta's flat geography and large plantations encouraged many farmers to mechanize before World War II. Not only did the number of mules decrease in the Delta, but so too did the number of farmhands needed to work a given patch of land. According to historian George B. Ellenberg, many large plantation owners were attracted to the tractor for what it saved them in the long run. "In the Delta region of Mississippi," explains Ellenberg, "preparing and planting a one-acre cotton field required 9.3 man-hours and 20.4 mule hours." Mechanization reduced those hours to "4.9 man-hours and 3.3 tractor hours." In addition, the federal government pushed plantation owners to transition from sharecropping to wage labor, making human labor more expensive. In sum, with tractors, fewer farmers were needed to work the land and a plantation-sized cooperative employing hundreds of individuals became obsolete.[20]

Before World War II, cooperators at Delta used both mules and tractors, and even tested one of the first models of the mechanical cotton picker. As wartime needs increased demands for efficiency and food, farms across the country used more and more machines. Coupled with an increase in urban jobs in the war industry, Americans left the farm in record numbers. Given the drastic changes in mechanization and immigration, a large-scale cooperative that employed a hundred or more farmhands was simply unsustainable. Although many observers figured that rural America would return to mixing stock and machines after the war, the economy continued to boom, and by the 1950s tractors had almost completely replaced mules and displaced untold numbers of farmhands. After all operations at Delta Cooperative were moved to Providence Farm, the endeavor only faintly resembled a cooperative, and the inhabitants, while still spending some time engaged in the intricacies of large-scale agriculture, now focused on issues that would mark the post–World War II South for African Americans: economics, education, health, and civil rights. The mechanization and labor changes that took place at Delta and Providence were part of sweeping changes occurring across the rural South.[21]

Mechanization forced many rural southerners to modify their interactions with the land and with each other. As the practice of sharecropping came under attack, as blacks joined the Great Migration, and as whites found work in the war industry, race and labor relations were altered to the point that they challenged the southern social stratification. Those engaged in opposing the social status quo experienced backlashes from southerners entrenched at the top. Planters and their allies based their hierarchy on white supremacy, plantation agriculture, and a capitalist, microlevel view of core–periphery exploitation. Simply put, planters exploited the labor of the poor and the resources of their region to line their own pockets. In the minds of plantation owners, the very presence of Delta and Providence farms, with black and white sharecroppers making dividends off of what they grew and sold, threatened to overturn white planter hegemony in the rural South. The planter class, however, was not the only group of southerners with ardent visions for the region's future.[22]

Delta Cooperative Farm and Providence Farm were two examples of how southern dreamers worked to widen the scope of democratic inclusion and possessed bold visions for the South that were consonant with a truly democratic society. Despite dozens of studies documenting various reformers and movements, their lessons and legacies remain largely obscured from a public more comfortable with seeing the region as intransigent and monolithic. This other South was very real and existed alongside the ubiquitous demagogues and segregationists. But southern dreamers were different; they were progressive, leftist, and often intensely radical. Although cooperative members at Delta and Providence steered clear of calling themselves "radical," so as to not raise the suspicion of their neighbors, they were living and working on a socialist-inspired interracial farm in Mississippi. Few large-scale endeavors were as radical as Delta and Providence.[23]

The radical spirit of the other South met the racial mutability of the rural South at Delta and Providence farms. From 1936 to 1956, residents embarked on a path that few Americans chose. At the time, the possibilities were endless and the individuals were hopeful that their communitarian vision for the region would spark new possibilities. The moment, born from the despair of the Great Depression, teemed with optimism.

Remaking the Rural South is organized into five chapters and an epilogue that relate a chronological narrative of the farms while weaving them into national and international events and trends. I have chosen this method because the history of Delta and Providence farms can best be told in a linear fashion, as a story of birth, death, and hope on southern soil. I divide the events at Delta and Providence into three periods: the Great Depression, World War II, and the postwar civil rights era.

Chapter 1 addresses the intellectual and ideological antecedents of Delta Cooperative Farm and Providence Farm and places them squarely in the context of an international cooperative movement. I argue that a blend of national and transnational cooperative ideas, given life by the immediacy of the Great Depression, converged in the mid-1930s and led to the founding of Delta Farm. The political, economic, and social institutions that most influenced farm founders also drove other reformers in the same era. Thus, the political economy of Delta Cooperative Farm figures into a simultaneous, if unsystematic, movement for human rights by activists around the world. Initially, the egalitarian tendencies of New Deal policy, however tepid, and the socialist belief that American infrastructure could be remade in the wake of economic devastation enabled white and black southerners to pursue economic and labor agendas that had heretofore gained little traction. Beginning in the late 1800s and ending just before Delta's founding in 1936, this chapter specifically traces the farms' origins in the Socialist Party of America, Reinhold Niebuhr's Christian Realism, and the international cooperative movement exemplified by efforts such as Toyohiko Kagawa's cooperative farming in Japan, which directly influenced Delta Cooperative Farm's founders. The 1930s served as the moment of opportunity for sharecroppers and their allies to bring together these ideas on southern soil. Born of the economic hardships of the Great Depression and political possibilities generated by the New Deal, the convergence of ideas made the groundbreaking at Delta a radical alternative to working-class life in the rural South.

Chapter 2 establishes and helps answer a central question of this book: How did an alliance of missionaries, labor radicals, and sharecroppers create an interracial community in a state plagued by racial violence and economic oppression? By deciding to set up shop in the Magnolia State, they "jumped from the frying pan into the fire," as one Delta trustee warned. Mississippi's oppressive race relations and the dominance of plantation agriculture gave Delta Cooperative Farm certain legitimacy in the eyes of the media and potential allies. If the farm could succeed in Mississippi, the founders believed, it could succeed anywhere. In answering that question, the chapter uses Delta Cooperative Farm to demonstrate how the national and transnational ideas of human rights movements functioned at the local level and focuses on the day-to-day lives of black and white sharecroppers. I explore the relationships among leaders, on-the-ground organizers, and local people; the challenges of interracial labor organizing; the navigation of local power brokers; and tension between outsiders and local people. This chapter focuses on these minute details in order to shed light on the tediousness of social justice work within the contexts of Deep South segregation and the tandem natural and economic disasters that swept the country in the 1930s.

Chapter 3 uses Delta Cooperative Farm as a case study to understand just how difficult interracial cooperation was within the context of Depression-era America as the country faced dramatic changes. Outlining the internal and external reasons why the endeavor at Delta declined beginning in late 1937, the chapter reveals how liberal paternalism, a persistent plantation mentality among former sharecroppers, and various suspicions from outside the community eroded interracial cooperation. As international war inched closer to the United States, more whites found work by joining the military-industrial war effort. During this time, most white residents left Delta. Simultaneously, the increased mechanization of farm labor led to a decreased need for field workers. Both developments altered the goals and scope of the cooperative endeavor at Delta, the social and economic lives of rural Americans, and the global cooperative movement. Coupled with an inability to compete with the region's well-established sharecropping plantations, Delta soon found itself near bankruptcy. Ultimately, however, Delta's brand of interracial cooperation suffered the most. With these major changes and setbacks, Delta's founders decided to start anew on a second parcel of land in Holmes County, Mississippi.

Chapter 4 positions Providence Farm as a microcosm of the broad changes rural African American activism experienced during and in the immediate aftermath of World War II. For the farm, the region, and the nation, 1942 was a transformative year. As the United States plunged headlong into war, the cooperative experiment in Mississippi experienced its largest turnover in residents and leadership while national apathy for the plight of landless blacks prevailed. Delta Cooperative Farm's economic woes carried over to Providence when large-scale cotton production—especially the socialized kind—ceased to be a viable economic endeavor as the Cotton Belt gave way to the Sunbelt in the postwar years. While whites—including most of the leadership—continued to flee the farm, the remaining residents and newly appointed leaders jettisoned socialist-inspired cooperative communalism and remodeled Providence Farm into a center of black human rights activism. Following trends in black communities throughout the South in the 1940s, Providence residents modified their human rights activism into localized, civic-oriented black self-help initiatives. They did so by continuing some of the old endeavors such as religious institutes for black leaders, summer camps for economically challenged children, and a racially integrated medical clinic. New approaches were also integrated into the farm's operations, such as a federal credit union where the rural poor could secure fair loans and interest rates without going into debt to plantation owners. These changes constituted the endeavors' most dramatic moment of modification.

Chapter 5 demonstrates the steady decline of the relationship between Providence and the surrounding community and the corrosive effects of white massive resistance that ultimately led to the farm's closing. When anticommunism and the backlash to the civil rights movement coalesced, the relative safety of the community changed dramatically at Providence. After the Supreme Court's 1954 school desegregation decision in *Brown v. Board* brought international headlines from the South, the Emmett Till murder one year later focused the nation's attention expressly on Mississippi. Headlines derided white Mississippians' intransigence and violence. In response, much of the state's white population closed ranks and insisted that "outsiders" had no business instructing Mississippians on the law or race relations. The Ku Klux

Klan became a powerful force once again and the white Citizens' Council was founded in Mississippi as the unofficial, "civil" arm of the more militant Klan. In many circumstances, these two groups had the full support of local law enforcement and religious institutions. In the weeks following Till's murder, and with increased calls for racial equality, the Citizens' Council and the Klan in Holmes County turned their anger to the curious farm outside of Tchula.

The epilogue chronicles the journeys that the land and the people at Providence have taken since 1956. Several black farmers and their families continued to live on the Providence parcel long after Eugene Cox—the resident director—and David Minter—the community physician—had left. Led by longtime resident Fannye Booker, the farm became a base for voter registration drives, Head Start programs, and other black self-help activities. Additionally, Cox and Minter sustained their relationships with these working families after leaving Mississippi while continuing to advocate for reforming rural labor practices and race relations. For their efforts, the Mississippi Sovereignty Commission opened clandestine investigations into Booker, Cox, and Minter. Sovereignty Commission investigators left an extensive paper trail, inadvertently demonstrating the important work each of the former Providence residents was doing long after 1956. The epilogue explains that to focus on strict interpretations of success and failure is to miss the point entirely. For twenty years the farms existed in perhaps the most economically and socially oppressive region in the country. That the farms existed at all is testament to local, regional, national, and global forces that came to rural Mississippi and, for twenty years, saw the South's rural poor work toward creating a more democratic vision for their lives.

CHAPTER 1

The Problems of Collective Man

I n 1934, the perennial Socialist Party of America's candidate for president, Norman Thomas, published a pamphlet titled *The Plight of the Share-Cropper*. Thomas, compelled by his affection for the working classes and having recently returned from a trip through the South where he saw the destitution firsthand, called sharecroppers the "most truly forgotten" Americans. Thomas's little book familiarized America with the sharecropping system, the sharecropper, and New Deal programs that worsened the situation for many landless farmers. The pamphlet was meant to tug at the heartstrings—and hopefully the purse strings—of its readers, establishing the sharecropper in stark tones. According to Thomas, he was "a man who raises cotton but cannot possibly afford proper underclothes for his children or sheets and towels for the family." Once Thomas established the picture of Americans living in the direst of situations, he turned his attention to eviscerating southern landlords and critiquing the Agricultural Adjustment Administration (AAA). Thomas, a Presbyterian minister who espoused the Social Gospel, called landlords no better than antebellum slave owners and labeled administrators in the AAA as dishonest bureaucrats who cared little for sharecroppers' well-being.[1]

Thomas laid much of the blame at the feet of the profit system of capitalism, and a "nationalistic capitalism at that." He knew, however, that a wholesale revolution in the market or in American culture was practically impossible. Instead, Thomas advocated for collectivism among sharecroppers who wished to stay on the land. Sharecroppers, believed Thomas, could use collective organizing to their advantage in two ways. First, they must organize into a labor union. "For this organization to be effective," counseled Thomas, "it must be of white and Negro share-croppers together." Second, sharecroppers should join cooperatives "which would get the benefit of expert guidance and a comprehensive plan" that would, in turn, pool their production and maximize their buying power. "Social ownership," concluded Thomas, would lead to the "emancipation" of the South's rural laborers.[2]

Thomas's missive, published by the League for Industrial Democracy (LID), an organization aimed at promoting socialism and labor activism in the United States, included a fifteen-page report on the "social and economic consequences of the cotton acreage reduction program" forced on farmers by the AAA. This report, directed by what Thomas called "the Amberson Commission," further indicted the Department of Agriculture's local administrators for pocketing government subsidies while evicting thousands of sharecroppers, thus denying the laborers "access to the land, and to the only labor that they know." In some ways, Thomas's essay on the sharecropper served as a preface to the devastating accusations leveled by the Amberson Commission. Every page of the report contained statistics, culled from over five hundred interviews with sharecroppers in Missouri, Arkansas, Tennessee, and Mississippi, which supported its argument that the AAA and plantation owners were in collusion to evict sharecroppers from their land and livelihood.[3] While intent to destroy the lives of sharecroppers was a matter of perspective, the actuality of the Agricultural Adjustment Act was that it left many sharecroppers on the verge of starvation.

The Plight of the Share-Cropper and the accompanying report coincided with a burgeoning interest among social scientists in the experiences of the southern sharecropper. Although University of North Carolina sociologist Rupert B. Vance had published his groundbreaking dissertation on cotton culture and the inequitable sharecropping system in 1929, Thomas's small publication five years later kicked off a legion of important works on the topic. In addition to Vance's continued work, Fisk University sociologist Charles Spurgeon Johnson published two of his seminal books, *Shadow of the Plantation* (1934) and *The Collapse of Cotton Tenancy* (1935), within months of Thomas's publication. Arthur Raper, who had studied under the eminent sociologist Howard W. Odum at the University of North Carolina, followed Johnson's publications with *Preface to Peasantry* (1936), a scathing critique of plantation agriculture, and *Sharecroppers All* (1941), which argued that continued reliance on sharecropping diminished the economic standing and social independence of all southerners. The numerous publications on sharecroppers began to influence public interest and, in turn, public policy. Even as Thomas wrote about the travails of sharecroppers, plans were under way to accomplish two of his recommendations: organizing a sharecropper union and establishing cooperatives.

The individuals engaged in the Amberson Commission, whose report had been published in tandem with Thomas's pamphlet, were members of the Memphis (Tennessee) Chapter of the LID and the tiny, fledgling Tyronza (Arkansas) Socialist Party. The latter was made up of two men, Clay East and H. L. Mitchell. By the end of 1934, East and Mitchell would organize the most important labor union in the Depression-era South. Two members of the Memphis Chapter of the LID who were central in collecting, compiling, and publishing the findings of the Amberson Commission were William R. Amberson, a physiologist whose meticulous scientific research methods made him the de facto head of the commission, and Blaine Treadway, a Memphis printer. While East and Mitchell were busy organizing sharecroppers for collective bargaining purposes and Amberson and Treadway set to work placing poor farmers into cooperatives, both groups tried complementary avenues to solve the problems faced by sharecroppers. Amberson, and Mitchell in particular, understood that the Depression and the AAA only worsened a decades-long battle over racial and economic hierarchy.

The Old South plantation system dictated the effects of the New Deal on southern agriculture. Following emancipation, landlords and laborers in the South struggled to develop a system of labor to replace slavery. Because of the resistance of ex-slaves, a gang labor system could not be enforced by postbellum planters. Gradually, planters developed a new system based on the family as the central unit of labor and sharecropping as the prevailing contractual relationship between laborers and landlords. By the early 1900s, the plantation system had evolved, under Jim Crow, into an exploitative relationship in which planters reaped the bulk of the benefit from the labor of their sharecroppers and tenants.

As Amberson, Mitchell, and East knew well, sharecropping kept both black and white landless southerners politically powerless and dependent on wealthy whites. "In the cotton country croppers have been driven from pillar to post for so long and have sunk so low in the human scale," wrote Amberson in the pages of the *Nation*, "that they cannot imagine any other type of life, and do not know how to resist exploitation." From Reconstruction to the mid-1930s, fueled by constant sources of cheap labor, southern planters perpetuated a separate agricultural system that kept the rural poor isolated from the rest of the nation. In the process, the South lagged behind in nearly every socioeconomic measure, including health and education. Tenants and sharecroppers on plantations faced plummeting cotton prices and a vicious cycle of debt. Borrowing "furnish" from plantation owners or crossroads merchants on credit meant that sharecroppers were almost always beholden to wealthy whites come selling time. Sharecroppers' minimal survival was based on constant borrowing. Sharecroppers and tenants had some of the grimmest living conditions in the nation. In Crittenden County, Arkansas, just across the river from Memphis, nearly 90 percent of African American males were sharecroppers or tenant farmers in the early 1930s. Amberson received word from a Poinsett County relief official in the winter of 1934 that approximately one-third of all county residents received federal relief. According to the 1930 census, over 150,000 tenants and sharecroppers lived in Arkansas and around 225,000 resided in Mississippi. Economist T. J. Woofter reported that roughly 6.5 million rural Americans, the bulk of whom were concentrated in the South, were eligible for relief from the federal government.[4]

Rural African Americans in the South, having secured emancipation only a few generations before, had few choices. They could join thousands of other African Americans and migrate northward in search of better living and working conditions, or they could remain in their home communities, toiling on the same lands their ancestors had. Sharecropping, compounded by Jim Crow, meant that rural black southerners experienced the bleakest situation of any laboring group in America in the early twentieth century. Although rural African Americans were never completely powerless, they lived under the constant threat of the unpredictable, and sometimes violent, whims of white supremacists. While some of their urban counterparts joined unions, rural workers languished in a backbreaking cycle of poverty and racism with few opportunities for collective redress.[5]

The New South offered only marginally more to white sharecroppers. The color of their skin did not shield landless whites from the same impoverished fate that befell their black counterparts. Despite the ideology of white supremacy, the fortunes of black and white sharecroppers were inextricably bound together before World War II. Amberson was keenly aware of this fact and believed that "white and colored croppers [would] work together when once they have seen that their economic interests are identical."[6]

Black and white sharecroppers kept an eye toward greener pastures somewhere down the road. When living and working conditions became unbearable, croppers sometimes had the freedom to vote with their feet and set out for a different plantation where another planter might, with luck, treat them better. Yet, usually this freedom was limited, as Gavin Wright has pointed out, since most sharecroppers moved only a few miles away in order to maintain a working rapport with local merchants who lent them furnish.[7]

The Great Depression threw sharecropping into the public conversation about the nation's ills. Precisely because the effects of the Depression made manifest the inadequacies and inequities of the southern political economy, Amberson and other leftists renewed their commitment to dispatch poverty and racism in the South. In the predicament of the southern sharecropper,

Amberson and other organizers saw a glaring critique of American labor and the urgent necessity for reform.

The transition for landless farmers from sharecropping to cooperative farming would not be easy. Proponents of reorganizing sharecroppers into cooperative communities began casting about for ideas on exactly how to accomplish what they considered a momentous transformation of the southern economy and social structure. One of the first to weigh in was E. B. "Britt" McKinney, the charismatic African American preacher and eventual labor union officer. Although McKinney was only passably literate, he was an exceptional speaker respected by white and black sharecroppers alike. He declared that all who toiled under the "hellish system" of tenant farming and sharecropping "were slaves." One way to attain freedom for these farmers, McKinney urged, was to create cooperative farming communities. H. L. Mitchell, William Amberson, and Blaine Treadway shared McKinney's belief in the redemptive possibilities of farming cooperatives and were well on their way to initiating one in the Mississippi Delta.[8]

McKinney took great pains to explain to Mitchell, Amberson, and Treadway the type of person who should be selected as the cooperative's first director. If the director was fair and friendly and did not adopt the moniker of "boss" among the tenants, McKinney predicted, the cooperative would accomplish its first goal: freeing southern tenant farmers from an oppressive cycle of poverty, psychological torment, and physical violence. Additionally, for the undertaking to succeed, "and to make it a cooperative in truth," McKinney believed, "it must consist of both White and black." Once the cooperative ideal was established, concluded McKinney, the South could boast that it was truly the "land of the free" because it had been "won by the brave." McKinney underscored the significance of the undertaking by pointing out that an interracial agricultural cooperative in the region had the potential to be a new model "for the whole south, if not the whole nation."[9]

McKinney fervently believed in the importance of creating an interracial community where blacks and whites would toil together in the fields, make mutual decisions on behalf of the entire community, and have equal stakes in their collective welfare. Even housing, he suggested, should be secured on a first-come, first-served basis, regardless of color. He did not, however, advocate complete intermingling of black and white in the cooperative. Foreshadowing Delta Cooperative Farm's measured approach to residential integration, McKinney contended "that the white and the colrd [sic] should not live together [sic] at this time." In McKinney's vision, the cooperative would be divided in half by a wide road. On one side African American farmers would reside with their families; the other side would be designated for whites. McKinney also proposed that a school should be constructed with a partition for separating white and black students, while each class would have a "teacher of their own race." The children, however, would not be as strictly separated by the boundaries of racial segregation and could play together. He hoped that this level of integration would mean that "the young minds will not be poisoned with the old chronic ills that the older ones are infected with."[10]

McKinney's suggestions not only succinctly summarized the hopes, desires, apprehensions, and reservations of the cooperative farms proponents, but also reflected the feelings of the sharecroppers who would make up the residents and laborers at the cooperatives. Given the climate of southern race relations in the 1930s, what McKinney advocated and what reformers put into practice in Mississippi was a forthright challenge to white planters' economic hegemony, the plantation's inequitable labor system, and the Deep South's racial hierarchy. In 1936, secular socialists and union activists, with help from Christian Socialists, came together to envision and establish a mode of agricultural production rooted in egalitarian collectivism. The reformers realized that the provisions put forth by the AAA and the mass eviction of sharecroppers in Arkansas and elsewhere exposed the gross inequities of the southern agricultural system. They moved to promote their own solutions in the form of collective farming.

The sometimes tenuous alliance of well-meaning activists and the rural poor that put into practice progressive ideas regarding labor, religion, race, and class at Delta Cooperative Farm and its successor, Providence Farm, suggests the degree to which the New Deal expanded notions of democracy and citizenship and, for a brief moment, allowed for radical reformers to dream of remaking America. At Delta Cooperative Farm reformers drew on American socialism and the theology and practice of Christian Realism to envision the uplift of southern sharecroppers, the nation's most marginalized working class. In the experimental spaces of Delta and Providence, reformers felt at liberty to imagine the possibilities of cooperation across the color line, challenging inherited notions of race and established labor practices. Reformers hoped that Delta and Providence would transcend the color barrier and directly confront the South's twin enduring dilemmas: poverty and race.[11]

Three men were the principal founders of Delta Cooperative Farm. These three first converged on Arkansas and helped make the horrible conditions of sharecropping front-page news, then led homeless sharecroppers into Mississippi to their new homes. The head of the Amberson Commission, William R. Amberson, a physiologist at the University of Tennessee Medical School in Memphis, a member of the American Socialist Party, an advisor to the Southern Tenant Farmers' Union (STFU), and the Tennessee secretary of the American Civil Liberties Union (ACLU), brought socialism and a passion for rural labor organizing to early discussions of cooperatives. Sherwood Eddy, a theologian, prolific author, and Christian missionary with socialist leanings, joined the discussion on starting farmers' cooperatives through his devout belief in Christian Realism—what he called practical Christianity—and service to the world's poor. Sam H. Franklin, a protégé of Eddy's, native of rural Tennessee, missionary, activist, and staunch believer in reforming the southern agricultural system of sharecropping through Christian cooperation, offered firsthand knowledge of cooperative enterprises. Although other notable reformers such as Reinhold Niebuhr and union activists Howard Kester and H. L. Mitchell were also involved with Delta Cooperative Farm from the early stages, Amberson had access to sharecroppers, Eddy provided the economic backing to get the cooperative off the ground, and Franklin directed the crucial legwork and manpower.

William Ruthrauff Amberson was born in Harrisburg, Pennsylvania, in 1894. In 1922, he received a PhD in biology from Harvard University. After researching for a brief time in Germany, in 1930 he joined the University of Tennessee Medical School in Memphis as chair of the Physiology Department. Amberson became familiar with a specific brand of German socialism in the 1920s. This type was different from the German Social Democrats who steered German politics in the era of World War I. Amberson was instead drawn to the pacifism and staunch internationalism of a splinter of the Social Democrats called the Independent Socialist Party.[12]

Amberson's socialism, then, differed in origins from that of Reinhold Niebuhr and Norman Thomas, whose socialism was rooted in Christian theology. For a time, however, their socialist critiques of the plantation system intersected. After being introduced to socialism in Germany, he worked with and advocated for the unemployed once settled in Memphis. He also joined the American Socialist Party, an affiliation that often put him at odds with university administrators while also bringing him in direct contact with the casualties of the Great Depression. In 1932, in conjunction with the Memphis Socialist Party local and the Unemployed Citizens League, a group he helped form, Amberson prepared an exposé of dishonest Memphis merchants, particularly grocers, who habitually short-weighted and overcharged welfare customers. Amberson's report caused a stir in Memphis and was his first taste of the activism that would shape the next decade of his life. Amberson then embarked on a mission to break down the rigid class and race boundaries that limited economic liberty in the South. He noticed that the majority of the unemployed who flooded urban Memphis came from rural areas south and west of the city. They told him of recent mass evictions of sharecroppers throughout the Delta. Amberson wrote Socialist Party standard-bearer Norman Thomas of his deepening concern for sharecroppers, concluding "I feel strongly that the socialist groups can do much . . . to aid these dispossessed people."[13]

Amberson soon found allies for his cause. In Tyronza, Arkansas, H. L. Mitchell, a dry cleaner, and Clay East, a gas station operator, witnessed first-hand the devastation of local sharecroppers. Mitchell, an activist-minded socialist and follower of Norman Thomas, gradually schooled his friend, East, in socialist ideology. Both knew Amberson from socialist circles in Memphis, a short drive from Tyronza. For two years Mitchell and East made futile efforts to aid and organize sharecroppers and to start a local socialist party. Mitchell even ran for local office as a socialist candidate, only to be disqualified from running on a technicality. Mitchell did not sign a pledge to eschew corrupt practices. He wryly joked that there was "great danger of the (Socialist Party) buying the election." After being removed from the ballot in his bid for local office, Mitchell wrote to Amberson and included a petition locals had started to get Mitchell back in the election. "The Class Struggle is a reality in Poinsett County as elsewhere," declared Mitchell. He and an African American socialist "were over at the election board meeting and you should have heard this old time Red—threaten them with a Communist Revolution. Keep the petition as I would like to show that as an illustration of what happens when Socialists try to elect men to office in Arkansas."[14]

Through their socialist activities and their attempts at labor organizing, Mitchell and East waded into a dangerous mess in Arkansas. The situation was particularly precarious for sharecroppers. In the Arkansas Delta, generations of clear-cutting for cotton production had denuded the Mississippi River's western floodplain of its trees. Timbering and cash-crop agriculture had been Arkansas's economic lifeblood since the end of slavery. Even by southern standards Arkansas planters and landlords were notorious for controlling their workforces through violence and intimidation. After World War I, the Arkansas Delta was infamous for club-wielding planters, gun-toting night riders, and law enforcement officers who practiced vigilante justice. In Poinsett, Cross, Mississippi, Crittenden, Lee, and Phillips counties, the rural poor during the interwar years faced some of the harshest and most oppressive conditions in the nation.[15]

As Amberson discovered, the onset of the Great Depression worsened already terrible working and living conditions. Through the AAA, the New Deal attempted to step in to alleviate some of the problems facing agriculture in the unpredictable 1930s. This recovery program called for farmers to participate in acreage-reduction programs that took portions of farmland out of production and allowed it to lay fallow. As compensation, the federal government paid farmers a fee for reducing their cultivated acreage. President Franklin

Roosevelt and Secretary of Agriculture Henry Wallace hoped that when crop production decreased, prices would stabilize. The crop-reduction regulation established by the AAA irrevocably changed the face of sharecropping in the South, though not in the ways Roosevelt and Wallace anticipated.[16]

While Mitchell and East could observe the ill effects of the AAA up close in Tyronza, Amberson witnessed some of the consequences from afar. Despite feeble attempts by the AAA to enforce a stipulation that sharecroppers not be forced off the land, planters immediately began serving eviction notices. After reviewing the AAA contracts, Amberson wrote to Norman Thomas that the planters were instructed to keep sharecroppers on the land "so far as possible." To Amberson, this constituted a "loophole as wide as the Mississippi River through which many plantation owners are moving to reduce the number of tenants." Thomas replied that the only thing standing between thousands of sharecroppers and near starvation was the landlords' "good faith." Thomas knew most planters would take the check and cut their sharecroppers loose. In mid-January 1934, a sharecropper and his family on Arkansas's Twist Plantation received a terse letter stating, "You are hereby notified that we demand that you quit, and deliver to us the possession of [the plot] now occupied by you on or before January 21 1934." This notice gave the cropper and his family only five days to vacate.[17]

By booting sharecroppers off their land, landowners were able to comply with the AAA's acreage-reduction program while hoarding the full federal payment they received for keeping the land fallow. In time, Amberson came to hold local AAA officials personally responsible for the mass eviction of croppers and possessed little faith that the New Deal agency would be able to do anything to reverse the wrongs perpetrated against landless farmers. Amberson expressed his displeasure in a searing critique of the New Deal in a 1935 article for the *Nation*. The Department of Agriculture "can get adequate investigations neither through its county agents, who, though technically competent, are yet unskilled in social relationships and closely bound to the landlords, nor through the hurried trips of harassed minor officials inspecting scattered cases on the run and unfamiliar with local situations." Amberson understood the situation the Depression had created. "In times of economic distress," he concluded, "we see the feeble hold of legal forms."[18]

Mitchell and East met with Amberson to address ways to help sharecroppers. By then Amberson was a member of the LID and chairman of the Committee for the Defense of Southern Sharecroppers, an advocacy organization affiliated with the American Civil Liberties Union. For months Amberson kept up constant communication with AAA officials and the sheriff in Poinsett County, pleading with both to stop sharecropper evictions. Neither tactic worked. Encouraged by the national headquarters of LID, an organization that promoted left-leaning democratic and socialist ideals, the three compiled a report on the conditions around Tyronza and other locales in the Delta. Amberson developed a detailed questionnaire card, asking sharecroppers about income, crops, housing, and treatment by landlords. When not traveling into the Delta himself, Amberson enlisted the help of Mitchell, East, and ex-sharecroppers to go house to house filling in the cards for the illiterate. Roughly five hundred sharecroppers participated.[19]

Strolling through the hobo haunts in downtown Memphis, Amberson befriended former sharecroppers seeking refuge in the city, hitting up passersby for their next meal. One panhandler in particular, Buck Jones, proved especially valuable to Amberson's research in the Delta. Ex-cropper Jones, Amberson figured, was someone who could infiltrate plantations without raising too many suspicions. Even though Jones was a northerner, he could speak the language of sharecroppers and certainly play the part. "Jones is a Michigan boy who 'lost his crop' last fall," explained Amberson. "He begged me for food on the streets of Memphis, having had nothing to eat for 24 hours." Amberson sent Jones to Oscar Johnston's sprawling Delta Pine and Land Company in Mississippi. Despite the name, Johnston, who was a Mississippi official in the U.S. Department of Agriculture, ran his operation as a plantation. Amberson specifically targeted Johnston because of his ties to the federal government. If he could paint Johnston as not abiding by AAA contracts, he would have a compelling case to take to the public and the courts. In Mississippi, Jones operated like a spy, clandestinely interviewing sharecroppers and taking pictures of empty shacks. Jones knew it was dangerous work and that he was "sitting on a box of powder with the fuse all ready to light." Once Johnston caught wind that a stranger was in the area asking suspicious questions of his sharecroppers, he had Jones arrested and jailed for several hours. Deputies attempted to extract information, pointing a pistol in his face while they demanded to know the names of his associates. Jones responded like a captured partisan, refusing to tell the authorities anything of substance except that he was there on orders from the American Socialist Party. Frustrated, the sheriff let him go. Jones was relieved and hoped "not to see any more guns for awhile."[20]

Emboldened by Jones's findings and despite his many obligations as an academic, Amberson threw himself headlong into the sharecropper research project, traveling throughout the Arkansas and Mississippi river deltas, interviewing landless farmers and enlisting the aid of national reformers to publicize their dismal situation. With the fire of a zealot, Amberson garnered a reputation as "the angry Prometheus of the sharecroppers' original revolt." Amberson, East, and Robert W. O'Brien, professor of sociology at Le Moyne College for Negroes, set up an official tour of Johnston's Delta Pine and Land Company. Not knowing that the troublemaker Jones had worked for Amberson, Johnston agreed to the delegation's visit. While stopped for lunch at a restaurant in Scott, Mississippi, the local sheriff arrested all three. The sheriff told the group that they were detained on suspicion of being John Dillinger's gang who were currently making headlines while on the lam for robbing banks and murdering police officers. The indignant Amberson considered this an excuse to round up outsiders who might be rousing trouble among the rural poor. They were released from jail when Amberson produced a written letter from Oscar Johnston and the plantation owner came down to retrieve them, but not before they came to a clear understanding of the dangers that awaited them in the Deep South if they drew attention to the plight of sharecroppers.[21]

The interviews and questionnaires Amberson gathered on his trips into Mississippi and Arkansas represented an overwhelming indictment of planters and the AAA. Amberson conveyed a straightforward account of his encounters with sharecroppers. "We have interviewed dozens of families who have been evicted, or in whose hands there are eviction notices," informed Amberson. "Many other families have been forced to move by pressure and intimidation, without service of papers. Most of these people are still living in the country, some in tents, some in abandoned houses, a few in such miserable shelters as corn-cribs and cotton houses. Many of them have drifted into the cities and towns, where they are dependent on direct federal relief." Norman Thomas published Amberson's findings in *The Plight of the Share-Cropper*. The Associated Press picked up his findings and printed them in newspapers and magazines across the country. Nowhere else in America, wrote Thomas, "is life on the average so completely without comfort for the present or hope for the future as among the share-croppers of the South." The results of Amberson's research led Thomas to increase the Socialist Party's focus on the South and inspired Mitchell and East to launch a collective bargaining union for sharecroppers. Amberson also mailed the results of the survey to Henry Wallace and other officials in the AAA. Despite handwringing and promises to investigate, government officials proved unhelpful.[22]

Inspired by Amberson's report and the ineffectual attempts by the AAA to stop evictions, Mitchell and East decided that the only way to directly aid sharecroppers was to organize them. In July 1934, when Hiram Norcross, a planter and local AAA official near Tyronza, expelled many of his tenants, Mitchell and East held an interracial meeting with several of the evicted croppers and officially formed the first chapter of the STFU. The union grew out of deep convictions of egalitarianism and drew on long traditions of rural African American organizing based on the family and the church. The STFU soon garnered the interest of liberals and radicals around the country, including clergyman Ward Rogers, a white graduate of Vanderbilt; his roommate, the charismatic preacher-activist Howard "Buck" Kester; and African American itinerant preachers E. B. McKinney and Owen Whitfield. The principal organizers called for interracial meetings, rallies, and strikes throughout the lower Arkansas and Mississippi river deltas, harvesting hostility from white planters and law enforcement officers. The STFU proved to be one of the notable exceptions to the paucity of labor organizing in the rural South.[23]

Many sharecroppers were eager to join the Socialist Party and the STFU when Mitchell, East, and other grassroots organizers ventured into Delta communities. Although labor movements and socialism had mainly lain dormant in Arkansas since the 1920s, the STFU found old activist networks through which to recruit new members. Socialists focused their recruiting pitches on one group of disaffected southerners in particular, southern Populists. Recently defeated in elections across the region, southern Populists were predisposed to join the Socialist Party as it moved southward. Targeting agrarian workers, socialists had made significant headway in parts of the Cotton Belt, including Arkansas and Mississippi, during the first two decades of the twentieth century. Efforts by socialists to recruit rural southerners were so successful that by 1937, when Prentice Thomas, a law student, STFU intern, and eventual lawyer for the NAACP, toured the Mississippi Delta, he was surprised to hear sharecroppers speak of socialism. In a letter to a sympathetic Farm Security Administration official, Thomas wrote that he was "surprised to learn that Marx and Engels are not wholly unknown here."[24]

Socialists had also established a handful of viable cooperative communities in the South. By the time the STFU organized, most of the communities had folded, but the living memory of these socialist colonies was fresh. Although socialist communalism came to America in 1825 with the founding of New Harmony, Indiana, by the Welshman Robert Owen, the rather hasty fracturing of the community and its Owenite sister communities led many cooperative supporters to abandon the socialist model. But the 1890s saw a resurgence in socialism as a political movement, which also resuscitated socialist communalism. The most successful of these communities was the Ruskin Cooperative Colony in Tennessee, founded in 1894. But like the Owenite communities seventy years prior, Ruskin eventually collapsed under the weight of individual grudges and intransigence. Only five years after the colony's founding, and struggling financially, colonists sold the Tennessee farm and relocated to rural Georgia to start anew. By 1901, the Georgia site and all the colony's assets were sold at auction to pay off farm debts.[25]

Arkansas socialists could also point to a contemporary experiment in cooperative socialism in the Deep South. The New Llano colony in Louisiana had emerged from the failed Llano Del Rio Cooperative near Los Angeles. While socialist cooperative communalism was quite common around the country in the late 1800s and early 1900s, New Llano and its California predecessor were extremely influential in the cooperative movement of the 1930s. From 1918 to 1938, because of the popularity of the colony's weekly newspaper, the *Llano Colonist*, New Llano acted as the intellectual hub of the cooperative movement in America. Publishing articles on international cooperatives, particularly in the Soviet Union, the *Llano Colonist* spread the popularity of socialist colonies around the country. The paper solicited articles from other colonies, and reciprocal networks emerged as a result. Through the pages of the *Llano Colonist*, cooperative communities across the country traded everything from advice to produced goods.[26]

The race question in the South, however, confounded American socialists. While their communist counterparts, after 1920, suggested that southern African Americans were a nation unto themselves, deserving of autonomy and full citizenship, socialists dithered on the issue, fearing the loss of white support or an all-out race war. Many white southern socialists treated African Americans much as their Democratic counterparts did—as workers in need of controlling, who had no business in the American political process. It was clear to northern socialists that the Socialist Party could successfully recruit southern African Americans only by removing Jim Crow from the equation, a task many socialists were not committed to undertaking.[27]

By the 1930s, however, prodded by the fear of losing membership to the Communist Party and emboldened by the liberal New Deal, southern socialists such as Mitchell and East saw interracial organizing as a route to success in the South. They believed, however, that STFU locals should be integrated not because of socialist ideology per se, but because of the need to communicate effectively and efficiently. "There couldn't have been much understanding if we had two unions," explained East, because it would have taken twice as long to hold segregated meetings. Organizers held initial meetings where they felt safe and where they thought they could reach the most sharecroppers—black churches and schoolhouses.[28]

Shortly after the STFU's founding, Mitchell informed Amberson that local planters were incensed by the new union meetings, particularly when they involved black members. "Norcross' manager Alex East has notified the negroes," reported Mitchell, "that their church and school buildings were going to (be) filled with hay and locked up if any more Union meetings were held." Over the next few months, tensions increased. When one white STFU member asked to borrow a wagon at the Norcross Plantation, the planter refused and questioned the man's racial loyalty for joining the union. When the sharecropper threatened to "slap the old devil," Norcross's manager, Alex East, drew a gun on the man. Mitchell wrote to Amberson that "Hell may break loose at any time."[29]

Threats of personal defamation and violence became more common. Amberson wrote an open letter published in the Memphis *Commercial Appeal* defending himself against slander that he was a communist revolutionary. Amberson, in fact, loathed communists. C. T. Carpenter, the STFU's attorney, hired armed guards to protect his house beginning in March 1935 after he was accused of being a communist and received threats. Nevertheless, the STFU continued to organize black and white sharecroppers and conducted integrated meetings whenever possible. Out of pragmatic necessity and after years of false starts and halfhearted gestures, socialists in Arkansas committed themselves to organizing interracial union locals.[30]

Southern interracial movements existed decades before the founding of Delta Cooperative Farm. The most prominent endeavors were Christian-oriented organizations such as the Association of Southern Women for the Prevention of Lynching and the Commission on Interracial Cooperation. While organizations like these pushed important conversations about race in America and had some practical successes to show for it, they were often plagued by a lack of black involvement and persistent white paternalism. Perhaps where southern interracial cooperation was most successful, and certainly most radical, was in labor unions of the late nineteenth and early twentieth centuries. From the Alabama coalfields to the Louisiana docks, unions organized black and white workers together as a unified front against exploitation.[31]

In the 1930s, unlike previous decades, labor union organizers had measured national support. The onset of the Depression focused the nation's sympathetic attention on poverty and labor. Hired by the Roosevelt administration to evoke compassion, photographers like Dorothea Lange and Walker Evans plied their trade around the region, taking pictures that would become iconic. Lange visited Delta Cooperative Farm in 1936 and photographed men working in the fields, an African American STFU organizer, and a biracial Fourth of July picnic. Mostly, though, Lange photographed the heartrending side of the 1930s. Through these photographs, the rural American became the hollow-eyed human face of the Depression. Franklin Roosevelt's New Deal zeroed in on those faces, and many government programs attempted to alleviate the gut-wrenching poverty experienced by rural southerners. If the New Deal could uplift the South, it could surely raise the entire nation out of ruin.[32]

This national attention gave the STFU a profile that previous rural labor unions in the South lacked. Rural Americans, particularly sharecroppers, were hit hardest by the Great Depression. Left behind by the prosperous 1920s, already struggling dirt farmers suffered from falling crop prices. As more and more farmers were evicted from the land, makeshift communities sprang up all over the rural and urban United States. Many large farms went into debt and foreclosed while sharecroppers and tenant farmers spiraled further into poverty and malnutrition. Attitudes toward labor changed dramatically during the 1930s and 1940s, although southern planters never fully accepted unionization of their laborers. Planters attempted to maintain their labor force through violence and other forms of intimidation. For a time, though, the STFU was able to take advantage of national sympathy for the sharecropper. New Deal liberals, who knew that the Agricultural Adjustment Act's stipulation of removing land from production to stabilize prices would hurt sharecroppers, debated the fate of landless farmers. Socialist sharecroppers in Arkansas seized the moment, formed the STFU, staged roadside pickets, and filed lawsuits on behalf of their members.

As the old labor and racial systems of the rural South further crumbled, cooperative models of labor and planned communities were tested by groups as disparate as religiously motivated utopian colonists and the federal government's Resettlement Administration, an umbrella bureaucratic program that placed the government in the role of landlord over rural agriculturalists in communities throughout the country. After all, Delta Cooperative Farm was only a few miles from the Dixie Plantation, a Resettlement Administration colony, and Providence Farm shared Holmes County with an all-black cooperative community named Mileston that later led the way in organizing Holmes County civil rights activists.

Many government and philanthropic individuals were inspired in the 1930s to pursue cooperative communalism by the emerging back-to-the-land movement. In the late 1920s and early 1930s, several groups promoted measures that repudiated industrial society in favor of living closer to the land. The philosophies of the Nashville Agrarians and the proclamations of the Rural Life Movement found popularity across the country as alternatives to what many Americans saw as the deprivations of urban life. Perhaps most influential to burgeoning ideas of rural homesteading among federal employees was New Yorker Ralph Borsodi. Borsodi and his family, having given up their home in Manhattan, moved to seven acres in rural New York and began living off the land. While the Agrarians "wrote about rural simplicity with great verve and imagination," Borsodi was willing to eschew his urbanite trappings and live "the aesthetic and spiritual satisfactions of rural life." In 1933, Borsodi published the influential book *Flight from the City* and began espousing his vision for rural homesteads to acquaintances in the federal government. While his personal involvement in government-backed homesteads was short lived, his ideas had a lasting influence on New Deal liberals and back-to-the-land movements.[33]

The crisis of the Great Depression, the rising popularity of the back-to-the-land movement, and the willingness of the New Deal to address that crisis through highly proscribed collectivism meant that the 1930s witnessed a boom in cooperative communalism. Drawing on an "inherited philosophy of agrarianism" that stretched back to Thomas Jefferson, the federal government sought to make the belief in the agrarian ideal a reality more so than any previous government endeavor save for the Homestead Act of 1862. The New Deal created approximately one hundred communities that directly affected nearly fifty thousand people. The Federal Emergency Relief Administration, the Division of Subsistence Homesteads, and the Resettlement Administration created the bulk of the colonies. They emerged all over the country, from Arkansas's Dyess Colony to Alaska's Matanuska Colony. Depending on local resources, governance, and which New Deal program they were associated with, there was often great operational diversity from colony to colony. Most communities, however, operated as cooperatives. Some experiments, like the highly successful Greenbelt community in Maryland, organized around consumer cooperatives. Other colonies functioned as producers' cooperatives. Dyess was typical of New Deal colonies because it was organized as a farming producers' cooperative that grew crops to be sold by the community at large. Still other communities diversified their producers' cooperatives by relying on local resources and distinctive knowledge. Gee's Bend, Alabama, a New Deal project, founded a wildly successful quilting cooperative.[34]

Although ubiquitous in the 1930s, cooperative labor communities were not foregone conclusions for fixing the country's economic woes. In the United States, where the national ethos of rugged individualism stood in stark contrast to communitarian-style cooperation, planned communities faced outside ambivalence and internal cleavages. Even at Delta and Providence, collective labor often proved as untenable as sharecropping. Unhappy with their meager dividends, many cooperative members complained to the trustees or left the endeavor completely. Although the moment was rife with hope that the farms would usher in a new kind of collective labor in the rural South, the difficulties of interracial, socialized labor presented at Delta and Providence proved vexing.

Still, thousands of poor black and white southerners took advantage of the opportunities that New Deal programs offered. Early in the Depression, even southern politicians apprehensive of federal intervention were convinced that their constituents needed help. That support would not last. Increased federal presence in public programs around the South meant a liberalization of social policies that the South had glimpsed only a few times in its history. While some of the rural poor found employment in Roosevelt's relief programs such as the Civilian Conservation Corp, others found aid in privately funded endeavors, like Delta and Providence, many of which proposed to go further in their social agendas than had the federal government. The Resettlement Administration, for example, refused to integrate its communities in the South, while Delta and Providence were open to both black and white residents.

At first officials in the federal government offered tepid support for the STFU, but after a shake-up in the AAA in 1935 the Department of Agriculture was no friend of interracial unionism. U.S. courts dismissed lawsuits brought by the STFU because the farmers were not considered direct parties to the contract between the Department of Agriculture and the landowners. Bolstered by the support of the courts and the AAA's inaction, planters evicted members of the STFU from their farms en masse, and local law enforcement officers began arresting union members and, in some cases, forcing them into peonage. The organized strikes that followed further enraged planters and resulted in additional mass evictions.

These setbacks, however, nurtured mounting interest in interracial farming cooperatives and prompted more reformers to join Amberson, Mitchell, and East in the fight to assist the sharecropper. Amberson convinced scores of his reform-minded contemporaries that the plight of the sharecropper was worsening under the New Deal and that something had to be done. One concerned observer important to Delta's eventual formation was the energetic and idealistic missionary Sam Franklin. Franklin, recently returned from a mission in Japan, was eager to bring his socialist activism and practical Christianity to the American South, eventually linking transnational human rights movements to Delta Cooperative Farm.[35]

Sam H. Franklin Jr. was born in 1902 in rural Tennessee and grew up on a farm near Knoxville. He attended Maryville College, McCormick Theological Seminary in Illinois, and the University of Edinburgh in Scotland. In the 1930s, he was ordained in the Presbyterian Church and left for a five-year mission in Kyoto, Japan. There, Franklin and his wife Dorothy witnessed deplorable conditions of the poor that "forced us to rethink our faith in a way that came to terms with social tragedy and injustice." In Japan, Franklin also met Presbyterian missionary Sherwood Eddy, who denounced Japanese imperialism and atrocities in the Sino-Japanese War. At Eddy's suggestion, the Franklins decided to take a furlough from missionary work in Japan and returned to the United States in 1934.[36]

While stateside, Franklin took graduate courses at Union Theological Seminary in New York City where he studied with influential theologian Reinhold

Niebuhr and again came into contact with Eddy. Eddy invited Franklin to become his assistant and travel the country as "a lecturer and preacher at large." This was exactly the opportunity Franklin wanted as he and Dorothy reflected on their time in Japan and decided whether they wanted to return. While traveling in January 1936, he met with William Amberson, H. L. Mitchell, and other officials from the STFU in Memphis to discuss cooperative models that Franklin had experienced firsthand in Japan and on mission trips with Eddy in Europe. Amberson brought the southern sharecroppers' plight to the young missionary's attention, and Franklin vowed to return and inspect the situation himself. Several months later, with Amberson as his guide, Franklin found the conditions in rural Arkansas "shocking." It was January when Franklin toured the roadside communities. After years of living in rural Japan, Franklin could hardly fathom the level of poverty he observed in his own country. For a time, the images he saw in Arkansas haunted him. Although the idea took several months to germinate, Franklin looked back on his January trip as an epiphany. He and Dorothy talked extensively about the important work that could be done in the South. Since intermittent warring between China and Japan made travel to Asia nearly impossible, Franklin resigned his position as missionary with the Presbyterian Church in 1936 and headed south to put his experience to use aiding sharecroppers.[37]

Amberson and Franklin were not the first social justice advocates or reformers to consider cooperatives as a solution for the problems of rural America. Almost always referred to as "experiments," cooperatives possessed long—but often hidden—histories in the United States at least two centuries before Arkansas refugees broke ground at Delta Cooperative Farm. Debates over the economic path of the country regularly encouraged cooperative movements. During the late nineteenth century, the South became the epicenter of the nation's efforts with over half of all cooperative colonies established in the region. North Carolinian Clarence Poe, for example, editor of the *Progressive Farmer*, was an advocate of the Populist and cooperative movements that swept through the countryside in the 1880s and 1890s. Populists, and the Farmers' Alliance before them, encouraged credit, purchasing, diary, and feed cooperatives in rural America. In the pages of the *Progressive Farmer*, Poe entertained the idea of reorganizing farming communities based on the cooperative principle. Most often, reform came from agriculturalists, like Poe, deeply rooted in Jeffersonian ideals, who railed against the changes wrought by modernization that eroded the position of agriculturalists.[38]

The political mobilization that shaped the era came mostly from farmers in the South and West, but support for cooperative farms in the early twentieth-century United States also drew inspiration from international sources. From his experience on missions in Japan and traveling to Russia with Sherwood Eddy, Sam Franklin had firsthand knowledge of international attempts at cooperatives. He brought that familiarity to Delta. Ultimately, cooperative farming initiatives that emerged in the United States during the New Deal, like Delta, had polyglot origins. Indeed, according to historian Daniel T. Rodgers, international reform currents, as much as the Great Depression, begat the New Deal. American reformers' interests in European cooperatives culminated in the formation of the New Deal's Resettlement Administration.[39]

STFU officials were well aware of the transatlantic cooperative methods. As early as 1934, Amberson and Mitchell discussed the possibility of organizing large cooperative plantations run collectively by former sharecroppers and hoped to earn the interest and aid of the Federal Emergency Relief Administration. Mitchell also endorsed the Rochdale Plan, a cooperative store model first envisioned in Rochdale, England, in the 1840s, as a possibility in Tyronza. Seeking an escape from insufferable working circumstances and squalid living conditions, nineteenth-century flannel weavers in Rochdale had started a cooperative store for the local working-class community. After its initial failure, a more diverse group of workers began a second cooperative store in the mid-1840s called the Rochdale Equitable Pioneers Society. The success of the cooperative store, as the only viable model for the penniless, was evident as similar initiatives took root across urban and rural Europe. Through cooperative advocates at home and abroad, the popularity of the Rochdale Plan eventually wound its way across the Atlantic.[40]

Foreshadowing what Sam Franklin would later start at Delta Cooperative Farm, Mitchell wrote Amberson about the Rochdale model and displayed a firm stance on the importance of the endeavor. "Clay [East] has had an idea that we might establish a co-operative store later on," wrote Mitchell. "Will you please have Co-op League send me details, I have heard of the Rochdale plan and understand that it is the only successful plan now in operation. We would have to have financing if it should be established anytime soon because as you know the share-croppers would hardly have funds enough at one time to take even a $5 share. . . . It is important that the co-operative store idea be developed for in the time of Revolutionary crisis a strong Co-operative system could feed the workers before the capitalist system of distribution could be rearranged." By the time Sam Franklin visited Amberson in Memphis in January 1936, the Memphis socialist and the STFU had decided that any cooperative farm they supported would operate on the Rochdale model.[41]

The emerging cooperative farms in Mississippi also shared a link with transpacific rural reform initiatives, and in some ways Japan's influence was even more direct than Rochdale's. Not long after arriving in Japan, Sam Franklin met Toyohiko Kagawa in Kobe. A Christian Socialist reformer and cooperative supporter, Kagawa was drawn to help rural Japanese at the height of the Depression. For Kagawa, rural lives had been destroyed by the atrocities wrought by a modernizing and industrializing Japan. For over thirteen years, Kagawa lived in the slums of Kobe in a small room that he sometimes shared with outcast residents of the slum, contracting diseases and facing arrests for "his fearless vindication of the rights of labor." Sherwood Eddy and Kagawa, whom Eddy called "the Christian Gandhi of Japan," had a working relationship that dated back to the 1910s when Kagawa was a student at Princeton and Eddy footed the bill for Kagawa's mission work. In Japan, Kagawa and Franklin were close associates.[42]

In the early 1930s, Kagawa set his vision of cooperatives to work in Japan and asserted that "through them the economic salvation of Japan could be effected." In the midst of a rural depression and on the heels of one of the worst famines in modern Japanese history, Kagawa preached the gospel of agricultural cooperatives throughout the countryside. Kagawa's experiences in the Kobe slums, involvement with some of Japan's first labor unions, crusades for rural reform, and passionate religious beliefs made him a particularly compelling figure for Franklin and other reformers all over the world. Admirers saw Kagawa as a mystic, a prophet who tapped into the gemeinschaft of the rural Japanese to create successful cooperatives at a time when Japan experienced heavy-handed government repression. To help drum up support for cooperatives around the world, Kagawa traveled to the United States in the mid-1930s. In 1936, Franklin received a letter from a friend in Wisconsin who enthusiastically anticipated Kagawa's visit and declared that the cooperative movement would soon sweep the nation.[43]

Sam Franklin's epiphany in Arkansas in January and his knowledge of international cooperative movements impressed Amberson and set into motion events that led to the formation of Delta Cooperative Farm less than four months later. Amberson had connections in Arkansas that could funnel destitute croppers to the farm and Franklin had the practical know-how to get cooperative farming operations under way. One last piece of the puzzle remained: funding. Franklin's close friend and mentor, Sherwood Eddy, often used a trust fund for worthy humanitarian initiatives and was trusted and admired by many wealthy philanthropists. Franklin knew that it was imperative for Eddy to come to Arkansas and see the devastated lives of sharecroppers firsthand. He hoped that Eddy would be moved to action. Eddy's arrival in Arkansas and his subsequent desire to help sharecroppers ensured that the envisioned cooperative community would be backed by his extensive funding networks.

Born in 1871 on the edge of the American West in Leavenworth, Kansas,

George Sherwood Eddy inherited wealth and a luxurious lifestyle from his parents. He attended Harvard, Princeton, and Union Theological Seminary in New York before setting off for his first missionary trip to India in 1896. His subsequent years as national secretary of the YMCA included continued missionary work in Asia, Europe, and the United States. As a Presbyterian missionary, Eddy witnessed firsthand the horrors of warfare around the world and vowed to devote his life to rooting out the evil that caused such bloody conflicts. Just before he turned his attention to the lives of the sharecropper in 1936, Eddy wrote, "I was driven in my pilgrimage of ideas to the inescapable conclusion that capitalism is doomed. I as a radical," Eddy continued, "must seek to build a completely new order. To seek by every reform the improvement of the lot of the workers and farmers, the employed and unemployed; and to begin to build, here and now, a new social order, using every possible means of education and of coercion short of the destruction of life by war, whether civil or international." Eddy saw socialism and the Gospel of Jesus as balms for the suffering world. Foreshadowing his work with the cooperative farm, Eddy declared in 1934 that "to build an economic and ethical society under socialism, I would push forward the triple organization of workers, consumers and voters."[44]

Through publishing and missionary work, Eddy and other reform-minded theologians set out to alter the way Christians expressed their faith. He and Reinhold Niebuhr "were deeply concerned with how to make Christianity relevant to an increasingly secular society and how to get Christians to think socially." Eddy hoped that Christians would use "personal faith as a foundation for social action," and would contribute their time, labor, and money to those less fortunate or in need.[45]

Eddy's Social Christianity had roots equally in the United States and abroad in the half century between Reconstruction and the New Deal. Social Christian activist James Dombrowski credited multiple circumstances for the creation of Social Christianity in America. But for Dombrowski, one factor caused the most important and dramatic developments. After the Civil War, the growth of organized labor activity, and the power gained by labor unions, pressured ministers and theologians in the United States and Europe to develop a Christian-based philosophy that incorporated support for social movements. Labor leaders criticized ministers who, they believed, encouraged their flocks to be complacent, docile workers resigned to their lot in a stratified society. Sociologist Liston Pope, for example, famously criticized the role that local churches played in supporting mill owners in Gastonia, North Carolina, during the 1940s. Labor unionists and ministers alike argued that American churches were in danger of being rendered obsolete by the growing popularity of labor organizations. The development of Social Christianity was a way for churches to be relevant in the altered American economic and political landscape.[46]

Gradually, some churches and seminaries, particularly in the North where labor unions were strongest, adopted the tenets of Social Christianity. These churches proved instrumental in spreading Social Christianity to Americans in the late 1800s. Seminaries at Princeton, Harvard, Andover, and Union in New York pushed the notion that tithing and charity work were no longer sufficient. Direct social justice advocacy was necessary to create the Kingdom of Heaven on Earth. At the turn of the century, the term "Social Gospel" gained wide use as a catchphrase for the burgeoning Social Christianity. In the American South and West, Social Gospel practitioners made headway through public health initiatives, settlement houses, and national organizations like the YMCA.[47]

Students and faculty who passed through New York's Union Theological Seminary were particularly influential in developing and reworking the Social Gospel. Union became the epicenter for the teaching of social ethics and exploring the divine plan and man's role in it. Sherwood Eddy first suggested Union hire Reinhold Niebuhr, one of the country's prominent theologians. Having no budget for a new position, Union balked until Eddy offered to pay Niebuhr's salary in the first year. During the interwar years, Niebuhr became one of Union's most influential and renowned teachers when he developed a course on social ethics that promoted the idea that "moral idealism" would save Western civilization. As a result of their close friendship and similar worldview, Eddy's and Niebuhr's brands of Social Christianity often evolved in tandem. Although at first Niebuhr furthered the espousal of liberal Christian idealism perhaps more than any other instructor at Union, he would begin to change his views in the late 1920s, inching ever closer toward socialism, taking Eddy with him.[48]

Throughout the development of the Social Gospel in America, invested observers noticed troubling shortcomings. For Eddy, Niebuhr, and other leftist Christians, a sense of futility set in. The positivist belief that society inched ever closer to utopian equality and that this perfection could be attained through continued moral suasion struck many radicals as naïve. Through their belief in the triumphant arc of history, liberal Social Christians adhered to pacifism and clung to their staunch belief that middle-class morals would save society. Liberal Christians had become complacent, Niebuhr believed, and written the historical function of sin out of their theology by sentimentalizing the Gospel of Jesus. The tragedy of history, as Niebuhr saw it, was that the working classes suffered brutal fates at the hands of a capitalist system run amok. Sin was all around us. To Niebuhr, liberal Christian doctrine was too self-congratulatory, was too wedded to capitalism, and made no real long-term progress at alleviating the problems of the poor. For Eddy and Niebuhr, like Union student-cum-socialist-politician Norman Thomas, their Christian Socialist ideology gave way to more applied approaches to their activism and faith.[49]

By the 1930s, both Eddy and Niebuhr noted the Social Gospel's deficiencies and moved to the far left of American politics. Niebuhr joined the American Socialist Party and the Fellowship of Social Christians while rejecting the pacifism of his old friends in the Fellowship of Reconciliation, a transatlantic pacifist organization that grew out of the horrors of World War I. In 1932, Niebuhr published *Moral Man and Immoral Society,* in which he ridiculed liberal Christianity and the old Social Gospel for being hopelessly naïve. The world demanded more aggressive measures, Niebuhr counseled. At this stage in his life, Niebuhr was an avowed Marxian socialist and Christian realist, lambasting capitalism, idealism, and pacifism.[50]

Taking a less doctrinaire—although no less uncompromising—tack, Eddy was similarly displeased with the inadequate state of Christian volunteerism and apathy toward the poor exhibited by most Americans. In his public speeches and publications he frequently displayed his socialist inclination while admonishing a complacent society for its lack of charity. He wrote in 1927 that "our social order is characterized by gross inequality of privilege; vast wealth unshared, side by side with poverty unrelieved; flagrant luxury and waste confronted by unemployment, poverty and want; costly homes and resorts for the rich, and reeking slums and disgraceful housing conditions for the poor." Eddy's mission work and extensive world traveling convinced him that humans were social creatures and religion was a social experience. "Love thy neighbor as thyself" and the parable of the Good Samaritan "who went out to bind up bruised and bleeding humanity" were Eddy's lessons wherever he traveled. Religion, Eddy demanded, must be dynamic, practical, and attentive to the brutality of human existence—what he and Niebuhr called "Christian Realism." Despite his wealth, Eddy condemned the privileged who would not better humanity by giving of their time and resources. Although he suggested personal lifestyle changes, his true goal was a complete overhaul of the social order, a redistribution of wealth, egalitarian race relations, and international peace.[51]

Niebuhr's and Eddy's newfound Christian Realism strongly influenced Christian-inclined social activists, particularly those who came through Union Theological Seminary. Among Christian realists, Niebuhr was notably moderate on the issue of race, yet his teachings on practical egalitarianism were translated by others into the espousal of racial equality. In spite of Niebuhr's ambivalence, Social Christians' commitment to overcoming racial inequality ran deep.

A movement of socially conscientious Christians in the 1930s was made up of mostly white clergy and black reformers who felt compelled to tackle issues of race and race relations. Howard Kester saw in Delta Cooperative Farm Niebuhr's espousal of practical Christianity wedded to social equality. Kester, one of Niebuhr's most radical understudies and a future STFU organizer, was a staunch believer in racial equality. Eddy, too, hoped to wipe out racism. "I will seek justice for every man without distinction of race or color," he wrote. "Especially I will strive for the fuller opportunity for the self-advancement of Negroes, Orientals, and all exploited races, seeking legal protection against lynching, and against all racial discrimination." Unlike Kester, Eddy and Niebuhr were intellectual peers and their theology often developed together. One of Niebuhr's closest friends and allies, Eddy developed Niebuhr's ideas about Christian Realism and put them into practice around the world, first in Asia, then in the cotton fields of the South. Through international missions, Eddy and others modeled an egalitarian form of Social Christianity that proved to be a precursor to Liberation Theology. This specific brand of the Social Gospel trickled down from Niebuhr to Eddy to Sam Franklin. As late as 1943, Franklin believed that the farms had put into practice a "sternly realistic" Christian philosophy in the Mississippi Delta that he believed eschewed "optimistic humanism [and] the psycho-pathic tendencies that threaten modern reformers." Franklin brought Kagawa's cooperative teachings to Delta, blended them with the Rochdale model, allied them with Amberson's socialist values, and wed them to Eddy's vision of dynamic Social Christianity.[52]

Sam Franklin's meeting with William Amberson and the other STFU officials in January 1936 began a complicated alliance of men with strong convictions and stubborn personalities. In late February 1936, Eddy arrived in Memphis where he met Franklin and Amberson. Any of the men present at the meeting could have ended up elsewhere, Amberson continuing to rally Memphis's unemployed, Franklin heading back to Asia as a missionary, and Eddy globe-trotting around the world preaching Christian Realism. Yet a sense of social and spiritual responsibility, empathy for sharecroppers, hubris, and a taste for adventure led all three across the Mississippi River and into the Arkansas bottomlands. Together they decided that the best way to acquaint Eddy with the sharecroppers' situation was to take a driving tour of the Arkansas Delta. The three men set out with inventor Mack Rust, who had developed a mechanical cotton picker and was interested in improving the lives of sharecroppers and cooperative farming methods, and Jack Byer, a reporter from the *Memphis Press-Scimitar*. During this trip a vision for collective cooperative farms began to coalesce.[53]

In a tumultuous and revelatory road trip that predated a similarly revealing journey taken by Agriculture Secretary Henry A. Wallace in the fall of 1936, the group toured Arkansas and observed evicted sharecroppers living in makeshift tents on the side of the road, some fleeing for their lives after being threatened for joining the STFU. Recalling the trip years later, Eddy labeled what he saw as "aspects of slavery, feudalism, and Fascism in the attitude of the planters and the landowners toward the evicted sharecroppers and tenant farmers, black and white." As the men traveled the area, speaking with displaced sharecroppers and learning of retribution lynchings, powerful whites also threatened the group. In Cross County, the local sheriff treated the carload to a few hours in a makeshift jail in a cotton warehouse for, as the sheriff saw it, stirring up trouble among black sharecroppers. As they sat detained in the warehouse, "a score of planters and men off the streets" came by to relay what they deemed "the truth about these damned niggers who won't work." Local whites told Amberson, Eddy, and Franklin that any black sharecroppers the group spoke with would be stricken with "sudden pneumonia," a euphemism for lynching, unless the three men left the Delta immediately.[54]

In Eddy's account of their travels, threatening whites evoked the specter of the bloody massacre that took place fifteen years earlier in Elaine, Arkansas. Radical changes in the Deep South had long been a dangerous undertaking. A 1919 massacre in Phillips County, Arkansas—only a few miles from the Mississippi border—served as a chilling notice of how far white supremacists in the Delta would go to keep Jim Crow and plantation labor intact. African American sharecroppers in and around the community of Elaine joined the Progressive Farmers and Household Union of America in an attempt to improve their bargaining power and share in rising wartime cotton prices. Before the operation could gather momentum, white planters broke up sharecroppers' meetings. After several white Phillips County residents exchanged fire with black guards outside a union meeting, deputized planters and federal troops fresh from the trenches of Western Europe roamed the county's towns and countryside looking for "insurrectionists" and engaging in bloody standoffs. Black and white veterans on both sides of the massacre remembered those events as a cautionary tale fifteen years later when the new STFU set to work organizing in Arkansas. Throughout the Delta, labor and civil rights organizing was perilous business, even in the New Deal's relatively labor-friendly milieu.[55]

The sheriff released the men after Eddy was permitted to send a telegram to his former college roommate, U.S. Attorney General Homer S. Cummings. The arrest and threats only increased Eddy's and Franklin's resolve to help the men and women living under the harsh conditions of sharecropping. "If it were the last act of our lives," Eddy declared, "if it took the last dollar we possessed; if we were ever to respect ourselves as American citizens, we could not accept this disgraceful situation 'lying down,' nor leave this shame and blot upon the honor of our country without doing all in our power to remove it." Both Eddy and Franklin had traveled extensively in Europe and Asia spreading the gospel as Presbyterian missionaries, lured from their homes to far corners of the world because they felt compelled to help where their work was needed the most, but never had they experienced a situation like the one they found in Arkansas. On this southern journey, Eddy and Franklin decided to lend their skills to Amberson's plans to help the sharecropper, not so much out of "divine guidance," said Eddy, "as of divine compulsion."[56]

The STFU and Amberson had ideas to purchase land in Arkansas to provide the displaced sharecroppers with a place of their own, a large plantation where land would be farmed collectively. Eddy and Franklin immediately took up the idea as the best way to blend their socialism, Christian beliefs, and commitment to the sharecropper. "We believe," preached Eddy, "that we can more nearly carry out [Jesus's] law of love through cooperative organizations than thru capitalism." Eddy decided to stay longer and find a suitable piece of land that could handle a resettlement community. Several days later, he and Amberson drove through Bolivar County, Mississippi on a tip that a large tract was for sale. There Eddy found "a gift from God"—a tract of 2,138 acres abutting the Mississippi River levee.[57]

Rather than stick their heads in the lion's mouth by starting a cooperative in Arkansas, Eddy deemed this tract in Mississippi to be the best location to create the new social order. Amberson remembered Eddy's conviction that this was the right place when they first saw the plot. "Near sundown we reached the 2,000 acre plantation which became Delta," recalled Amberson years later. "Mobley turned East on the road which runs the length of the farm. At its end he stopped and we all got out of the car. Looking toward the setting sun Eddy was in ecstasy. 'God has brought us to this place. He has guided me before. I will buy this farm as soon as possible.'" Eddy made a down payment out of his own pocket, subsequently subsidized by a trust fund set up specifically for his Social Gospel endeavors. On March 26, 1936, Eddy finalized the purchase for $17,500. One-third of the plot was ready to be cultivated, and approximately 160 acres could be timbered for the use of a Rochdale-style building cooperative. Amberson and Mitchell criticized Eddy for being hasty with his purchase and prophetically warned that if Arkansas was the lion's mouth, Mississippi was surely the lion's den. Despite these concerns, Eddy and Franklin were anxious to build their vision onto the landscape.[58]

In the late winter and early spring of 1936, Amberson, Franklin, and Eddy felt that the tides of labor and race in the South were changing. In April of that year at Lookout Mountain, Tennessee, southerners converged for the second meeting of the Southern Policy Committee (SPC), a politically liberal, purely advisory body that hoped to shape the direction of southern politics and labor practices. Some of the most influential southerners of the Depression Era, including sociologists from the University of North Carolina at Chapel Hill as well as the Vanderbilt Agrarians, represented most vocally by Allen Tate, were present at the meeting. William Amberson and officials from the STFU also attended.[59]

Discussion at the meeting centered on federal passage of legislation aimed at aiding tenant farmers—known as the Bankhead-Jones bill—and debate over small, self-sufficient homesteads versus large cooperative farms as the most viable livelihood for ex-sharecroppers. The Nashville Agrarians favored small, individually owned homesteads while the STFU favored plantation-sized cooperatives; the debate was often heated. The intellectual confrontation between Tate and Amberson that occurred at the meeting led H. L. Mitchell to later write that it was the end of "Southern Agrarianism, which had sought to turn back the pre–Civil War days of moonlight and magnolias." In a clash of ideology and practicality, Amberson thoroughly discredited Tate's romantic notions of the agrarian lifestyle as "pretty-poetry foolishness" and "nothing but a plan to reduce the people to peasantry."[60]

In an article for the *Nation*, the Tennessee socialist later expounded on his argument, saying that the individual homesteads advocated by the Agrarians were unsustainable in the present economy and a naïve throwback to the "Golden Age of the Republic." "Forty acres and a mule," said Amberson, would only produce more tenants in time. Without access to all the modern farming amenities that big planters possessed, small homesteaders would not be able to compete and the large plantations would eventually take over. "The big planter across the road," declared Amberson, "with his tractor and four row equipment and his superior credit facilities, cultivates his cotton at $5 an acre, while the mule, dragging a half-row plow, runs the bill up to over $14." "The frontier is gone," he thundered, "it is gone not only horizontally but vertically."[61]

There was, Amberson suggested, a "'middle way' for the agricultural South, steering between plantation exploitation on the one hand and the inefficiency of the small homestead on the other." Amberson's "middle way" was "large-scale cooperative farming ventures." Some bureaucrats in the Farm Security Administration agreed and established cooperative farms that were "a continuation of the plantation tradition of the South" and "represented an almost complete break with free enterprise." Amberson's suggestion was a moment of modification in how many of the major players in rural reform had approached the problems facing sharecroppers. At Lookout Mountain, all Tate could muster were feeble attempts to paint Amberson as a communist.

By the end of the impromptu debate, Amberson had won the crowd over and "even Tate's friends grinned" in support of the fiery STFU advisor. The debate at the Lookout Mountain meeting further confirmed to Amberson and his reform-minded circle that they were riding a tide of activism that would remake southern society.[62]

Yet from the outset, the founders of Delta Cooperative Farm were hampered by the reality of the endeavor not living up to the lofty plan. Most notably, African Americans were conspicuously missing from the early stages of a supposedly interracial endeavor. Although Amberson, Eddy, and Franklin informally consulted labor unionist E. B. McKinney, his assistance mostly came sporadically via correspondence. Franklin and the STFU specifically targeted African American farmers as potential inhabitants, but they did not significantly enlist blacks to contribute to the intellectual development of their endeavor. The fact that no African Americans were included as major players in the founding of Delta demonstrates the contradictions implicit in starting an interracial cooperative with only whites at the top. Once Eddy and Franklin entered the scene, establishing the farms was hasty, but ambitious. The first challenge for Amberson, Eddy, and Franklin, however, was to secure the lives of sharecropping families by moving them to the recently purchased tract of land in Mississippi.

CHAPTER 2

From the Frying Pan into the Fire

In the late winter of 1936, Sam Franklin carried the cooperative idea to a handful of starving and destitute sharecroppers in Arkansas. Franklin ducked into dilapidated, dusty cabins and makeshift tents where whole families crowded into a space meant for only two or three, to deliver a message of hope. Despite his experience in the slums of Japan, the conditions he observed in Arkansas appalled Franklin. When he visited future white cooperative member Nute Hulsey, he found a family begging for help. "In the middle of a great muddy field was a wretched shack," Franklin remembered. "There was no floor in it, but the wind, for it was February and cold found plenty of holes thru which to pour. In the center of the room sat a young woman holding a baby on her knee, its little legs covered with sores, on the floor played a beautiful three year old child and both had but one garment to cover them. Nute was not at home that day, having walked some three miles to find firewood, as he was forbidden to get any nearer the shack." Before Franklin could secure transportation for the Hulsey family to move to Delta, they were evicted from the spartan shack and spent their last few weeks in Arkansas living in a seven-by-seven tent on the banks of a muddy stream. "The hygienic conditions were so bad," regretted Franklin, that Nute and his wife had "contracted a bad skin disease." As he explained the nascent ideas for an interracial farming cooperative to the gaunt and hardened faces, their near-starving children looked up at him expectantly. For the remainder of his life, Franklin would remember the "distended stomachs of some of the little children." When the Hulseys finally moved to Delta, "not even a comb could be found to help them look more respectable."[1]

Following networks already established by the Southern Tenant Farmers'

Union (STFU), Franklin spoke to sharecropping families about Christian brotherhood, socialism, racial egalitarianism, and cooperative communalism. He assured each family that these methods were the answers to their long-standing problems under the plantation system. These meetings also acted as interviews, and Franklin, future trustee William Amberson, and STFU secretary H. L. Mitchell often decided who would make productive members of the cooperative. By visiting these sharecroppers, Franklin confronted some of the social and economic issues facing the nation's rural communities. Once Franklin deemed them suitable, he extended invitations to move to the parcel of land in the rural Mississippi Delta that Sherwood Eddy purchased only days before.

Here, Sam Franklin, a few staff and volunteers, and over two dozen sharecropper families moved in the spring of 1936 to start over. They took their stand in Mississippi, a state notorious for its lagging economy, antiquated labor practices, and harsh social and racial norms. Along the Mississippi Delta, where slavery evolved into sharecropping but cotton remained king, white and black dirt farmers often lived hand to mouth in backbreaking destitution. Yet these sharecroppers and tenant farmers still found spaces to challenge the plantation mentality and carry out strategies they hoped would foster economic parity and fair labor practices.

That white and black sharecroppers would go beyond forming an interracial labor union and cast their lot with an interracial communitarian experiment demonstrates a clear moment of modification in the struggle for Depression-era human rights. While many of Delta Cooperative Farm's residents, both black and white, continued to cling to corrosive racialized beliefs, they understood that economics and dehumanizing labor practices had intertwined their fate. It was an auspicious moment in twentieth-century race relations generated by pragmatism and desperation.

The colossal, meandering Mississippi River—"beneficent and dangerous by turns"—forms the Delta region's border to the west while dramatic bluffs and the Yazoo River mark its boundary to the east. Beyond the eastern edge of the Mississippi Delta, topographical maps depict ridges, river basins, and rolling hills. On the same maps, the geography of the Delta, in comparison, is implausibly flat, with no hint of the slightest crests or valleys. The soil, though rich from sediment deposited by flooding, challenged cultivators with its tendency to become viscous in the rainy season and concrete-hard during droughts. This was the land that Sam Franklin, Nute Hulsey, and dozens of sharecropping families heaped their hope on in the spring of 1936.[2]

In that year, as now, Highway 61 pierced the delta landscape through Vicksburg, Cleveland, and Clarksdale before reaching the sprawl of Memphis. Between hamlets like Panther Burn, Arcola, Hushpuckena, and Alligator, Route 61 often seemed as desolate as a desert highway. Sharecropper shacks and unadorned churches dotted the landscape. "These people must have great Faith in the Lord," noted one traveler from the North, "because you experience the feeling that the least sign of a breeze might topple the churches over. I believe the expression 'impending Heaven' might aptly be applied here." In Clarksdale, relocating sharecroppers turned west from Route 61 and drove directly toward the Mississippi River, bounded by raised levees that could easily be seen from a distance of miles if not for the lush cypress, sycamore, pecan, highwood, ash, elm, oak, and gum trees that choked the roadside. In Rena Laura, travelers turned southward on graveled Highway 1 for a few miles before reaching a place in the road where the Mississippi River bowed toward the highway, just over the Bolivar County line near the tiny Hillhouse Township. It was here that Presbyterian missionary and theologian Sherwood Eddy purchased the 2,138-acre cooperative. On Eddy's farm, the experiences of rural southerners reflected a nation and a region undergoing rapid and profound change in race and labor relations, industry, and economy.[3]

William Amberson had appointed Sam Franklin as the first resident director of Delta Cooperative Farm because of Franklin's experience with farming cooperatives in Japan. Franklin's strong personality, devotion to Christian activism, and previous hands-on farming knowledge doubtless endeared him to Amberson, who played a major role in finding suitable staff for the new cooperative. "Franklin is really a distinguished personality," Amberson gushed, "and will ultimately be recognized as one of the really significant Southern leaders." Amberson, Sherwood Eddy, Howard Kester, and H. L. Mitchell considered Franklin to be the "most competent and enthusiastic leader for this venture we can find." To grease the wheels and get the cooperative under way, Eddy agreed to pay Franklin's salary for the first six months.[4]

When Franklin's interests had shifted away from rural Japan, where war with China made it difficult to return, he and his wife, Dorothy, had quickly agreed to move to the Mississippi Delta and carry on their work of uplift through Christian Socialism. Franklin accepted Amberson's job offer, stating that he was eager to show "men the revolutionary gospel of Jesus instead of the soporific of bourgeois Christianity." The resident director position required all manner of responsibilities, only the first of which was traveling through Arkansas and interviewing possible candidates for membership in the cooperative. Franklin soon found himself involved in a bevy of duties, including answering all mail to the farm, sending out donation requests, greeting all visitors and sometimes hosting them overnight, speaking to interested groups in Mississippi, Arkansas, and Tennessee, and assisting in the planting of crops and raising of structures. His busy schedule was not aided by the fact that he was a micromanager who often critiqued the work of cooperators then continued to spend hours working side by side in the fields to make sure the work was done to his liking. In a cooperative communal environment based on the tenet of social equality, Franklin certainly situated himself as the unquestioned leader of the community. Even in the fields, he sported a collared shirt and tie and jodhpur breeches, meticulously tucked into his knee-length leather gaiters. Strolling around the farm, dolling out orders, the typically genial Franklin must have resembled a cavalry field commander from a distance. Franklin wrote to Eddy after less than a month on the farm detailing an industrious scene of cooperators hard at work, and confirming just how busy he had become since taking the position at Delta. "Your reference to being so busy making history that no time was left to write it," disclosed Franklin, "has held true pretty well of me."[5]

Amberson and STFU officials decided to name Blaine Treadway as associate director. Treadway was a secretary and organizer for the STFU, was executive member of the Socialist Party of Tennessee, and had worked on the Amberson Commission documenting how the Agricultural Adjustment Administration had negatively affected sharecroppers. Treadway's close associate Howard Kester recommended Treadway for the position. Before arriving at Delta, Treadway managed a print shop in Memphis, and in the early and mid-1930s he was one of four editors for the independent literary publication the *Observer*, which published submissions from poetry to literary criticism. The *Sewanee Review* considered the *Observer* to be the organ of a small but important literary movement in Memphis that had the potential to rival the Nashville Agrarians. Treadway, observed the *Sewanee Review*, was "interested in literature as propaganda for the class struggle." A devout socialist, Treadway considered socialism, union organizing, and cooperative farming to be the cure for problems facing southern sharecroppers. As Delta's associate director, he was in charge of farm operations when Sam Franklin was away from the cooperative. In addition to his duties as associate director, Treadway took charge of Delta's community store, which sold goods to its members and the surrounding community. A good-natured man, he "appeared to have his feet flatter on the buckshot earth than anyone else on the plantation," mused visiting journalist Jonathan Daniels. He was as dedicated to the cooperative effort at Delta as Eddy, Amberson, or Franklin, though his hands-off, pragmatic nature often contrasted with Sam Franklin's dynamic, and occasionally overbearing, leadership style.[6]

Franklin and Treadway embodied the two principal ideological influences at Delta Cooperative Farm: the Social Gospel and American Socialism. At the outset, these two approaches to reforming life in the rural South worked in harmony. Treadway certainly had strong socialist convictions, and Franklin, as a missionary, knew a thing or two about the Gospel of Jesus. Both the STFU and the American Socialist Party advocated for cooperative approaches to American labor and economy while Franklin's brand of activist, practical Christianity had espoused cooperative communalism all around the world for many decades. Now the two men were poised to put their respective ideologies into practice in the Mississippi Delta.

Sherwood Eddy cobbled together a board of trustees in the spring of 1936 that assisted Franklin and Treadway in making some of the larger decisions regarding the cooperative's direction. Eddy hoped that national luminaries like Eleanor Roosevelt, Norman Thomas, and William Alexander Percy would serve on the national advisory board of Delta Cooperative Farm, but quickly scrapped those names in favor of a board that had direct experience with race, labor, agriculture, socialism, and the Social Gospel. If not as influential as the first names suggested, the eventual board members were more accessible and could easily give advice on the farm's progress and goals. Joining Eddy and Amberson as trustees were Bishop William Scarlett, mechanical entrepreneur John Rust, and theologian Reinhold Niebuhr. As bishop of the Episcopal Diocese of Missouri, Scarlett was a tireless advocate for sharecroppers and the poor in Missouri and an old ally of Eddy's. With his brother Mack, John Rust had developed a mechanical cotton picker—around the same time as the International Harvester Company—that they hoped would revolutionize agriculture. Both brothers supported cooperative communalism and planned to use the proceeds from their cotton pickers to replicate communities like Delta Farm around the country. As a prominent theologian, socialist, and member of the Fellowship of Reconciliation with Norman Thomas, Niebuhr brought name recognition to Delta Cooperative Farm. Although Niebuhr's Christian Socialist theology was an important ideological foundation of Delta, he mostly remained a figurehead throughout his service on the Board of Trustees. Each trustee served specific purposes, and Niebuhr's was to bring legitimacy. Of them all, Amberson had the most direct contact with sharecroppers from his travels through the South while Eddy provided the bulk of the funding.[7]

The parcel was already home to approximately ten African American sharecropping families who had worked for the Staple Cotton Association, the previous owners, and lived in dilapidated homes scattered around the farm. Eddy and Franklin gave these families the option to stay, which most elected to accept. They would become some of the most valuable community members because of their intimate knowledge of the cooperative's land. Two of these African American families became charter members of the farm. George Smith and Monroe Whitney, who were brothers-in-law, lived and worked at Delta Cooperative Farm throughout most of its six-year existence. Smith, who had farmed the area for the past decade and possessed valuable abilities as a carpenter, drew up plans for buildings and became an elected leader among the cooperators. Smith also fully embraced socialism and labor organizing as an integral member, and eventual president, of the farm's STFU chapter.

Like Smith, Monroe Whitney seized opportunities created by the arrival of a cooperative farm. Whitney "had been studying poultry bulletins for two years and dreaming of someday having a poultry farm of his own." The cooperative, needing the meat and eggs that chickens could provide, offered Whitney the opportunity by acquiring "750 day-old chicks." Whitney raised them in a brooder he built from an oil drum and eventually brought them to "frying size, losing only 19." Whitney was temporarily set back in December, however, when a thief nabbed 117 of his prized chickens. He vowed to track down the offender. His single-minded determination to find the thief compelled Sam Franklin to write prominent lawyer and renowned Mississippi poet William Alexander Percy in case Whitney needed legal representation.[8]

Delta's Board of Trustees, on advice from Amberson, decided that preference would be given to STFU members when determining who could join the farm. Following connections established through the STFU and the two-year-old Amberson/Thomas field study, representatives from the union and the farm traveled to Arkansas identifying some of its hardest hit members and judging their ability to work and live in a cooperative capacity. Franklin identified potential members for being in acute physical danger or on the verge of starvation. A few of the original cooperative member families were previous Resettlement Administration clients on a plantation project in Earle, Arkansas. They told STFU and government interviewers that they experienced near starving conditions on both resettlement farms and private plantations. The rural resettlement division of the Resettlement Administration, a New Deal agency, relocated thousands of sharecroppers to tracts of land that resembled rural communities. Wilburn White, who along with his wife and six children was chosen to live at Delta, told STFU interviewers that his family lived on a government farm and "went hungry most of the time." When a union organizer visited the Whites and admitted that she had never known real hunger, the children remarked "your father must have been a very rich man." By the end of March 1936, Amberson boasted that the STFU offered invitations to over twenty families who possessed a "proven devotion" to the Union.[9]

Although the producer cooperative model of farming sounded worthwhile to most prospective members, some wanted to know more about the founders' designs to make the farm interracial. Franklin assured both black and white sharecroppers that interracial interactions would mainly take place in the context of work and that all other interracialism would be mainly voluntary. Franklin thought he noticed that African Americans in particular seemed relieved that they would not be forced into more intimate forms of interactions with whites. Black and white sharecroppers already had plenty of experience working side by side, but their interactions were typically limited to the fields. Southern custom and law segregated social gatherings, like meals and church meetings.

Southern African Americans were often as invested in keeping these events separate as whites, but for markedly different reasons. For blacks, the separation was necessary to cultural survival where white hegemony was the norm. "We just want economic equality," African Americans told farm organizers, "we don't care to have socials with them." Despite the devout commitment of the cooperative's socialist organizers to promoting interracialism, sharecroppers had a much more ambiguous understanding of and commitment to that founding tenet. Because of the ideological differences between farm managers and most of the ex-sharecroppers, race relations would prove to be one of the most difficult tasks facing the cooperative effort at Delta.[10]

As soon as the land was secured in March 1936, destitute sharecroppers, many of whom were refugees from the Dibble Plantation near Parkin, Arkansas, began moving to Delta. Planter C. H. Dibble had been in negotiations with the STFU to sign a collective bargaining agreement when H. L. Mitchell gave a fiery speech in which he issued Dibble an ultimatum to either sign the agreement or face a labor strike on his plantation. Newspapers in Tennessee and Arkansas quoted Mitchell's speech, and suddenly influential whites pressured Dibble to evict his sharecroppers with STFU affiliations. Threats of foreclosure and economic boycott of his plantation forced Dibble's hand, and in January 1936 he evicted approximately one hundred sharecroppers from his land. Mitchell had inadvertently worsened the situation and alienated a potential ally in Dibble. The sharecroppers set up a tent colony, many sleeping in their cotton sacks, along the roadside between Parkin and Earle. Many of these refugees were the first to arrive at Delta Cooperative.

By early April 1936, threatened with destitution, starvation, and violence, the families who resided at Delta included those from the ruins of the Dibble calamity, former Resettlement Administration evacuees, those identified through the interviews that Franklin and STFU organizers conducted, and the few African American families who already resided on the original parcel. Joining families like the Whitneys and the Smiths were Bennie Fleming, his pregnant wife, and their young child. Fleming, an African American and president of the STFU local on the Dibble Plantation, was evicted by the plantation owner and threatened by local officials with death if he did not give up his union affiliation. Instead, Franklin and the STFU gave the Flemings a chance to start anew at Delta. After only a few months on the farm he became "a transformed man," noticed Sam Franklin, "again holding his head erect and unafraid." When their second child was born, the first on the cooperative, the Flemings chose to name him Sherwood after the cooperative's benefactor.[11]

Other members came from similarly dire situations. James H. Moody, a white sharecropper identified by the STFU as a potentially valuable resident, was an STFU member and socialist of the Norman Thomas ilk. He and African American cooperator George Smith often worked side by side on carpentry responsibilities, demonstrating the residents' early embrace of interracial labor. Moody's daughter, Shirley, displayed considerable musical talent and was placed in charge of entertainment and recreation. Two white cooperators, brothers Jess and Hubert Erwin, and their families impressed Sam Franklin by their work ethic, and "they were soon driving tractors and trucks and taking other assignments of special responsibility." Jess Erwin's family had been residing "in the most forlorn slums imaginable" with "no window glass in their shack." Their six-year-old daughter was severely malnourished upon arriving to the cooperative, and Franklin learned that she had been whipped frequently at school "probably because she hadn't the strength after the fifteen mile bus ride in an overcrowded bus to keep up with the other children." White sharecropper Jim Henderson's stubborn nature had served him well on a plantation "where both Negro and white workers were in the habit of being taken to the barn for beatings when the boss-man was displeased." Learning of the opportunities at Delta, Henderson emotionally asked Franklin, "Do you really mean that I can learn to read and write?"[12]

Plantation owners, overseers, and law enforcement officials, often threatened at gunpoint croppers and union members for relocating. When Jim Henderson decided to leave his previous plantation, the planter threatened violence. Instead of acquiescing, Henderson grabbed his shotgun and stood guard while union members helped him load all his belongings in a truck bound for Delta. While interviewing a female sharecropper whose husband had been killed by white vigilantes in Crittendon County, Arkansas, Sam Franklin was approached by a pistol-brandishing plantation owner and ordered to leave because the planter believed he was "interfering with labor." When Franklin simply said he was doing his duty as a Christian minister, the planter ended the conversation by proclaiming, "I'd shoot you if you was Jesus Christ himself."[13]

Like Henderson, most new residents traveled to the farm via transportation that Franklin and the STFU secured for them. Amberson received word from Franklin in mid-March that he had helped thirteen families move in one week. In all, thirty families, eleven white and nineteen black, were admitted to Delta as members in its first year. Accounting for adults and children, the farm housed 111 individuals, not including the Franklins, Treadways, and other staff and volunteers.[14]

Most sharecroppers in the 1930s were peripatetic, choosing to vote with their feet and moving to new farms from year to year. Census data from 1940 demonstrate that sharecroppers often did not reside on the same plantation as they had in 1935. The same nomadic mentality followed many ex-sharecroppers to Delta. Because some residents stayed on the cooperative only for a year or less, the community was in a state of constant flux. The population's fluid nature speaks to the fact that, though there existed a degree of self-selection among farmers at Delta, they did not arrive with necessarily the same convictions or hopes that drove people like Sam Franklin, Sherwood Eddy, and William Amberson. Organizing a cooperative was a tactic that activists hoped would lead to economic equality for both white and black. For Christian missionaries and most socialists, interracialism, socialism, and practical Christianity were ideologies they hoped to put into practice. For many ex-sharecroppers, choosing to move to Delta Cooperative Farm was simply a choice born of desperation or hope for a fresh start.[15]

Staff members and the relocated farmers began, hastily but optimistically, to get their project under way near Hillhouse, Mississippi. The need to provide destitute sharecroppers with food and shelter dominated the early days of breaking ground and moving families to the cooperative. Pragmatism, however, took a back seat to ideology. Although the cooperative idea had percolated for several years in the minds of many involved in organizing Delta Cooperative Farm, no one took much time to explain the day-to-day vision to the relocated sharecroppers. The reality was that despite any earlier experiences as overseas missionaries or as union organizers, no one knew precisely how a farm like Delta—founded on interracialism—would operate. In essence, the blind led the blind. Yet optimism prevailed among trustees, managers, and farmers. Cooperator Virgil Reese, a teenaged early resident of the farm, told a reporter that "we are going to make a go of this," and he hoped, "we're all going to be getting something out of" their decisions to move to the new experiment. In the face of the brutal violence and near constant intimidation sharecroppers had previously experienced at the hands of plantation owners, overseers, and law enforcement, it was easy to view Delta as a beacon of hope.[16]

Mayhem and violence in Arkansas drew the nation's attention to the plight of sharecroppers and increased the profile of endeavors like Delta Cooperative Farm. Sherwood Eddy made a return trip to Arkansas in May to investigate the accusations of peonage labor, intimidation, and murder against Crittendon

County Sheriff Paul D. Peacher. He was appalled by what he saw and heard. He interviewed thirteen African American "prisoners" in the county jail who all told him what he already suspected, that Peacher had murdered several share-croppers and that the inmates were incarcerated without cause. Eddy learned that Peacher had arrested other African Americans on vagrancy charges and forced them to work as free labor on his cotton plantation.

Upon returning to the Peabody Hotel in Memphis, Eddy, still seething from his visit to Arkansas, drafted a letter to U.S. Attorney General Homer Cummings. He and Cummings had been roommates at Yale, yet Eddy wasted no time on cordial greetings. "Our histories should be revised," insisted Eddy, "in misleading us that slavery was ever abolished in Arkansas." In a threatening tone, probably in the hopes that it would galvanize his old friend, Eddy declared that if the federal government refused to look into the matter he would "rouse public opinion from coast to coast over the national disgrace of lawless Arkansas." The Peacher ordeal would drag out for several months, but the STFU's lawyers eventually convinced a federal court that, while sheriff, Paul Peacher had engaged in peonage labor, which federal statute strictly outlawed. A federal court found Peacher guilty of seven counts of false arrest and peonage labor. He was sentenced to two years in prison, but had it reduced to probation when he paid a $3,500 fine imposed by the court. For the STFU, Christian activists like Eddy, and the federal government, Sheriff Peacher embodied the malevolent side of sharecropping in the Deep South. Eddy, Amberson, and Franklin were now more determined than ever to see their cooperative communalist endeavor to fruition.[17]

Because of the violence in Arkansas, the Board of Trustees accepted "refugee residents" who were not accorded full cooperative membership but deemed by the STFU to be in grave danger. The most famous of these refugees was Vera Weems, the wife of STFU "martyr" Frank Weems. In May 1936, Frank Weems, an African American member of the STFU, helped organize striking farmers near Earle, Arkansas, as they protested evictions, demanded work reinstatement, and agitated for wage increases. Local law enforcement officials and plantation owners did not appreciate the sight of empty fields while black and white sharecroppers betrayed the bonds of white supremacy to picket side by side. Violence erupted as thugs beat or shot at picketers. A white mob cornered Frank Weems, severely beat him, and left him for dead. His friends and family assumed his body had been disposed of by his attackers. When Weems disappeared, he became an immediate martyr, and his story attracted national and international attention.[18]

Weems's disappearance became emblematic of the chronic violence that sharecroppers faced in Arkansas. Two African American sharecroppers, Jim

Reese, a founding member of the STFU, and Eliza Nolden, were also beaten by the same group of vigilantes who attacked Weems. Neither Reese nor Nolden would fully recover from their beatings. Reese suffered psychological damage for the remainder of his life, and Nolden died not long after in a Memphis hospital. White activists like minister Claude C. Williams and Willie Sue Blagden, both with the STFU, were severely beaten in Earle when the two were on their way to attend Weems's funeral. *Time* magazine reported that Weems's apparent death and other beatings, maimings, and murders "swung the spotlight of national attention on the 1936 Arkansas sharecroppers' strike which had been fumbling along unnoticed for four weeks."[19]

Vera Weems, assuming her husband dead and wracked with fear for her own safety, found sanctuary at Delta. She and her children moved to the farm while the media frenzy around her husband's apparent death reached a fever pitch. Members of the interracial cooperative met to discuss her situation and, echoing the brotherhood of the STFU and the Christian charity advocated at Delta, resolved that "Weems gave his life in our cause, and we'll take care of his wife and children." Sympathetic cooperators even suggested that each able-bodied member pitch in on Saturdays to build the refugee family a new home. Vera Weems and her eight children resided on the farm until 1937 when news reached them that Frank was alive. STFU activist and musician John L. Handcox was performing at a sharecroppers' charity event in Chicago when Weems found Handcox. Still fearful for his life, Weems refused to go back to the South and reunite with his family. Not long after, Vera Weems and her children left Delta with a widower in search of other employment and a new home.[20]

Like Vera Weems, desperate sharecroppers from Mississippi, Arkansas, Tennessee, Georgia, Missouri, and Illinois sent letters to STFU officials or directly to Delta Cooperative's managers and trustees attempting to plead their way onto the farm. A handwritten letter to H. L. Mitchell from Harvey Barton, a white farmer in Truman, Arkansas, revealed similar hopes among sharecroppers that Mitchell could help their families join the cooperative. Barton began the letter by addressing Mitchell as "dear comrade" and stressed that he was a socialist since 1910 as well as a charter member of the Truman STFU local. To make themselves attractive to the cooperative endeavor, Barton, his wife, and three children offered their hard work and a "Jersey Heffer." Barton ended the letter by declaring that he had "been in a destitute condition for two years and if it had not been for the boxes of clothing that was sent to" STFU organizer Charlie McCoy "we would have been necked." Mrs. Jim Thunderberg from Ruleville, Mississippi, pled directly to Sherwood Eddy during the summer of 1936: "Dear Sir, Would you give us a crop on your farm? We have had not crop in 3 yrs. Have 5 children. My husband has walked all over this Delta hunting a crop. At least 10 families here would be glad to get a crop with you." Inarticulate and haggard from years of destitution, scores of farmers from all over the Southeast and Middle America found hope in Delta's existence. The vast majority, though, had to be turned away for lack of facilities and resources. Franklin wrote to H. L. Mitchell only days before Mrs. Thunderberg made her request, lamenting that the cooperative wanted to take in more sharecroppers, but no longer had space to do so.[21]

An aggressive publicity and fund-raising campaign, mainly executed by Eddy, brought the interest of another constantly changing population to the cooperative: college-aged volunteers. Prompted by Eddy's extensive speaking engagements and article-writing campaign, offers to volunteer from young men and women inundated his YMCA office, the farm's post office box, and the desk of Rose Terlin, the YWCA's National Student Secretary for Economic Education of the National Student Council. White and African American students wrote to volunteer from institutions as wide ranging as Berea College, Hanover College in Indiana, Washington University, Garrett Theological Seminary in Illinois, the University of Texas, the University of Georgia, the University of Kentucky, North Carolina State University, Emory College, Spelman College, Morehouse College, and Gammon Theological Seminary in Georgia. In some cases, interested volunteers, like one white male college student who hitchhiked down from Madison, Wisconsin, to lend a hand for the summer of 1936, showed up unannounced. Because volunteers usually stayed for only a few months, often during summer break from college, they proved both helpful with their labor and entertainment and a hindrance due to their constant turnover.[22]

A letter Franklin received from Warren H. Irwin, a twenty-two-year-old white resident of Loranger, Louisiana, was typical of the requests Delta received. Irwin was a "single, young, non-smoker, non-drinker, without race prejudice, nor fear of hard work" and enthusiastic to help in an endeavor he viewed as a religious undertaking. Volunteers arrived from every corner of the United States, and most of the early volunteers at Delta Cooperative were drawn to the farm because of what Eddy termed "Christian cooperation." Though some volunteers came to Delta because of their belief that the farm would help them "get a real understanding of the problems of the common people," most were called to act through their commitment to Christian service. Signing his letter, "Your [sic] for practical Christianity," Irwin typified the majority of young, eager volunteers who came to Delta.[23]

Despite similar enthusiasm from African American college students, however, Sam Franklin and the trustees decided that no African American male volunteers should be accepted at the farm during the first few summers. Any African American volunteer would have to "adjust themselves to a race policy which while daring in this section falls short of what both they and we would desire." "For this reason," rationalized Franklin, "it will be necessary to choose only those who will bear with us patiently and make adjustments." Franklin was even more obtuse to YWCA secretary Rose Terlin. "I believe that it will not be advisable to take negro men this year on account of housing and other problems," he told her. What Franklin feared most however, was that black men from outside the region would be in danger in the Mississippi Delta and, in turn, endanger the farm's residents. Franklin's reticence was also clearly a result of what he thought college-educated African American men might find at Delta, a social experiment that, at times, was not as progressive as it was billed. Fearing backlash to their racial policies, Franklin informed the female volunteers that under no circumstances were black and white girls to live "under the same roof" and mix "intimately on a social plane." Franklin concluded that in all other areas female volunteers could mingle as they pleased, but rooming together "would unduly complicate the situation at this time."[24]

Although drawn to Delta through liberal Christian activism, most volunteers were typical college students of the era who worked hard and blew off steam in their free time. Volunteers paid a lodging fee of fifteen dollars per month and funded their own travel expenses. Terlin suggested to volunteers who came through her office that they dress appropriately for the work at hand. "Galoshes" were needed to deal with the Delta mud, and women were instructed to wear cotton dresses so they would not stand out from the poorer female farmers; slacks and trousers were similarly discouraged for female volunteers. The male volunteers typically helped clear fields and repair buildings, while their female counterparts ran a summer school for the children and helped female residents in "activities having to do with the care of a home." During breaks on summer days volunteers visited the farm's swimming hole, where they occasionally did not abide by the surrounding community's moral standards. One volunteer reported that "the ladies in the community do not approve our nudist tendencies." On weekend evenings, after long workdays, volunteers attended farm dances, sang "mountain ballads," played horseshoes and checkers, or collapsed into their cots from exhaustion. Occasionally they drove to Clarksdale or Memphis for entertainment in the way of minor league baseball and movies. Wanting to keep up a relationship with the farm, the STFU sent young, energetic union secretary Evelyn Smith during the summer of 1938. The other college-aged volunteers quickly deemed Smith their unofficial leader.[25]

To train and oversee college students who came to the farm, Eddy asked the American Friends Service Committee (AFSC) to establish a summer work camp beginning in 1937. The AFSC sent brochures to college campuses all over the country calling for students "conscious of the serious limitations of our economic structure in meeting fundamental human needs" and searching for "constructive patriotism (as compared with military service). This generation of students," stated the brochure, "must face a world threatened by war, torn by class strife, and thwarted by poverty in the midst of plenty. They can be defeated by the thought of entering such a world," it continued, "or they can be challenged by it to start, during their student days, the building of a better world." The brochure informed applicants that at Delta Cooperative Farm they would be "building a work-shop, a road, and clearing land for the Delta Community" over the course of two months. In the summer of 1939, the nearby Mound Bayou newspaper reported that "twenty-two young white representatives" from all over the United States and Jamaica came to volunteer at Delta's summer work camp.[26]

As a result of the student volunteer summer work camps, the number of Quakers and political activists concerned with pacifism and racial equality increased at Delta. Quaker activists and utopian community advocates Wilmer and Mildred Young arrived with their children from Pennsylvania in September 1936 to assist with the cooperative endeavor and the summer work camps. The Youngs, recently enamored of cooperative communalism, came not as volunteers or staff but as full-fledged cooperative members with the same labor and community responsibilities as the other cooperators. Mildred took charge of a women's social circle while Wilmer lent his services to constructing houses and overseeing the community garden. Their children, previously accustomed to middle-class amenities, participated in the same educational and recreational opportunities as their neighbors.[27]

The stresses of embarking on a radical endeavor did not always consume the lives of Delta residents, volunteers, and staff; they fell in love, raised children, celebrated weddings and birthdays, and suffered sicknesses and deaths. The first wedding at Delta, between the children of two white refugee sharecropping families, the Hendersons and the Moodys, took place in January 1937. Newlyweds Shirley and Jim Henderson and their extended families would be longtime members of the cooperative. Reverend Sam Franklin presided over the wedding of cooperators Birvin Mason and Margaret McKee. In December 1936, Mildred Young's sister, Dorothy Binns, visited Delta Cooperative Farm to spend the holidays and volunteer at the makeshift medical clinic. While there, Binns met the handsome, hardworking, and idealistic Blaine Treadway. By the next summer, Dorothy and Blaine were married and she had moved to the farm full-time. A year and a half later, they gave birth to their first son.

Longtime Delta residents George and Leola Smith gave birth to their daughter, Mary Alice, seven days after the Treadways welcomed their child. Quaker volunteers Art Landes and Margaret Lamont from Oklahoma and New Jersey, respectively, met at Delta in February 1939 and were married by June.[28]

When not hard at work and engaging in the prosaic lives of 1930s families, black and white cooperators spent their free time at Delta engaged in various activities, some segregated and some integrated. Increased participation in varied entertainment and leisure activities marked a shift in the lives of many sharecropper families. Cultural events of a wide array took place in the farm's community building. Delta acquired a motion picture projector in 1938 and showed free movies in the community building, an early showing for African Americans and a late showing for whites. By the end of the year, twelve families on the farm owned personal radios. Music was apparently very popular among cooperative residents and neighbors who frequented events at the community building. The cooperative did not have its own musical instruments for cooperators to use until 1937 when staff member Constance Rumbough sent away to Sears and Roebuck for a fiddle and guitar. After Delta acquired several musical instruments, the community center hosted a square dance every Saturday night. Social life on the farm sped up as families became more settled into their environs. County extension agents sponsored segregated home demonstration clubs for women while Delta sponsored its own Women's Club that mostly promoted the making and selling of clothes at the cooperative store. Adults encouraged young girls to join a social circle of their own that focused on sewing, bookbinding, and cooking. Save for the rare event, most leisure activities reinforced racial boundaries and adhered to the letter of the Mississippi law.[29]

Although on the surface the lives of residents at Delta were not so different from those of other rural Americans, the cooperative nature of the endeavor had a profound effect on their daily lives. Franklin, Eddy, and the other trustees intended the cooperative to be a viable, long-term community, and the organization of the farm was an extension of that goal, with a chain of command to help operations run smoothly. Once enough families were in place, farmers chose a democratically elected council, selected every six months, to govern all farm decisions and appoint individuals to specific tasks in the spring of 1936. Reflecting a commitment to interracialism, the five-person council could not consist of more than three members of the same race.

The council answered to the farm members but could be overruled by the resident director and the Board of Trustees. This hierarchy set up an unequal balance of power and resulted in many contentious council meetings. Decision making could often be a long, arduous task. A visiting *Washington Post* journalist witnessed a council meeting firsthand. He watched "the two colored members and the three white members quietly and with crude parliamentary precision plan the work for the next week," the journalist reported, "patiently arguing out the problems associated with pioneering." First, the farm council had to speak on behalf of the cooperators. Then Sam Franklin could weigh in, often using his veto power to overrule the council's decisions. Finally, for major decisions, the Board of Trustees entered the equation and, at times, overruled the will of the members. To the cooperators, Franklin seemed to be the mouthpiece of the Board of Trustees, carrying out the will of absentee white men. The complicated and hierarchical chain of command sometimes fostered suspicion and hard feelings among ex-sharecroppers whose only comparison to the situation was the hated riding bosses and absentee landlords of their former lives. In the beginning, however, Franklin and the trustees considered this process to be the most democratic and egalitarian way to proceed.[30]

Franklin, Treadway, and the council set to work delegating tasks for each farming family to accomplish in the hopes of getting the farm off to a productive start. The cooperative had three goals in its early weeks. The first was to begin making money. Cooperators cleared approximately three hundred acres and put them into cotton and staple crop production by mid-April. Once farmers properly prepared the soil in late summer, they planted Delta's other main staple crop, alfalfa. Acreage not covered in timber or staple crops was sown with tomato, potato, corn, and other seeds for the expansive community garden. Subsistence crops were augmented by beef, poultry, and dairy production. The Board of Trustees also pushed to establish a sawmill on the farm, but equipment and knowledgeable operators proved hard to come by in the initial weeks. Still, within a few months, Delta operated a small sawmill that quickly grew in production. Otto C. Morgan, a white tenant farmer and journeyman born in Mississippi County, Arkansas, during the 1880s, arrived sometime in the spring with his family, and Franklin put him in charge of all sawmill and timber operations at Delta. Morgan's work ethic and rapidly acquired acumen eventually led to the sawmill eclipsing cotton production in financial returns, although it could not sustain itself indefinitely because of the finite availability of timber on the farm.[31]

Last, cooperators built new structures and renovated existing houses to accommodate the newly arriving cooperative members, staff, and volunteers. Houses were initially primitive, but offered several amenities that most sharecropper had not previously enjoyed, such as sanitary toilets, attached to the back of each home, and mosquito-proof screening to reduce the threat of malaria. Each house was equipped with either a kerosene- or wood-powered stove for cooking. To adhere to local custom and law, housing was segregated along the main road through the farm. Whites lived in homes along the north row, and African American families lived across the road on the south row. The houses, however, were identical and provided to families on a first-come, first-served basis.[32]

Cooperative laborers finished the community building, capable of holding approximately one hundred people, in April 1937 as they continued construction on individual housing. Renowned sociologist and former member of the Commission on Interracial Cooperation Arthur Raper, who became a member of the Board of Trustees in 1938, thought that the community building was the heart of cooperative living. "For it was here that all the families met for the Cooperative business meetings," Raper extolled, "here that the people gathered to celebrate a good crop, to meet with some visitor who wanted to hear what the farmers themselves would say, to hear and see entertainment provided for them, and to complain to the Staff, or the Trustees, about something that went wrong. Here was a common meeting place for any and all members of the community." For both egalitarian and expedient reasons, business and union meetings were integrated in the community building. Aside from business dealings, music often echoed from the building from the community radio, the old piano, or Saturday night square dances. The building served as the backdrop for many of the most important events at Delta.[33]

Because of the farm's location bordering the levee and the rich alluvial soil that washed down river, the 2,138 acres that Sherwood Eddy purchased seemed the perfect location to begin building a new agricultural society and accomplish the first task of getting a good crop in the ground. The soil, however, was Sharkey clay, known regionally as "buckshot." Presumably the soil earned this name because when it dried, it broke off in clumps and farmers considered it more fit for loading a shotgun than growing crops. Sand and silt washed in from the Mississippi River usually made up about 40 percent of buckshot soil. The other 60 percent was clay that possessed high water retention and was slow to drain. In practical terms, when buckshot saturated during winter and early spring, it became a mire of knee-deep mud. One farm resident remarked that "if he would stick to the earth in summer, it would stick with him in winter." When the soil dried, it developed wide cracks that threatened the integrity of seeds and roots. Fortunately for the cooperators, the first year's crops were successful despite the deficiencies of buckshot soil.[34]

The first year was a busy time for all involved with the cooperative. As important as work projects, Delta's residents and managers were trying to figure out their identities and roles in this new endeavor. In fact, no one had yet decided the name of the farm. Between March and April, it was referred to variously as the People's Plantation, Rochdale Cooperative, Delta Cooperative, and Sherwood Eddy's Cooperative. In keeping with his modest character, Eddy made it clear that if his name were used in the farm's title he would resign as its trustee and treasurer. Eventually the council and the Board of Trustees settled on Delta Cooperative Farm as the official name, perhaps because "People's Plantation" conjured the specter of communism, an association Franklin and Eddy tried doggedly to avoid because of virulent anticommunism in Mississippi. Often though, residents referred to their home as Rochdale, in homage to the British Rochdale Equitable Pioneers Society, the 1840s groundbreaking cooperative that launched the modern transnational cooperative movement.[35]

On the surface, the little community at Delta might have been a microcosm for any community in America. Jess Erwin's young wife took over teaching Sunday school classes, while other women took to beautifying the area around the community building. Staff and volunteers offered evening classes for adults in reading, writing, and arithmetic. Sawyer Otto Morgan was "going to night school and is learning long division for the first time, although he stands at the saw and estimates log footage as few college professors could." The farm also offered a library, socials, outdoor sports, children's story hours, a choir, and educational forums for adults on various topics including Japanese culture and socialist communalist pioneer Robert Owen.[36]

By the spring of 1937, a year after breaking ground, Delta Cooperative Farm resembled a small village. It claimed thirty families, a community building for social, educational, and religious functions, a makeshift medical clinic, several rows of mosquito-proof houses, a post office, and over one thousand acres in alfalfa, cotton, and various cover crops. In the late summer, Sam Franklin spoke to a journalist as he looked out over the thriving cooperative. "Within 10 years," Franklin proudly mused, "we hope to have 75 to 100 families here." He envisioned Delta as a lively hamlet built on a cooperative model that would be replicated by cooperative communalists across the nation. Franklin and the other trustees hoped that their experiment could change the face of poverty in rural America, "wipe malaria out of the county, foster higher education," and produce leaders from the impoverished families who now lived at Delta.[37]

The founders of Delta Cooperative Farm also conceived of the endeavor as a remaking of plantation agriculture. In reality, Delta operated much the same way a plantation would. Although it borrowed strategies from cooperative models and completely cut out the profit that usually flowed into the pockets of plantation owners, Delta's operations replicated many facets of the plantation. The endeavor paid skilled laborers more than unskilled laborers, and farmers realized very little real income in the process. In fact, the trustees knew that small farms could not compete with large plantations, so Delta was conceived as a "large plantation on the cooperative model in order to compete with privately owned large plantations." Economist T. J. Woofter, a keen observer of sharecropping and the plantation system of agriculture, remarked in the late 1930s that "there can be little doubt of the similarity of the economic arrangements of the plantation share tenant and those of the worker on a co-operative farm." For Woofter, the only differences between these two types of laborers were that "the tenant does not have any voice in management policies and receives a smaller proportion of the total income" while the cooperator, in theory, enjoyed both practices.[38]

Still, Delta Cooperative Farm unambiguously borrowed from cooperative communitarian endeavors. Blaine Treadway established and operated a consumers' cooperative, patterned after the Rochdale model. That the founders of Delta relied on the Rochdale model spoke to the international roots of the farm and the sheer influence of the 1840s British cooperative. Began by skilled weavers who felt squeezed by the industrial revolution, the Rochdale cooperative store diversified their products and collectivized their earnings.

The cooperative store at Delta sold meat, homemade ice cream, and vegetables from the community garden, including tomatoes, melons, onions, corn, cane, cabbage, and several varieties of potatoes, to both residents and nonresidents. Additionally, the consumers' cooperative sold garments fashioned by female cooperators and goods received from outside that sharecroppers normally procured from a plantation commissary or crossroads store. Tobacco, coffee, salt, sugar, fat meat, and basic provisions were also available at the store. A volunteer at Delta remembered that some residents came to the store at six o'clock to get breakfast before heading off to conduct the business of the farm. The store sold "soft drinks" and, in order to boost the store's profit, shoppers were charged one dollar for cups for the water cooler. "They thought that was expensive; thought it robbery to have to pay for water," the volunteer remembered. "They would buy a paper cup and park it on the shelves to use it next time. The shelves were dotted with the cups!" Each member of the farm was automatically a member of the consumers' cooperative and, every six months, had to buy five-dollar shares in the cooperative until they reached a total of ten shares. Members also received dividends on what they purchased and the total of what was sold. For many people in and around Bolivar County, the consumer's cooperative store became their only interaction with the peculiar farm near Hillhouse. Blaine Treadway and a small group of young female members and volunteers usually worked as store clerks and fostered good relationships with some local whites who may have had doubts about the endeavor.[39]

A producers' cooperative conducted all business related to Delta's production and operated in tandem with the consumers' cooperative storefront. The producers' cooperative sold goods to the consumers' cooperative at wholesale prices and also conducted business off the farm, selling cotton and other crops to outside buyers. Members received dividends proportional to the quality and total of their work output. When the farm failed to produce a profit, which was likely at Delta because overhead costs were high, there were no dividends to distribute.[40]

Recognizing the uncertainty of Delta's income, the trustees established the Cooperative Foundation, Inc., a nonprofit that raised money for the farm. The Board of Trustees, including Sam Franklin and Blaine Treadway, all agreed that the trustees, through the foundation, would own the land for an undetermined number of years, eventually turning it over to the ex-sharecroppers. The official charter stated that the trustees could "sell or transfer any part of the property to the cooperative farmers who have been awarded permanent membership in the cooperative farms." "Our land is held in trust by the trustees," reported William Amberson to the *Christian Register*. "Our members are building an equity in the property through their own labors," he continued, "and they will ultimately own the farm, as a co-operative group, together with all improvements which they make upon it." Eddy hoped that after the staff and volunteers established the cooperative model at Delta and ex-croppers took up all responsibilities, the trustees could turn over all ownership to the cooperators. Franklin predicted that "in four or five years we will be able to turn it over to the people."[41]

In 1936, Eddy embarked on a speaking tour around the country to raise money for the Cooperative Foundation. At churches, colleges, chambers of commerce, and town hall meetings, Eddy spread the gospel of interracial communalism. He often scheduled lunch or dinner meetings with groups and charged a fee per plate. Although Eddy fronted the money to purchase Delta and the new residents agreed to repay the acquisition price of the farm at 2.5 percent interest, he knew that his personal trust fund was insufficient to sustain a long-term venture. Aid in the form of small donations trickled in from individuals and religious organizations from as far away as Quebec. Some national organizations gave generously, including a $2,000 donation from the New York City–based Church Emergency Relief Committee.[42]

Eddy courted influential Americans, including theologian and social activist Warren Wilson of the Union Theological Seminary and First Lady Eleanor Roosevelt, both of whom pledged support and promised to rally like-minded individuals to their cause. Eddy also published dozens of articles and wrote scores of introduction letters on behalf of Sam Franklin to recipients as diverse as officials in the Works Progress Administration (WPA) and Mississippi author William Alexander Percy. Almost all received news of the farm with enthusiasm. Cordell Hull, the U.S. secretary of state and Tennessee native who would help establish the United Nations and win the Nobel Peace Prize in the next decade, wrote to Eddy expressing his admiration and support. By June 1937, donors had given Eddy's fund over $10,000 for educational, agricultural, and medical projects while also providing Sam Franklin's salary. Eddy's speaking schedule truly was a kind of evangelizing on the farm's behalf. When economic times worsened on the farm and uncertainties loomed, northern philanthropy almost single-handedly kept the cooperative afloat.[43]

Eddy often began his public remarks by situating Delta as an alternative to the Resettlement Administration's policies toward sharecroppers. He liked to compare Delta Cooperative with the Resettlement Administration's Dixie Plantation just a few miles down the road. Eddy felt certain that farmers at Delta were getting a squarer deal than those at Dixie, who rented the land at a higher rate and complained that they could not get the aid they needed because of government "red tape." In fact, at least two families, the Wilkinsons and the Holmeses, migrated from Dixie to Delta. Eddy also bragged that "the Government at Washington" offered to build the houses at $1,000 a pop but because of the timber on the land and the presence of the sawmill, the houses at Delta cost $33 to build. Additionally, he claimed that Bolivar County produced more cotton than any other county in America "if not in the world," thus situating Delta on a prime piece of land purchased for approximately $5 an acre and worth, Eddy assured his audience, well over ten times that amount. Audiences came away from Eddy's remarks with the overwhelming feeling that government aid was inept and only endeavors like Delta could succeed. On this issue, Eddy and William Amberson were in complete agreement. Amberson pointedly critiqued the Roosevelt administration and the New Deal overall as unable to address the plight of sharecroppers. Amberson believed that the administration favored "small individual subsistence homesteads" that could not possibly address the needs of every destitute sharecropper or compete with large plantations. Because of the large number of tenant farmers, approximately two hundred thousand new families each year, Amberson insisted that agricultural cooperative communities were the only solution.[44]

Eddy tugged the heartstrings of his audience by belaboring sharecropper hardships while underscoring the hope that Delta represented. "The Negro Fleming," declared Eddy, who was forced out of Arkansas, now plies his trade as a carpenter to help others build their own houses at Delta. He explained how Jim Henderson felt like a free man for the first time in his life after working on a plantation where black and white tenants were "whipped" and, when evicted, had to "rescue his furniture only with his own rifle." Eddy bragged about the accomplishments at Delta and conjured a bustling little village with an apiary, a busy sawmill, Holsteins acquired "at a bargain," "two tractors plowing furrows, four men spreading fertilizer, other crews logging, building houses, sowing cotton and corn and planting vegetables."[45]

Addressing many of the pressing issues that brought about Delta's formation, Eddy assured his audiences that the Rochdale model of cooperation was the best way to accomplish an overhaul of the crumbling economic system. More important, Eddy conveyed the clear message that Delta's organizers were serious, smart men who were tapping into and building on a long history of cooperatives of which they were acutely aware. The founders hoped, through the consumers' cooperative and the producers' cooperative, that the undertaking in Bolivar County would duplicate the success of cooperatives in Europe and Asia.

But the Mississippi Delta was a long way from England and Japan. In Delta's cooperative model, members would have to come to grips with an increasingly mechanized system. Eddy put great faith in the Rust Brothers Cotton Picker and prayed that Delta would "be the first in our district to have its cotton picked by machinery." Amberson joined in Eddy's sentiment and hoped that Delta Farm would be the "proving ground" for the Rust Cotton Picker. In 1936, Mississippi's Commissioner of Agriculture observed a demonstration of the Rusts' invention and was none too impressed. He objected that the machine occasionally picked green leaves with the cotton and that the picker sometimes missed high-grade cotton, knocked it to the ground, and trampled it. The first demonstration at Delta, however, generated much ambivalence. Observers considered the coming of the mechanical cotton picker as a blessing and curse for sharecroppers. Mechanizing agriculture meant that long hours in the field could be reduced but also that many sharecroppers would be rendered redundant. To mitigate such fears, the Rust Brothers formed a foundation that sought to subsidize a number of cooperative efforts around the world, especially in developing regions, using the proceeds from the cotton picker to finance these efforts.[46]

The Rust brothers and their cotton picker embodied one of the great contradictions of the farm: it was a cooperative model using capitalist measuring sticks. As a result of the trustees' ownership of the farm, the cooperators were, in some ways, like employees. The problematic and disjointed chain of command left members feeling completely disconnected from the Board of Trustees, who rarely visited the farm. Most damning was that members saw very little monetary compensation for their labor. Trustees pledged to turn the land over to the cooperators eventually, but in the interim most of the money the farm made went into paying overhead costs like equipment and seed or reimbursing Sherwood Eddy, who had fronted the initial seed money from his trust fund.

Although Delta's challenge to the plantation system was not as radical as the founders hoped, the presence of an interracial STFU local, a rarity in Jim Crow–era Mississippi, demonstrated that the cooperators were committed to contesting unacceptable labor conditions that confronted black and white alike. H. L. Mitchell authorized an official charter for a new STFU local based at Delta Cooperative Farm less than a month after farmers arrived. He sent the necessary paperwork for STFU Local 146/UCAPAW Local 127 to African American resident Bennie Fleming, a union leader evicted from the Dibble Plantation and charter member of the cooperative. STFU officials like H. L. Mitchell, Howard Kester, Evelyn Smith, and Claud Nelson kept in touch with their union members by paying frequent visits to the farm.[47]

Apparently Kester thought enough of the endeavor at Delta to ask Sam Franklin for ten pounds of Mississippi Delta soil to be used in his new "Ceremony of the Land," a ritual performed at large STFU gatherings which drew from notions of Christian brotherhood, socialist class solidarity, African American call and response, and a reverence for the earth. Kester's ceremony, which he wrote with Evelyn Smith, was his attempt to reach out to the STFU's rank and file through a participatory ceremony that echoed what many would have experienced in church. Asking for soil from Delta signaled that Kester felt the cooperative could play a role in the earthly salvation of downtrodden sharecroppers. STFU membership fluctuated at Delta, but in February 1938 Local 146 had thirteen white members and four African American members. George Smith, one of the original members of Delta, was its president and Quaker Wilmer Young was the secretary.[48]

While raising money for the foundation, Eddy stressed that collective bargaining was the right of all laborers at Delta and that he was working closely with the STFU to ensure worker rights. Yet he was careful to distance himself from more radical approaches to labor and race relations. "If we should desert" the STFU "and the Communists should capture the organization and inject the element of violence and race war," declared Eddy, "the weaker race will be further crushed and the Union will be destroyed." This sentiment demonstrated both Eddy's loathing for communism and his belief in the importance of protecting Delta from it. Socialists and communists were often at odds, especially since communism had garnered a mainly negative image in the United States. Strictly in a political sense, Eddy knew that associating the farm's endeavor with communism could jeopardize the whole affair. But it was not merely a show; Eddy was a staunch anticommunist who often critiqued communist governments around the world. He hoped that he would be able to distance his own socialist views and the cooperative's egalitarian spirit from the more radical approaches of communists.[49]

Eddy's commitment to egalitarian socialism trickled down to the farm. Fair labor practices had a lasting impact on the cooperative's members and their children. The council, with the full support of the Board of Trustees, decided that children under twelve were forbidden from laboring in the fields at Delta. Those children were instead paid a small sum by the cooperative, amounting to just a few cents each day, for babysitting their younger siblings and neighbors. The cooperative organized those not babysitting into "clean-up squads" who busied themselves doing odd jobs around the cooperative grounds. In a move that must have pleased the STFU local and amused their parents, the children formed a "Junior Union," elected their own president, and lobbied the Cooperative Council for fair, age-appropriate wages. Additionally, the council instituted a ten-hour workday, although members typically put in longer hours, especially when the farm was in its infancy. Although the eight-hour workday was in vogue among labor unions and socialists, rural laborers such as farmers were mainly excluded from such hours because their work was closely tied to the rising and setting sun and fluctuations of agricultural production. Instituting a ten-hour workday in 1936 demonstrated Delta's progressive approach to rural labor and preceded by two years the eight-hour workday law established under the Fair Labor Standards Act.[50]

While Delta Cooperative Farm certainly challenged southern labor practices, the specter of white supremacy shadowed the farm and soon confronted the trustees, staff, volunteers, and cooperators in ways that threatened the existence of the endeavor altogether. Writing in 1934, Charles S. Johnson observed that rural blacks who lived in areas dominated by plantation agriculture engaged in "almost complete dependence upon the immediate landowner for guidance and control in virtually all those phase of life which are related to the moving world outside." And, for better or worse, Johnson continued, African Americans were "seriously affected when the relationship fails." Both sharecroppers and plantation owners found the plantation mentality difficult to cast aside, even by the mid-1930s.[51]

The plantation mentality infected nearly every interaction in the rural South, including efforts to bring poor whites and blacks together for labor and economic rights. Egalitarian class solidarity proved easier to preach than practice. Southerners interested in maintaining the status quo had so thoroughly quelled meaningful cooperation among the working class that many poor whites accepted white supremacy. Forging equitable race relations proved a constant headache to Delta's residents.[52]

The most vexing and delicate of all the endeavors at Delta was interracialism. On this subject, Eddy was candid and, despite his paternalistic tendencies, demonstrated a complex understanding of African American and labor history. "Are we here rushing in where angels fear to tread?" Eddy asked his audiences. "I for one refuse to believe that there is no solution for this perplexing question. If the Communists of Russia and the Moslems can solve it, is it insoluble only for Christians? We, or our ancestors, raided the African's villages long ago and against his will dragged the Negro here in slavery. Every other civilized slave-owning country, except our own, freed its slaves without bloody war. Russia gave land to all its liberated serfs, but we never did to our freed men. As long as the owners could play the Negroes and the poor whites one against the other, both have remained more or less in economic slavery. But at last they have seen that their interests are one." Though his explanations were brief, Eddy understood the harsh legacy of slavery, sharecropping, and Jim Crow. Additionally, he assumed that the changes that Delta represented would be accepted by the majority of white southerners only if they were ushered in by fellow southerners. Eddy made a point of highlighting the leadership of southerners in the venture. Referring to them, Eddy stated that Delta Cooperative Farm "was born in the hearts of Southern white men [who] absolutely refuse to run it on 'Jim Crow' lines of racial segregation and exploitation. Their vision and courage," he concluded "are putting us Northern men to shame."[53]

Eddy and most of the trustees understood the roots of historical, class-based racism in the South. He gave priority to economic justice for southerners, regardless of race. The finer points of Mississippi's racial caste structure would eventually give way if the system of economic injustice was reformed. Eddy declared that he refused to "draw a red herring across the trail by raising the moot question of 'social equality' which is now purely academic for these half-starving" sharecroppers. "The Negroes want bread and basic economic justice; a chance to live without fear and insecurity and degradation," Eddy believed. "They want rudimentary education and a right to work as self-respecting members of their own Union that demands elemental justice and liberty. The racial policies of these Cooperative farms (for we hope that this is only the first of a chain of such farms) will never be determined by Northern 'Yankees,' but by Southern men. It was Southern white men who found both colored and white families evicted by the side of the road in Arkansas and took them in. Both are now working like beavers, happily and harmoniously together." Eddy and the other farm organizers presumed that cooperators would embrace class solidarity. "The Negro and the poor white man today," noted one early pamphlet from Delta, "are the victims of economic injustice" who have been "pitted against each other by those who wished to make money out of both of them." The managers and Board of Trustees attempted to incorporate this understanding into business and interpersonal relationships on the farm in the hopes that it would trickle down to the farmers. In an early letter to a donor, Sam Franklin noted that white men who worked under black men were getting along well and engaged in productive work.[54]

Delta residents breached Deep South racial conventions in another important setting: church. The physical space of the worship service was one conspicuous location where cooperators transgressed southern racial mores. Franklin and the staff integrated previously segregated rural church services at Delta, particularly for significant religious holidays. "We held our Easter services in Fleming's house," wrote Sam Franklin. "I suspect it has been a long time since whites and blacks sat down to celebrate the resurrection of Christ together in this part of the country." Sunday school and adult "Christian education groups" were never officially segregated. Cooperative members proposed separate services for whites and blacks, but the practice never caught on and worshipers of either race were free to attend all services and "sat where they pleased." For Franklin, the worship service was a space that embodied two of the main aspects of Delta Cooperative Farm. He hoped that Christian practices would meld with interracial cooperation inside the church door and serve as the lifeblood of the community.[55]

In addition to interracial church services, Delta also hosted interracial meetings and conferences that fostered cooperation across the color line beyond the farm's borders. In the fall of 1938, continuing its commitment to practical Christianity, Delta held a Negro Ministers' Institute in which African American ministers from the region came to attend courses offered by managers, trustees, and guest lecturers such as the chaplain at the Tuskegee Institute. Classes at the institute focused on an array of topics including "Christianity and Modern Social Problems, the Minister's Use of the Bible, and a Reorientation in Theology." STFU official Howard Kester spoke on the broad topic of race relations (in exchange for which Sam Franklin offered to cover his travel expenses and, he joked, "an honorarium in the way of a check for $10,000 payable when the new social order is established"). The Southern Socialist Conference began holding their annual integrated meetings at Delta in the late 1930s. Southern representatives of the Socialist Party hoped that the "primitive surroundings" would help them "get in the right mood for an attempt at dealing with the tremendous problems of the southern area."[56]

Yet Delta's residents faced reactionary responses to interracialism outside the farm and had far from solved the race problem on it. Eddy's public remarks often reflected a balance between his egalitarian nature and Mississippi's racial caste structure. Sam Franklin recalled that the most knowledgeable and efficient member at Delta was George Smith. Smith was indispensable to all cooperative endeavors and a leader in the STFU local, and later spoke about the cooperative effort at national meetings of the NAACP. Yet because of the color of his skin, white members would often ignore Smith's suggestions, even when it came to carpentry, in which he was highly skilled. Franklin was sure that the fact that, on the farm, "his abilities would never be rewarded to the same degree that they would if he were white rankled within him." Though Franklin was aware of discrimination against Smith, he apparently took no action to alter such behavior.[57]

William Amberson reported to Fisk University president and sociologist Charles S. Johnson that as early as December 1936, the cooperative was "hitting angles of the race problem which have been a revelation to us. We had once thought that the addition of a colored worker in the higher administration staff might ease the strain" among cooperators, admitted Amberson, "but recent indications suggest that this might be just the wrong thing to do." He gave no specific account of the "recent indications," although a survey of several white members at Delta revealed that they still harbored racist views. The unnamed members believed that "Negroes were like brutes" who were unhygienic and sexually promiscuous. One white cooperator assured the interviewer that "we don't hate the Negro; People in the North think we hate the Negro. We don't," he continued. "The negro is just different, that's why we don't mix. They don't dance or sing like we do." Volunteer Constance Rumbough remembered that racial integration "didn't go far at all." The main goal, in her experience at the farm, was that the members achieve economic equality only. Full integration of social activities did not seem to be vital to the community's mission.[58]

Delta Cooperative Farm operated on what Jonathan Daniels called "a queer compromise" between the trustees' "Christian consciences" and Mississippi's "dangerous prejudices." "They want to take the Christian attitude toward race," observed Daniels, "but they do not want to complicate the cooperative experiment unduly by unnecessarily alarming Mississippi." The thirty-five-year-old Daniels was uniquely positioned to observe and comment accurately on race relations in the South. As the son of Josephus Daniels, an architect of turn-of-the-century white supremacy campaigns in North Carolina and later a secretary of the navy who almost unilaterally sanctioned the occupation of Haiti as a white man's burden, Jonathan Daniels could have turned out very different. A committed New Dealer and eventual race relations advisor to President Roosevelt, Daniels, by the time he was in his thirties, was his own man. In 1923 he had begun the task of taking over the Raleigh *News and Observer* from his father. It was from this platform in the 1890s that Josephus Daniels had launched his attacks against black voters and promoted the violent white supremacy that swept the state in 1898. Jonathan, however, often wrote about racial inequality and violence perpetrated on black southerners. Like most liberals of the 1930s, Daniels supported the maintenance of segregation, but he became an advocate for equal opportunities for African Americans. In 1937, Daniels decided to put his journalism skills to good use and took a long, circuitous road trip while documenting the South. He stopped at Delta Cooperative Farm in May 1937 and found it fascinating, but ultimately overburdened by the idealism of the venture. He would later publish his findings in a 1938 best seller, *A Southerner Discovers the South*.[59]

Not long before Daniels arrived to Delta, in December 1936, African American cooperators called an "indignation meeting" to address what they perceived as racial discrimination. Housing was a limited commodity on the farm, and when two African American families vacated Delta, black cooperators felt that the families had been forced out and were concerned that their houses would go to white families. The incident prompted William Amberson, despite his acute sensitivity to the downtrodden, to comment that "the race difficulties are much more in the minds of the colored group then in the white. The racial problem is evidently tremendously more difficult than any of us had dreamed," he continued, "yet thereby it becomes an even greater challenge."[60]

Despite obvious fissures in race relations at Delta, the "indignation meeting" demonstrated that African Americans would not hesitate to advertise their grievances to the managers and other cooperators. White residents noticed that African Americans with whom they had worked side by side for many years in the plantation system and who normally answered only with simple and deferential responses now stood up to any indignities that came their way. White cooperator Jim Henderson remarked to African American cooperator Jim Billington how much the latter had changed since arriving at Delta. "When you first came here, all you did was say, 'Yas suh' to everything a white man told you," Henderson continued brazenly. "The riding boss could call you a 'damned nigger' and tell you to hurry up and finish the job or, 'I'll kick your behind for you' and all you'd say was, 'Yas suh.' Now here you talk a lot." Delta Cooperative Farm provided the space in which African Americans no longer felt compelled to accept the indignities or everyday performances of Jim Crow that had previously defined much of their lives.[61]

Indignation on the part of poor farmers was well founded. Franklin was constantly concerned that his authority would be usurped by cooperators, thus he occasionally undermined the farm council's decisions and often ignored Delta's egalitarian principles. On several occasions, black and white farmworkers and outside observers accused Franklin of heavy-handedness in his management of the farm. Although Franklin was frequently praised for his efficiency and generosity by Eddy and distant onlookers, members of the farm did not always see him in such positive light. By most accounts, Franklin hovered over cooperative laborers, making suggestions, prodding them to work harder and increase production. Upon walking the length of the property with Franklin and observing his interactions with working cooperators, Jonathan Daniels reported that "there is undoubtedly a fire in the man." It seemed clear, too, that Franklin held paternalistic attitudes toward the poor agrarians at Delta. "I look forward to the day when all of them, black and white, will call me by my first name," mused Franklin. "But we must remember," he conceded, "that we are dealing with rough, passionate men." One observer, who was sympathetic to interracial cooperatives but unhappy with Delta's leadership, called Franklin a "paternalistic dictator" and refused to support the endeavor.[62]

Paternalism, even from the most well-meaning racial progressives like Franklin, hampered interracial and cross-class movements from abolition to civil rights. In the paradoxical practices of white southern progressives, they displayed the "often erratic behavior of reformers: how they embraced uplift and progress, yet believed in a hierarchy of race and culture; how they were fervent advocates of democracy, yet also endorsed measures of coercion and control." The liberals at Delta in the 1930s and 1940s displayed similar tendencies. By calling African Americans "the weaker race" in public remarks, Eddy conveyed his continued paternalistic views that were all too common among many liberal white men of his day. A letter to Sherwood Eddy from a woman who hoped to find employment teaching at Delta demonstrated the contradictions in the attitudes espoused by many liberals during the 1930s. Norma Nelle Bullard, from Aurora, Illinois, assured Eddy that she knew "a good bit about the darkies, for we have had them in our home. However," she tempered, with no sense of irony, "in those days they served us; it would be my joy to now serve them."[63]

Reflecting on Delta Cooperative Farm thirty years after it closed its gates, former trustee Arthur Raper commented that the South's rural poor possessed "no tradition of taking part in community affairs, or even in decisions directly affecting their own lives." Raper, antilynching activist, sharecropper advocate, and member of the Commission on Interracial Cooperation (CIC), saw rural African Americans as helpless because they possessed, as far as he knew, no history of self-organizing or community activism. Raper was blind to a rich, if often furtive, tradition of African American activism. But before the classic civil rights era, this point was lost on many whites of all political persuasions.[64]

The manifestations of cultural superiority were harmful to the cooperative effort at Delta. For example, although integrated church services had the larger goal of racial understanding and cooperation in mind, they ignored rural religious practices. While religious holidays were often celebrated together, very few farm residents attended church services because white missionaries did not preach the kind of rural prophetic religion that interested many premillennialist sharecroppers. One staff member thought that integrated services were "a painful experience [because] the two races had been used to different forms of worship." Most educated staffers shared the opinion that the "white sharecropper is one of the most unchurched groups in the country and the general level of Negro church life in the cotton belt is . . . such as not to commend religion to thoughtful members of the race."[65]

Indeed, many pastors and missionaries on the Christian left held rural prophetic Christianity, like Pentecostalism, in contempt for being a nascent, "unstable" denomination and its members for exhibiting "extreme or emotional" behavior. Although the rural poor who lived at Delta readily understood the sermons, the services held by educated white missionaries lacked other similarities vital to rural church services. For instance, Reverend Franklin laced services at Delta with Presbyterian restraint, a scene wholly unattractive to sharecroppers used to the fervor of tent revivals. By not taking complaints of racial discrimination seriously, by holding interracial church services that were vastly different from the rural prophetic religion of which many black southerners were accustomed, and by generally imposing Christian or socialist ideology, white volunteers, managers, and activists at Delta overlooked the long history of cultural autonomy and community-based activism present among rural African Americans. The staff and the trustees often treated the members as their children who could not be trusted to make sound decisions for themselves.[66]

To explain Sam Franklin, Arthur Raper, and other whites' attitudes only as paternalistic, however, simplifies them and removes them from their historical contexts. Scientific racism still held considerable influence during the Great Depression. For most white and black residents at Delta, given the prevailing opinion of the day, it was "natural" to separate residences and recreational activities. Additionally, while the New Deal was one of the most liberal government undertakings in American history, it could also be antiegalitarian and procapitalist, especially as conservative southern Democrats pushed back against many of Roosevelt's reforms. Delta Cooperative Farm could not escape the limitations of its time nor the sociopolitical climate of the New Deal.[67]

In the same ways, the New Deal made Delta what it was. First, the Agricultural Adjustment Act pushed the moment to its crisis and brought increased national attention to the labor and economic exploitation of sharecroppers. Second, Sherwood Eddy and his circle were, in the main, supporters of Roosevelt's administration and admirers of Eleanor Roosevelt. They were encouraged that the Resettlement Administration attempted to implement the cooperative model too, though disagreements about how to best carry out the endeavor persisted. It is plain, however, that Roosevelt's hope for a pluralist society did not always equate to egalitarianism. The complicated and contradictory limits of New Deal liberalism were equally reflected in the day-to-day activities at the cooperative.

Pragmatically, Eddy and the other trustees knew that interracialism in the Mississippi Delta had to be handled carefully. For people involved in interracial activities or upending established labor practices, Mississippi was as dangerous as Arkansas. The STFU's H. L. Mitchell, in fact, said that rescuing Arkansas sharecroppers but relocating them to an interracial communal endeavor in Mississippi was like "jumping from the frying pan into the fire." Exactly one year before Delta was founded, Reverend T. A. Allen, an African American minister and sharecropper activist, was murdered and his body thrown into a river near Hernando, Mississippi. Planters apparently killed Allen for organizing one of the state's few STFU locals. Even the appearance of interracial labor or organizing had to be handled carefully. After all, the *Chicago Defender* likened Delta to a volatile "keg of dynamite" that threatened to blow southern race relations and labor practices to smithereens. The *Defender* hoped, however, that Delta would prove to be the harbinger of "the new social order that will soon sweep the South."[68]

Delta Cooperative Farm, in fact, was somewhat of a cause célèbre in the regional black press, especially for Associated Negro Press (ANP) reporter William Pickens, who actively covered Delta Cooperative Farm in the 1930s. As a southerner who was born to ex-slaves, as well as a Yale-educated ranking member of the NAACP, Pickens found the interracialism at Delta to be a radical challenge to Mississippi's backwardness. Between 1936 and 1956, the black press wrote approximately twenty articles about Delta Cooperative and its successor Providence Farm. The attention Delta Farm received from the ANP meant that readers in every major black population center could learn about the farm's interracial practices.[69]

Hoping that the *Defender* had been right about Delta leading a new social order in the South, and continuing to push for interracial cooperation, Sherwood Eddy published a small booklet titled *A Door of Opportunity; or, An American Adventure in Cooperation with Sharecroppers*. Ostensibly, Eddy conceived of this booklet as a way to not only raise funds for the cooperative but also introduce many southerners to the farm. Eddy laid out the four tenets of Delta Cooperative Farm and stated that the endeavor grew from a deep desire and conviction to aid evicted sharecroppers. Eddy expounded on the third tenet of interracial equality at length, wedding the idea of racial equality with economic parity but stopping short of advocating for the integration of social activities. "We aim to be loyal to the principle of inter-racial justice in enlisting the cooperation of the white and Negro races in economic activity designed to bring about their mutual betterment," the pamphlet explained. "Without raising the question of 'social equality,' the teaching of which is forbidden by the laws of Mississippi (Statute No. 1103 of 1930), we endeavor to develop a sense of solidarity and to bring workers of both races to a realization of the necessity of facing their mutual economic problems together."[70]

The booklet straddled the knife's edge between promising what the local community wanted to hear and upholding Delta's tenets of interracial cooperation and justice. Eddy continued, however, to state that "the Negro is doubtless the acid test of America's principle of democracy. The Negro is also the spiritual test of our country." He stressed that all decisions made on the farm, especially on matters of race, were made by southerners. Eddy was also quick to point out that the farm manager, Sam Franklin, was a native Tennessean and devout Christian, and that white and black farmers were cooperating in work and economy, yet conducted separate social lives. He closed by assuring southerners, and Mississippians specifically, that the cooperative would adhere to the racial customs of the region as much as possible.[71]

On several occasions Eddy attempted to seek out the support of "men of good will" in Mississippi to combat rumors of communism or miscegenation at the farm. In the Mississippi Delta, as elsewhere in America, white segregationists saw communism, labor organizing, and black empowerment as inextricable challenges to white hegemony. Above all Eddy feared accusations of interracial sex. The perceived sanctity of white womanhood, Eddy knew, was the third rail of southern race relations. He envisioned a scenario that was all too common in the southern past. In a letter to Sam Franklin, Eddy wrote, "Some white girl will get in trouble. To avoid punishment she will point out some negro as having attacked her. The man may be lynched before there is any trial or inquiry or anything of the kind. I think we must get sponsors and the backing of men of good will before such an incident occurs, before they start the inevitable propaganda that we are a bunch of communists teaching free love."[72]

The recent trials of the Scottsboro Boys hung in the air as a reminder of the kind of danger Delta Cooperative Farm could encounter. In 1931, nine African American teenagers were arrested and accused of assaulting two white women on a train near Scottsboro, Alabama. When the Communist International Labor Defense committee stepped in to represent the teenagers in the hopes of a fair trial, white moderates and conservatives were incensed by the "meddling" of radical "outsiders." Eddy and his associates did not want to contend with the kind of foment that the Scottsboro Boys trial produced, nor did they want to confront the ire of conservative or moderate white southerners. On the contrary, Eddy hoped that the cooperative would gradually create racial harmony.

Friends warned Eddy to "exercise very great care in the realm of interracial relations lest all that you seek to do . . . be neutralized by too bold a move in the sphere of interracial activities." Delta trustee Bishop William Scarlett implored Eddy to use only southern men on the cooperative; "the experience of the Scottsboro Defense Committee shows how they resent northern attempts to step into their affairs." The more support Eddy sought, the more he realized that Delta Cooperative was both an enormously important and a dangerous endeavor.[73]

Correspondence among Delta's staff and the trustees in the first year spoke of unnamed threats to the farm and its residents. Supporters of the farm were fearful that farm enemies would use the slightest excuse to mount a violent campaign against the farm. On a visit in September, STFU organizer and budding folk singer Lee Hayes sent a letter from Delta Cooperative to friends back east describing his desire to have "a strong escort of about a hundred armed union men" to protect cooperative residents. The letter somehow made it into the hands of a local planter and raised even more suspicion about the curious farm. Howard Kester sent off a furious letter to Hayes, haranguing him for being "negligent," "irresponsible," and "thoughtless," and for providing "perfect ammunition for our enemies." Kester admonished Hayes that his statements and others like them had "given us our greatest troubles and permitted the planters and officers of the law to accuse us of being insurrectionists."[74]

Although Sam Franklin seemed to dismiss the idea that mob violence would befall the cooperative, William Amberson warned Franklin to take threats of violence seriously. Amberson outlined plans for mitigating future intimidation and defending the cooperative, and he suggested that Blaine Treadway be deputized in order to get on the good side of the local sheriff and to have some authority if an angry mob descended on Delta. In case of attack, Amberson begged Franklin to place an alarm on the boiler and erect a guard house on the most remote end of the property. Last, Amberson told Franklin that he and the cooperators must be ready to take up arms if necessary to defend their endeavor. Residents discussed at length whether or not members should be armed. Some ex-croppers supported this idea, saying that nonviolence had not worked for them yet. Others suggested that only whites be allowed to defend the cooperative while black members would be corralled into a hideaway. None of these steps were taken, but Amberson's suggestions and subsequent discussion underscored the serious threats directed against Delta. Amberson, lacking the religious foundation that Franklin possessed, reacted much the same way that rural farmers, who were no strangers to firearms or violence, might have reacted. Despite Amberson's best efforts to mitigate threats, fear of attacks and sabotage continued.[75]

Buttressed by his faith in humanity and Christian principles, Franklin's rosy outlook persisted. "Our cooperative meetings in which negroes and white people sit together have of course brought our race policy before the community," Franklin revealed, "and there has been some criticism from the illiterate lower class of white people." Yet Franklin did not want to betray his own efforts by painting too bleak a picture. "In general," he continued, "we have been amazed at the friendliness of the reception we have had." The goodwill between the outside community and Delta, however, was often little more than a shroud of civility. Although the cooperators often received support from Bolivar County public services, especially with health and sanitation projects, neighboring white planters were unfriendly, openly suspicious, and even hostile when they spoke about the goings on at Delta. Most planters agreed that the land Eddy bought was substandard and had ruined at least two previous planters.[76]

More exasperating than the staff's farming ignorance, though, was the interracial nature of Delta. Racial equality found its way into day-to-day courtesies when farm residents took to calling each other "Mr.," "Mrs.," and "Miss." Those who knew each other intimately would use informal greetings. ANP reporter William Pickens marveled at the formalities. "What a civilization it is! when we have to record as 'news' that whites address the Negro" formally, declared Pickens. He continued sardonically, "someday gaping posterity will marvel that we even mentioned such an ordinary exhibition of courtesy— ordinary in civilized places, but not in Mississippi." Right on cue, a white Mississippian proved Pickens correct. "Crazy," one exasperated local white critic spat, "mistering niggers in Mississippi."[77]

At an early "opposition meeting" held in Memphis in 1936, local community leaders had accused Delta of doing more than "mistering niggers." Sam Franklin attended the meeting and found a minister, "adept in old-fashioned Southern pulpit oratory," who was "dwelling on the horrors of attacks on white girls by Negroes, and presenting the case very luridly." The minister accused Sherwood Eddy, who was not there to defend himself, of being a communist who believed that white women deserved to be raped by black men. Franklin attempted to defend his friend and the undertaking at Delta but was cut off when another minister declared "if I was calling him a liar he would step outside with me and settle it." Franklin perceived that "others seemed anxious to get me outside in order to have a part in punishing me for my temerity." Franklin ultimately escaped the meeting without a physical confrontation. Coupled with internal problems of racism, opposition from outsiders impeded Delta's progress.[78]

Although articles, speeches, and pamphlets positioned Delta Cooperative Farm as a model for the South and the nation, the reality was less promising.

Audit records show that the farm could not continue to survive on its current financial footing. Delta made a net profit of over $8,000 during its first year of operation in 1936. Profits drastically fell every year thereafter. While profits in 1936 exceeded expectations, a series of harsh, soaking winters and hot, dry summers turned the soil at Delta alternately into a quagmire and then a cracked, barren wasteland. To make conditions worse, some of the farm volunteers and employees were inept at their jobs. Well-meaning volunteers from small-town and urban America came to Mississippi to lend a hand at Delta. Most had never lived or worked in such conditions and impeded the progress of production. When Jonathan Daniels visited Delta in 1937, he concluded that the volunteers and missionaries were "Robinson Crusoes washed up by good will on the Delta of Mississippi where they were applying their city brains and missionary Christian enthusiasm." Yet their "intellectual ignorance" toward daily farming operations, lamented Daniels, "seemed to me then . . . to be the tragic flaw in the Delta Cooperative Plantation."[79]

Contradictory approaches to interracialism and hastily established agricultural and economic structures weakened Delta Cooperative Farm out of the gate. To be sure, starting an interracial farming cooperative in the Deep South that supported labor organizing was a radical and admirable undertaking. Although a society built on white planter hegemony stacked the deck against them, cooperators made small but remarkable progress at Delta in the mid- and late 1930s. Not long after farmers were settled on the farm, however, internal racial and financial problems began taking tangible tolls. Time would tell if the struggling cooperative could withstand internal deficiencies and external disapproval to accomplish what it set out to do in March 1936: find economic solutions to sharecroppers' dilemmas through egalitarian, interracial, and Christian means.

Delta Cooperative Farm residents and neighbors celebrated Christmas 1936 on a cheerful note. On Christmas Eve, the cooperative's children performed a manger scene and pageant. Some of the staff dressed up as Santa Claus and distributed gifts—many of them donated—to their young residents. At the end of the night, one African American resident stood and, alone, sang "Lift Every Voice and Sing" the "Negro National Anthem." The residents had had a good year. Together they had lifted themselves out of the mire. Their fortunes as destitute sharecroppers seemed changed for the better. Their positive outlook would not last the decade.[80]

Delta Cooperative Farm, "The Old Council," undated (ca. 1936).
Left to right, front: Jim Henderson, Sam Franklin, Matt Smith;
left to right, rear: Clyde Erwin, George Smith, Wilbur White, Blaine Treadway.
(Allen Eugene Cox Collection Photographs, Mississippi State University
Special Collections, Manuscripts Department)

"King Cotton. Happily at work." Photograph by Dorothy May Fischer.
(Allen Eugene Cox Collection Photographs, Mississippi State University
Special Collections, Manuscripts Department)

"One of Delta cooperative farmsteads after a year of operation. Hillhouse, Mississippi." Photograph by Dorothea Lange.

(Dorothea Lange, U.S. Library of Congress, Farm Security Administration, Office of War Information Photograph Collection)

"Christian Democracy. Members of the Cooperative. The people are getting the most valuable kind of adult education in facing their practical problems as they arise. Cooperative meetings are held twice a month." Photograph by Dorothy Mae Fischer.

(Allen Eugene Cox Collection Photographs, Mississippi State University Special Collections, Manuscripts Department)

"Children at Hill House, Mississippi." Photograph by Dorothea Lange.
(Dorothea Lange, U.S. Library of Congress, Farm Security Administration,
Office of War Information Photograph Collection)

Jim and Shirley Henderson,
parents of Mary Ellen
Henderson, Providence
Farm residents, early 1950s.
(Allen Eugene Cox Collection
Photographs, Mississippi State
University Special Collections,
Manuscripts Department)

Fannye Booker, Providence Farm resident, fiftieth anniversary,
Southern Tenant Farmers' Union, Little Rock, Arkansas, March 16, 1984.
Photography by Georgia Lloyd.

CHAPTER 3

The Limits of Interracialism and the Failure of Delta Cooperative Farm

The cooperative's first calendar year ended on a positive fiscal note. Sam Franklin estimated that the farm had harvested 150 bales of cotton in 1936, roughly three-fourths of a bale per acre, or about 375 pounds of cotton per acre. This was well above the rate of production for the average American cotton farmer, who produced an average of just under 190 pounds per acre, but fell far behind neighbor Oscar Johnston's behemoth operation at Delta Pine and Land Company, which yielded 638 pounds of cotton per acre in the same year. The *New Republic*, which gained access to Delta's bookkeeping records, reported that the cooperative made more than $18,000, mainly from cotton and timber production. The overhead for the first year amounted to $8,000, and another $1,000 were paid toward the loan used to purchase the original acreage. On average, this left $327 in cash income for each member family. Cooperative member income was more than double the $122 the Works Progress Administration (WPA) reported the average sharecropper household received in 1935. Additionally, the WPA deduced that sharecroppers' cash income was only 30 to 50 percent of their real expenses and did not factor in shelter, food, and other necessities. "Applying these ratios," concluded the *New Republic*, "the total real income of Delta Cooperative Farm families would range from $655.06 to $1,091.76," which approached the income of the average employed American laborer. For the *New Republic*, these figures were evidence that "white and Negro sharecroppers, organized cooperatively, can raise their standard of living above anything the South has previously known."[1]

Yet when visiting Delta Cooperative Farm the same year, author and newspaper editor Jonathan Daniels peered through the thick Mississippi heat and saw the endeavor for all its shortcomings. While praising all involved for their efforts and genuinely impressed by what he saw, Daniels rightly observed that staff and volunteers were "better grounded in social and religious doctrine than in agricultural science." The same could be said for the absentee trustees, who often made decisions that affected Delta's residents. Amberson admitted to a staffer that he "never actually saw [the cooperators] in the fields." More damning to the cooperative method, though, was that Delta "still hung dependent upon capitalistic philanthropy," not "upon the cooperation in brotherhood of the common man." For Daniels, cotton and timber were not the source of Delta's income. "The one dependable cash crop is rich Yankees of soft heart," declared Daniels, who "stir in sympathy to the churchly sound of Christian Cooperation."[2]

Daniels was right about the donations that rolled in from mainly northern philanthropists. Most donations were solicited by Sherwood Eddy, but all the staff at Delta used their connections to increase the funds the farm had at its disposal. Dorothy Franklin sent a letter to a friend in Amherst, Massachusetts, who in turn read the letter to a group of her friends. "I can assure you," her friend replied, "that we had a group of women weeping real tears." The women—Daniels's "rich Yankees of soft heart"—promptly donated to the cooperative effort. If not for donations, Delta might have closed in its second year.[3]

The years between 1937 and 1942 saw the death and eventual rebirth of a social experiment in the Mississippi Delta. The rosy public perception of Delta Cooperative, portrayed by the *New Republic* article and shared by distant observers eager to praise a worthy cause, belied myriad underlying problems that Jonathan Daniels only glimpsed. The excitement of a productive start among cooperators soon gave way to harsh realities. Natural disasters and race and class antagonisms hampered the efforts at Delta, impeding residents' dreams to remake southern society.

First, farming was difficult under the best of circumstances. But during the Great Depression, the unpredictability and frustrations of working the land were exacerbated by poor weather and even poorer financial returns. The first productive year at Delta proved to be an exception across the rural South. The remaining years, when the cooperative struggled, were typical of the hard lives eked out by agrarians everywhere living hand to mouth.

Second, Christian and socialist ideologues like Sherwood Eddy, Sam Franklin, and William Amberson chose to experiment with their radical visions for America in this harsh environment. The trustees did not fully consider the cruel realities of farming in the Deep South. Their new hope for America blinded them to their own ignorance of exactly how to implement their vision in an unpredictable and unforgiving land. The failures that followed were

both human and institutional, and they exacerbated race and class antagonisms that already existed just under the surface but were largely pushed to the
margins during the cooperative's successful start the year before. Amberson,
Eddy, Franklin, and scores of sharecroppers made a leap of faith at Delta and
ultimately fell short. The social experiment at the cooperative underscores the
failure of many utopian communities when ideologies were put into practice
while the material realities of those living the experiment were not given foremost consideration. Out of Delta's failure, however, grew a new community.
Remaining members revised their vision for a cooperative community and
fashioned new solutions to the problems of the rural poor.

To the dismay of everyone living along the Mississippi River in 1937, rain
indeed followed the plow. Torrential rains fell on the farm not long after cooperative residents celebrated their first New Year's Day at Delta. In the first few
weeks of 1937, the Mississippi River Valley received the most rainfall since the
deadly 1927 flood that displaced thousands of Delta residents. By late January,
the farm was reduced to a muddy bog, and floods upriver threatened to over-
whelm the levee nearest Delta Farm. The same rains that threatened the farm
also wreaked havoc up and down the entire Mississippi River flood plain. At
the Resettlement Administration's Dyess Colony in Arkansas, excessive rainfall
and frigid temperatures left the colony a flooded, frozen mess. Colony managers sent colonists to live with relatives in the area or put them on trains to
Memphis. Homeless flood victims faced freezing temperatures and influenza,
which relief workers feared would spread rapidly among refugees housed in
close quarters. As a precaution, Delta Cooperative's women and children were
evacuated to Memphis like thousands of other refugees from Arkansas, Mississippi, and Missouri. Delta's evacuees found refuge in a vacant café, two private
homes, and the Rust Brothers' factory. At the factory, the Red Cross assisted
Delta's refugees, and local Memphis bakeries donated loaves of bread. Meanwhile the men secured what they could and built evacuation boats in case the
levees broke. William Amberson made the trek from Memphis to help evac-
uate cooperative families. Several staff families, including Sam Franklin's wife
and children, temporarily moved in with the Ambersons in Memphis.[4]

By the time the water began receding in mid-February, the 1937 flood had
covered more than eight million acres and killed nearly four hundred people.
The Red Cross mobilized its largest effort to that time and estimated they attended to over eighteen thousand refugee families who fell victim to the rising waters and disease. After a month of waiting out the rain, the women and
children returned to find production already behind schedule. "As we start
plowing," Sam Franklin confided in farm trustee Reinhold Niebuhr, "I can see
that we are up against quite a problem if we are to get this damp soil ready for

planting on time." To lift their spirits, cooperative residents sang "We Shall Not Be Moved" at the conclusion of a February community meeting.[5]

The flood in the winter of 1937 marked the beginning of Delta's downward financial spiral. Not even a year old, Delta Cooperative Farm began to confront financial and agricultural problems that proved difficult to overcome. The flood had set agricultural operations behind by a month. Cooperators did not plant cotton on the farm until mid-April. Slow production and inadequate financial returns put additional pressure on an endeavor struggling to find stability. As tensions rose due to harsh weather, poor crop yields, and economic instability, misunderstandings and disagreements among farm residents followed, further exacerbated when cooperative members were not immediately paid for their work. Most of this unrest manifested in racial and class antagonisms.

Each group involved with the cooperative effort was often oblivious to the travails of others. White cooperative residents were unsure what to make of black residents advocating for rights they had heretofore been denied, while black ex-sharecroppers were concerned that whites were getting better financial returns and preferential housing at Delta. Additionally, Resident Director Sam Franklin and the Board of Trustees often viewed former sharecroppers as a primitive community who needed to be shepherded along the path to socialism and were not yet capable of running the cooperative. Dorothy Franklin decried the lack of "moral suasion" and abundance of spiritual "superstition" among African American residents. "The stealing and lying among our Negroes are appalling not to mention their ignorance along truly religious lines," she complained. "We sometimes feel," she continued, "that we are in the heart of Africa." "The white families have more quickly grasped the meaning of the farm," Dorothy confided in a friend near the end of 1936, "but it is a terrific struggle for the Negroes to have even a modicum of faith in us or what we are trying to do." Ex-croppers, particularly African Americans as Franklin suggested, were sometimes skeptical of the motives of the manager, volunteers, and trustees. Used to conniving planters who had cheated them out of money by "figuring the accounts with a 'crooked' pencil," sharecroppers had learned not to take whites in positions of power at face value.[6]

Sam Franklin, like his wife, also approached the ex-sharecroppers with skepticism. According to Franklin, the "rough and passionate men" who populated the farm did not have the knowledge and discipline to run the cooperative themselves. Franklin ruled over each minute decision and micromanaged farm tasks. Yet publicly Franklin portrayed a different attitude. "I believe it remains for farms like ours," he told a potential donor, "to disprove some of the easy generalizations regarding the low mentality of the white and colored rural workers and their inability to manage their own affairs." Franklin's socialist ideology and paternalistic tendencies were often at odds. A naturally reflective man, Franklin was aware of his shortcomings as farm manager. Franklin wrote a colleague about the "pitfalls that await idealists in the field, especially if they lack the special technical training that the work required." "I have known this handicap myself," he conceded. Interracial cooperation among white and black ex-sharecroppers faltered as did the implementation of egalitarian Christian Socialist ideology from leaders like Franklin. The majority of these tensions happened between the members of the cooperative, who were hypersensitive to unfair treatment, and the paid staff like Franklin who understood his role as director in terms of mission work.[7]

Adding to these tensions, Sam Franklin had to inform several members that they were no longer welcome on the cooperative for various reasons. Some members who had fallen out of favor with Franklin had been antagonistic, while others simply produced poor work or conducted themselves in a manner contrary to the cooperative's founding Christian principles. Franklin asked African American croppers Clarence Wilson and Eugene Williams and their families to leave in 1937. Ernest Strong, a renter who had stayed on the land when Delta was established and who had offered keen insight into local agriculture, was also asked to leave. Franklin gave no reason except that the endeavor did not "want him next year although he is related to some of our people and would very much like to stay." Henry Williams and James Henderson were put on probation for the poor quality of their work. Member Clarence Oliver was asked to make changes in his negative attitude or else he would be forced to leave. Another member, Ben Baker, had suffered a serious illness and gone into debt with the cooperative in order to meet some of his medical bills. Baker left in the middle of the night, taking furniture and other items that belonged to the cooperative as he fled.[8]

Financial and agricultural problems persisted and put pressure on race and worker/manager relations at the farm throughout the late thirties and early forties. To solve many of the problems at Delta, the trustees authorized the purchase of a new farm in 1938 where old problems at the first farm could be corrected. However, the trustees put the new location, Providence Farm in Holmes County, under the same leadership. Gradually members, volunteers, and staff moved all operations from Bolivar County to the new site in Holmes County. For nearly four years, Delta Cooperative Farm and Providence Plantation existed together as dual challenges to the Old South's racial and economic structures. Staff and volunteers, however, stretched themselves thin between the two sites, and internal problems continued. In these years—1938 through 1942—the farms experienced crises of identity as structural changes occurred from top to bottom. This four-year period was a slow, painful moment of modification for the cooperative communal venture in Mississippi. At the end of 1942 and 1943, a kind of punctuated equilibrium occurred that made Providence a different sort of community than Delta Cooperative Farm. Still, in 1937, Delta Cooperative Farm's history was unwritten.

All farming, outreach, and social activities at Delta expanded in 1937 and 1938. One of the largest needs among black children at Delta was education. To receive the state-funded eight months of schooling, white children at Delta rode a bus to nearby Gunnison, where white teachers collected considerably more pay than their African American counterparts elsewhere in the county. In contrast, in 1936 and 1937, African American children at Delta walked nearly two miles to a nearby plantation where they received four months of state-mandated education in a one-room schoolhouse taught by an underpaid African American instructor. As was customary in most rural communities in Mississippi, Bolivar County did not have a high school for African American teenagers. In an early show of interracial communion, the cooperative council voted to educate African American children in all grades. The funds, however, were lacking.

Sam Franklin began contact with the Julius Rosenwald Foundation in early 1937, asking for money to help build a school at Delta. The Rosenwald Fund, which began as a philanthropist organization to provide monetary support for black communities building their own schools, had first built schools in Alabama in the 1910s, and by the 1930s had helped build rural schoolhouses throughout the South. Franklin argued passionately for an African American school at Delta, promising that the farm would supply all the material and human labor if the Rosenwald Fund would provide only the monetary means for construction. Writing to the fund, Franklin made a persuasive case. "I still think the matter of especial importance that we should have such a school, since our Negro youth are growing up in a different economic atmosphere and will therefore be better fitted to serve as leaders for their own race in meeting the social and economic problems which they face today," Franklin argued. "It will therefore be a double tragedy if we can turn them out with but little more schooling than the state of Mississippi now provides. The four and one-half month term is now in session, and they are supposed to be attending daily, but only a week or two ago the school was closed for several days for lack of wood to keep it warm. On other days we often see the teach[er] arrive at ten o'clock, and other evidences of a very low educational level." President of the fund, Edwin R. Embree, answered Franklin's letter directly, recognizing "the unfortunate condition of the Negro school," but acknowledging that his hands were tied because the fund had "to work chiefly through the higher sources" in Mississippi.[9]

In the wake of the Rosenwald Fund's refusal to help, Sherwood Eddy began a fund-raising campaign for building the school. The fund-raisers worked, and on September 21, 1937, Delta Cooperative Farm held a fish fry to celebrate the official opening of the new County Colored School on the farm. Delta hired a local teacher for $37.50 per month to offer four additional months of schooling for black children, marking the first time in the history of the county that both white and black children attended school for eight months. Seventeen-year-old Virgil Reese expressed the hopes of many young cooperators when he told a newspaper journalist that everyone was having their specific needs met at Delta. "Maybe I'll even go to school this fall." "I've only been as far as the sixth grade," he continued, "and haven't been to school in four years."[10]

Some white teachers and volunteers, however, were less than egalitarian in their dealings with white and black children at Delta. Constance Rumbough, Delta's Sunday school teacher in 1937, remembered that when she taught African American children she was "distressed to find them so very primitive, ignorant and seemingly retarded." Rumbough meant her comment to be an indictment of Mississippi's education of African American children, yet she also demonstrated a marked difference in perception between black and white children.[11]

In 1938, Delta held its first summer camp for area children, charging a small registration fee. The *Co-Op Call*, the cooperatives' monthly newsletter, announced an essay contest for resident children who would write on the "beginning and growth of cooperatives" in the United States or abroad. The announcement encouraged children to use the books in the cooperative's library as resources and win free admission to the camp. Split into four camps divided by both gender and race, forty-two children from six towns attended Delta's first summer camp. Camp offered a fun and educational experience to the area's children. An advertisement circulated in Mound Bayou, Mississippi, in 1938 announced that summer campers could "develop skills, initiative, and self-confidence" and "learn to make things by their hands, learn of nature, go hiking and camping." The Delta summer camps were also a place where trustees and volunteers hoped area children would receive "a better understanding of the whole cooperative movement"; where children would embody the visions of socialism, Christianity, and egalitarianism that adults had for Delta's future. Even William Amberson, a cautious pragmatist, acknowledged that Delta would "ultimately recommend this type of organization to the whole south."[12]

To outside supporters, whom trustee Sherwood Eddy courted for financial support and publicity, Delta Cooperative Farm seemed to be a successful model of interracial cooperation. Local, regional, national, and international publications ran stories about Delta, while New Dealers like Colonel Lawrence

Westbrook, a WPA official who supported cooperative communities, pointed to it as an example of Roosevelt's promotion of a pluralist society. National figures like photographers Marion Post and Dorothea Lange, socialist presidential candidate Norman Thomas, playwright and future best-selling novelist Elia Kazan, and past leader of the unemployed Coxey's Army, octogenarian Jacob S. Coxey, joined hundreds of curious visitors from all over the world. Gunnar Myrdal stayed overnight at Delta Cooperative Farm in the fall of 1938, among his first research trips that would produce the groundbreaking *An American Dilemma: The Negro Problem and Modern Democracy.*[13]

In midsummer 1939, Delta Cooperative Farm was a featured topic at the thirtieth annual conference of the NAACP in Richmond, Virginia. Delta resident and secretary of the local Southern Tenant Farmers' Union (STFU) chapter, George Smith, spoke to a session of young people about the merits of the farm, presumably to gain more working volunteers. Delta trustees and allies Charles S. Johnson, Howard Kester, and Arthur Raper all spoke at the convention on topics pertaining to Delta Cooperative Farm. Other speakers such as Thurgood Marshall, Charles Houston, and Walter White spoke on issues ranging from health to education while Eleanor Roosevelt presented operatic singer Marian Anderson with the NAACP's esteemed Spingarn Medal less than three months after Anderson staged her iconic protest performance on the steps of the Lincoln Memorial. Yet despite these prestigious guests, "economic security" for African Americans in the rural South dominated conference discussions. The fact that the cooperative effort in Mississippi was central to the conference signaled that Delta was considered by its allies to be part of the solution to challenges African Americans faced in the midst of the Depression. The reality was that Delta promised rural agrarians, black and white, chances to enact a better life for themselves. Yet not everyone realized these opportunities as progress was stunted by racism, financial problems, poor leadership, and inadequate agricultural production.[14]

The farm continued to draw more volunteers and staff as agricultural operations and activities increased. Trustee Sherwood Eddy's tour of college campuses and churches reached thousands of young volunteers, most of whom would stay only for a season or a year. Speaking at Texas Christian University in 1936, Eddy met a young idealist who subsequently became the farm's longest resident, and gradually shaped the cooperative effort by his vision. Upon hearing Eddy describe the cooperative movement, Allen Eugene "Gene" Cox became immediately interested in Delta Cooperative Farm. A deep devotion to practical Christianity led Cox to Delta and kept him there for the next twenty years. In 1931, Cox had entered TCU with just enough money for one semester. Over the next four and a half years he worked a series of odd jobs, including stints as a social worker with the Texas Relief Commission and as a community preacher, earning five dollars per week, in order to pay his way through school. When Eddy sought him out on recommendation from a mutual associate, Cox accepted the paid staff position of accountant and bookkeeper. Cox had not obtained his degree from TCU, but felt the opportunity Delta Cooperative Farm offered was too good to pass up. He arrived at Delta in late April 1936 and permanently settled at the cooperative in June of that year. A seminary student at TCU, Cox was "more interested in good works than preaching" and arrived at Delta "fully intending to make it his life's work." He eventually became as inseparable from the cooperative movement in Mississippi as Eddy or Franklin.[15]

In addition to gaining needed staff, Delta Cooperative Farm gradually added amenities after its first year. The U.S. Postal Service established the Rochdale, Mississippi, post office on Delta's grounds in September 1937, and the Farm Council asked Cox to serve as its first postmaster. Through rural electrification initiatives, Delta received electricity in 1938, although some residents elected not to have their individual homes wired and, instead, continued using kerosene lamps. Other residents, after having electricity installed in their homes, noticed that the lights attracted more mosquitoes than kerosene lighting and returned to using only oil lamps.[16]

Interracial and community events continued at the farm, too. Community celebrations, like the one-year anniversary party for the farm, were well attended. Delta residents celebrated the anniversary with horseshoes, checkers, a fish fry, a barbecue, singing, speeches from the earliest members, several competitive races, and a "husband-calling contest" for the women. Efforts at interracial understanding and black self-help also continued. A farm-wide community night in April 1937 featured a presentation called "What Do You Know about the American Negro?" An advertisement for the evening in the farm's organ, the *Co-op Call*, invited cooperative residents to attend. "If you want to hear about some of America's greatest educators, poets, authors, who are negroes," read the ad, "come to the Forum Thursday night at 7:40."[17]

In addition to the educational needs of the residents, the health of the cooperators and their sharecropping neighbors was long a concern of the trustees and staff. White staff had been appalled by the folk medicine practiced by some of the residents. Dorothy Franklin was particularly dismayed by "our old woman who tells fortunes 'by the Holy Ghost, the Virgin Mary and hoca-poca!' and puts hoodooes on people, as well as performing abortions, we believe, and affecting other cures." Another African American woman, the community's midwife, had prescribed a mixture of cockroaches, garlic, and herbs to be applied to a woman who had suffered a vaginal infection after childbirth.[18]

Just before the end of 1936, a young nurse named Lindsey Hail, the daughter of Christian missionaries in Asia whom Dorothy and Sam Franklin had known while serving in Japan, arrived and began nursing work on the farm full-time. One of her first patients was the farm's accountant, Gene Cox. Co-operators noticed that their normally reticent and business-like accountant immediately took to the attractive, single, and—according to one letter of recommendation—"impulsive" Miss Hail. Nine months after meeting, they were married, and lived the next twenty years of their lives in service to the cooperative effort, eventually taking over as trustees and resident directors.[19]

Gene Cox was only one of many patients Lindsey Hail Cox attended as cooperative nurse, and she often spent sleepless nights moving from house to house tending to the ill. In one incident that left a lasting impression on Hail, she played "the role of mother to a Negro baby for two weeks." The two-month-old infant, named Mildred, had been born to an unwed mother who left the newborn in care of the delivering midwife. The midwife, having experienced only delivering babies but not raising them, fed the child a steady diet of "raw cow's milk, undiluted." When the child arrived in Hail's care, the nurse thought the baby was dead. "Her eyes were sunk deep in her head and the eyelids were partly open and the eyes were glazed," Hail observed. "You could not see or hear her breathe. Wrinkles around the mouth and forehead made her appear ridiculously like a very old woman. . . . She reminded me of a baby crow with no feathers! The skin over her chest showed the outline of every rib. The abdomen was distended and looked like a round black drum. Her arms and legs had loose flesh hanging on the thin bones She was so dehydrated the flesh when pinched up remained that way instead of springing back in the normal manner. Her tongue had the appearance of white fur." Hail nursed baby Mildred for two weeks, waking up several times each night to feed her. When she deemed the child well enough, Mildred was returned to the mother who had originally given her up. The mother lived in a household "overflowing with children of various ages, all very dirty." When she gave the mother evaporated milk to feed her baby, the rest of the children seemed to covet it and Hail wondered "if little Mildred will not be sharing her diet." Despite her misgivings, Hail left her in the crowded home. "Perhaps if Mildred lives," Hail hoped, "she will grow up to be another Marion Anderson [sic]." Like many malnourished babies in Depression-era America, Mildred did not live beyond infancy.[20]

Among the duties that Hail immediately took on in late December 1936 was to supply experimental birth control to farm residents. Sam Franklin had been in contact with Dr. Clarence J. Gamble, heir to the Procter & Gamble empire and staunch advocate of birth control and eugenics. Gamble, eager to test new spermicidal jellies in the population, supplied boxes of diaphragms, lactic acid jellies, and applicators to the farm. As the only nurse, Lindsey Hail Cox was charged with dispensing the contraception and keeping copious notes to send to Dr. Gamble. With the new charge from Dr. Gamble, Hail was overburdened at Delta. One nurse could do only so much. It was not until a traveling health clinic sponsored by the African American sisters of the Alpha Kappa Alpha Sorority, INC. first visited Delta in 1937 that sharecroppers in the area and the farm's residents received adequate health examinations and immunizations.[21]

Alpha Kappa Alpha, a sorority for middle- and upper-class black women, placed a high premium on service. In the mid-1930s, they identified the black populations of the Mississippi Delta as in acute need of medical care. Dr. Dorothy Ferebee, of Howard University Medical School, headed up the project that began in 1935 in Holmes County, Mississippi. They were to make their headquarters at the Lexington-based Saints Industrial School. When the women arrived for their six-week clinic in the summer of 1935, however, they found that most plantation owners had refused to let their sharecroppers leave to attend the clinics. The women figured that if the sharecroppers could not come to them, they would go to the sharecroppers.[22]

Originally, the women of AKA had planned to take the train from D.C. to Mississippi, but they were refused service at Union Station by the ticket agent. The women instead organized a carpool and drove themselves to Holmes County. Using personal vehicles they had driven from Washington, D.C., the women traveled throughout Holmes County in 1935. The next year, however, they decided to move their base of operation to Mound Bayou in Bolivar County, figuring they would meet with more support in the all-black community. They were right. Thousands of patients visited their clinics in Mound Bayou that summer, and the AKA volunteers received additional support from an eager Bolivar County Health Department. The traveling health clinics continued as well, and for the next five summers AKA volunteers, nurses, and doctors set up temporary clinics in schools, churches, community buildings, and fields. In 1937, in addition to immunizing for diphtheria and smallpox, the sorority added a dental staff. Like all health care, access to orthodontia was limited for rural blacks. One Holmes County mother remembered that in the 1930s when she took her two sons to a white dentist to inquire about having them fitted for braces, the dentist flew into a rage. He refused to look at the boys' teeth and kept declaring that the mother would not be able to afford two sets of braces anyway. She left without the braces, and without knowing how much they cost. "I have always thought," she remembered bitterly, "that his apparent anger just meant that a black person shouldn't have the audacity to ask a white doctor for braces."[23]

The AKA-sponsored Mississippi Health Project collaborated with the medical clinics at Delta Cooperative from 1937 to 1941. In an attempt to address black health care and the "social welfare needs of the poor," AKA members traveled to Delta each summer as volunteers, bringing with them state-of-the-art medical devices, doctors, nurses, dentists, and social workers. The health clinics most likely continued providing birth control to Delta residents as well. Dorothy Ferebee, the physician who headed the summer health project in Mississippi, understood that black men and women were at the mercy of paternalistic white doctors when it came to gaining access to birth control. As a result, Ferebee became a proponent of providing birth control to rural blacks in Mississippi. Because of the health clinics, many black Delta residents went from having no medical facilities to being able to access some of the most modern clinics in the rural South. Still, residents at Delta needed medical attention above what Lindsey Hail Cox and the summer clinics could provide.[24]

In the late summer of 1938, a white doctor, David Minter, arrived at Delta to be the cooperative's permanent physician. Minter was dedicated to the type of missionary work that a clinic at Delta offered. The steady influx of college-aged women at the summer volunteer camps also offered the handsome and single doctor opportunities to find a wife. Minter had been visiting the farm to decide if the place was right for him when he met his future spouse, Sue Wootten. A recent college graduate, Wootten, from Evansville, Indiana, was a volunteer at the Quaker summer work camp that year and immediately fell in love with the Delta. Indianans, thought Wootten, did not have anything like the Delta's landscape, and she loved every aspect of her new environment. In her early twenties, Wootten was several years junior to Minter, but the two quickly took to each other. Both had unusual senses of humor that made them fast friends. Wootten was most attracted to the doctor's quiet but affable manner and the near constant practical jokes he played on residents at the farm. But it was not until she overheard a conversation between Gene Cox and Minter that she began to fall in love with the farm's doctor. One day Cox and Minter, thinking no one was within earshot, argued good naturedly over the color of Wootten's eyes. Minter was adamant in his belief that her eyes were brown, while Cox, being noticeably less interested, thought they might be green. Minter was right and Wootten knew she would soon be courting the doctor. The Minters married in December 1940 in Delta's community building, while Gene Cox played songs on the cooperative's Victrola. After a brief honeymoon, Sue moved to the farm permanently.

Cooperators spent most of the summer of 1938 building a new, two-story medical clinic to prepare for Dr. Minter's full-time arrival. Sherwood Eddy established a clinic fund and subsidized all medical needs at Delta, although patients had to pay for their own medications. Through donated funds and in cooperation with the AKA, the clinic possessed resources considered state-of-the-art in rural Mississippi. Not long after Minter arrived, the clinic was dedicated with a religious service presided over by trustee Bishop William Scarlett. The clinic had an integrated staff during the AKA summer clinics, which bucked the segregated custom of nearly every medical clinic in the South. White doctors did not employ black nurses, and when the rare African American doctor, often educated at black-only Meharry or Howard, set up a clinic in the rural South, the staffs were all black. In rural Mississippi, this was the prevailing practice. Often, though, the waiting room was reserved for whites only. Black patients visiting a white doctor's office in the rural South had to wait outside or in a hallway before they were seen. At Delta, the waiting room was integrated.

The clinic offered the most benefit, however, for area African Americans who did not have year-round access to a physician until Minter arrived. Most rural blacks still relied on home remedies and "conjure doctors" who practiced folk medicine. The health situation for many rural blacks was serious. In 1929, the mortality rate for southern African Americans was 59 percent higher than that of southern whites. Even into the 1940s, to contract tuberculosis was usually a death sentence, and most rural victims lived out the remainder of their days sequestered in "TB shanties" so as not to infect family, friends, and neighbors. Before Dr. Minter arrived and while Sam Franklin was away from the farm for a few weeks, Blaine Treadway wrote him of the deteriorating health of residents. "The health situation is still a major problem," warned Treadway. "Mr. White has had a bad case of blood poisoning in his arm which has prevented him from working. We have had him visiting the dentist while he has been out. Lando Hollman and family are having a siege of boils. Dr. Weidener has ordered Lando to bed. He says that one of the boils which he has, conceivably could cause instant death if its progress is not checked immediately. John Will Henderson was bitten by a spider on Friday, and before we could get Dr. Day here he was have serious convulsions. However, after two injection intravenously of magnesium sulphate he is able to work again. Tom Jones and Annie Belle Billington are both in bed with chronic cases of Gonnorhea. Lee Phillip's baby has a case of malaria." Travelers even had to receive typhoid and small pox vaccinations before venturing south to Delta Cooperative. From a public health standpoint, living in the rural South before World War II, when many communities did not have regular access to medical care, was akin to living in the Old World. Having a doctor and nurse on the farm—when they did—saved more than a few lives.[25]

Despite productive initiatives like summer camps and medical clinics, steady agricultural production and economic stability eluded the farm. As the land turned against them, cooperators began to raise questions about how race and labor were structured at Delta Cooperative Farm. Sam Franklin told Reinhold Niebuhr in March 1937, the one-year anniversary of the farm, that he had heard rumors of a "coming sit-down strike on the part of some of our women when the cotton-chopping season begins." The women believed that they were not making as much on the cooperative as other cotton choppers were on nearby plantations. When a similar event had happened months before, Franklin had remarked that the situation "indicates that some of the Negroes are abusing their new freedom." Demonstrating the extent to which the cooperative had not solved the issue of plantation labor, the women were "under no contract to work, so they cannot strike," Franklin reassured Niebuhr, "and I think the matter will be ironed out before the time comes." Franklin ironed it out, however, by sending cooperative member George Smith to Clarksdale to hire cotton choppers to come to Delta. When the day laborers arrived, Franklin paid them at the rate that other hired laborers in the area fetched. In addition, Franklin sanctioned the women who had participated in the strike by not allowing them "credit at the cooperative store nor to participate in the distribution of gift clothing that was sometimes sent to us." In response to Franklin's harsh measures, some of the women returned to work while others moved to nearby plantations. Some of the staff were furious at Franklin's actions. Mildred Young, a Quaker who joined the farm as a full member, protested side by side in the field with strikers in order to show her solidarity.[26]

The idea of cooperative labor, socialism, and interracialism proved difficult to implement. Some white cooperators expressed their desire to have "a separate project for the colored." Race and class antagonisms trumped interrace and cross-class cooperation when the day-to-day operations did not operate smoothly. White and black members accused Sam Franklin and other staff of unfair treatment and withholding payments. Black ex-sharecroppers charged whites on the cooperative with racism over housing, labor details, and fair wages. Racial tensions and accusations of paternalism added to an already difficult endeavor.[27]

The 1930s presented a crucial moment of modification in race relations. More than any previous economic event, the Great Depression had leveled differences of race and given poor whites and blacks common cause. What the 1930s did not do, however, was obliterate race. Charles Spurgeon Johnson, writing two years before Delta Cooperative was founded, observed that race "has an emotional content which persistently obscures its meaning." Anthropologist Hortense Powdermaker lived in Sunflower County, just sixty miles from Delta Cooperative Farm, as a participant observer for two years in the 1930s. Powdermaker concluded that "certain articles of faith, constituting a creed of racial relations, are held almost unanimously by the Whites in our community." She reduced these "articles of faith" into certain familiar phrases repeated by whites. Foremost, "negroes are innately inferior to white people, mentally and morally." Beyond this old canard, the orthodoxy became more specific. Important to the endeavors at Delta were proclamations about the "place" of African Americans. "Any attempt at any kind of social equality," Powdermaker reported, "would result in some disaster so overwhelming that it is dangerous even to talk about it and so terrible that it cannot be thought of concretely." A related creed declared that "because the Whites are so seriously outnumbered, special means must be taken to keep the Negro in his place, and anyone who opposes those means is dangerous."[28]

Jim Crow, however, was not a static phenomenon, nor did it operate the same way from locale to locale. A side-by-side examination of neighboring Mississippi Delta counties reveals the erratic and unreasonable nature of segregation. Delta Cooperative Farm sat just inside the Bolivar County line, only a few miles from Coahoma County. Racial customs in these two counties displayed the confusion and absurd idiosyncrasies of Jim Crow culture. In the late 1930s and early 1940s, sociologists observed that blacks could play athletics or billiards with whites in Bolivar but never in Coahoma. In Bolivar, blacks had to give whites the right-of-way on sidewalks and could not touch a white man without causing resentment or anger. In Coahoma, however, those customs were more elastic. Additionally, blacks served on juries occasionally in Coahoma, but never in Bolivar. Blacks had separate waiting sections in all stores in Coahoma, but whites and blacks waited together in Bolivar. The peculiarities and randomness of Jim Crow made navigating race relations a confusing—and often dangerous—undertaking.[29]

The simple fact that it was an attempt at cooperative farming also made Delta contentious. Establishing cooperative communities in a capitalist society was no easy task, even in the cooperative-friendly milieu of the New Deal. Ultimately, those in charge of keeping Delta financially viable could never reconcile that cooperatives were counterintuitive to American agrarian ideals of democracy and individual ownership. The trustees knew that a plantation-sized cooperative with thousands of acres in production was needed in order to keep Delta financially competitive. This was not always the preference of cooperative members. After sharecropping and tenant farming had proved to be so destructive for black and white croppers in the years since the Civil War, many preferred to seek out a plot of their own where they would not answer to a plantation owner or, in this case, a board of trustees. Several critics of the farm concluded that residents were not completely behind the cooperative model and did not take to sharing their work and profits with their neighbors. One early visitor was impressed with Delta on the whole, but surprised at the scant knowledge the average cooperator possessed about the principles in place on the farm. "The members need a clearer understanding of the nature and function of the Cooperative," he wrote. Another more critical visitor accused Franklin of running a "paternalistic dictatorship."[30]

Taken together, the early criticisms of Delta Cooperative exposed Franklin and implicated the Board of Trustees as misunderstanding the very people they were so eager to help. Often critical of liberals as milquetoasts on the race issue, Franklin, Eddy, Niebuhr, and other socialists were nevertheless ill-prepared to put ideology into practice in the Mississippi Delta. Franklin, educated at several seminaries, approached his role on the farm as missionary, teacher, father figure, and task master. His relationships with many of the cooperators were often abrupt, tense, and condescending. In spite of his efforts to help sharecroppers, Franklin and the board members carried prejudiced assumptions about how race and class operated in 1930s America. Ex-sharecroppers could not possibly be expected to take care of themselves, thought Franklin, because they simply were not culturally ready.

The cooperative suffered from a crisis of identity as a result of the communication gap between races and classes. Initially this crisis was most evident in the tenuous relationship between the STFU labor leaders and Christian missionaries who were quick to get the farm off the ground but often quibbled about the ideological focus and day-to-day operations. Yet the disagreements between the union and the cooperative paled in comparison to the criticisms that disgruntled trustee William Amberson began to level at his fellow trustees, particularly Sam Franklin and Sherwood Eddy. Beginning in the late spring of 1935 William Amberson gradually drifted away from the Socialist Party, feeling he had been "taken for too many rides" by fellow comrades looking for money, devoting more of his time to the STFU and his role as a trustee for Delta Cooperative Farm. The STFU, Amberson explained to Socialist Party leader Clarence Senior, was "the only significant Socialist work in this section." The Memphis socialists, he complained, were "faint-hearts" and not fully or financially committed to the socialist cause. Amberson's disgust with southern socialists was partly based on interpersonal squabbles and disagreements. But ruptures plagued the national party, too.[31]

The years 1934 to 1937 marked a major decline for the American Socialist Party. The party split into various factions and interest groups while longtime socialists were forced to choose ideological sides, cannibalizing their overall strength at the polls. The Popular Front had initially been a boon for the acceptance of socialism in the South. Yet cooperation among socialists, communists, and other leftists proved difficult and socialists often disagreed among themselves over how to best utilize the viability of the antifascist Popular Front. While some embraced cooperation, other socialists remained hard-line anti-communists. Instead of getting swept up in the heated and often unproductive arguments over the direction of socialism in the United States, many, like Amberson, simply disengaged from party politics.[32]

Amberson believed that his experience with the STFU had altered his and Howard Kester's approaches to aiding leftist reform movements. His previous "position was more theoretical than practical, and the experience of the field," Amberson realized, "has made us, not less radical I hope, but less doctrinaire." Amberson dove headlong into the organizing effort, spreading the STFU's aims around the South. He soon realized, however, that political action was moot without economic advancement and security for southern farmers. Soon disillusioned by the STFU's protest tactics and wanting more tangible successes for sharecroppers, he felt that striking and marching were empty gestures without serious plans for how to replace the plantation system of agricultural labor. The STFU, in his view, was gaining no political ground and had "no chance whatever to succeed for some years yet." The only viable answer Amberson saw was to support cooperative communities. When ex-sharecroppers found economic stability and competed in the agricultural market, Amberson believed, only then could they truly have their voices heard. Instead of the direct political action of the STFU, he was drawn more to the cooperative model at Delta, though he knew that this would be seen as acquiescence by many leftists. "I have reached the point where I am willing to accept half a loaf," conceded Amberson, "rather than go without bread at all." In this way, Amberson was different from many intellectual socialists of the 1930s. Doctrinaire ideologies often hampered the national party and blocked practical strategies for overhauling capitalism and American democracy. In 1937, Amberson still had high aspirations for socialism in practice and realized that the endeavor at Delta Cooperative Farm represented a fighting chance for rural socialists to enact their own vision for America.[33]

Gradually, though, Amberson became antagonistic toward the cooperative's trustees and management just as he had with the Tennessee Socialist Party. Financial and interpersonal disagreements led him to question his fellow trustees. Initially an admirer of Franklin's, Amberson accused both him and Eddy of not having the best interests of the poor in mind and, worse, embezzling money. His biggest concern, though, was that the other trustees had no intentions of allowing the cooperators to ever own the land outright on a collective basis, thus undermining the cooperative effort.

When Amberson's friend, fellow socialist, and cofounder of Commonwealth College A. James McDonald arrived to Delta as Franklin's secretary in March 1937, he immediately began criticizing his new boss and the day-to-day operations. McDonald was argumentative, hardheaded, and apt to think he knew best how to run a cooperative community and socialize the farm's economy. He had experience living on the New Llano Cooperative Colony in Louisiana and worked closely with the Rust Brothers as they developed their cotton-picking machine. Keeping up a steady correspondence, McDonald served as Amberson's informant on the farm. Most appalling to McDonald, an atheist, was the kind of Christian philosophy espoused by Eddy and employed by Franklin. McDonald considered practical Christianity to be unrealistic and naïve. Despite being personally attended to by Cox and Franklin when he came down with malaria, McDonald continued to loathe most of the staff, as well as the practices at the farm, and to pass his observations on to Amberson. McDonald's letters only fueled Amberson's displeasure with Franklin and Eddy.[34]

Through letters to associates and the other trustees, Amberson accused Franklin of being foolish in his expectations and Eddy of being dishonest, especially in terms of raising money for farm "improvements" and then pocketing the money to cover his purchase of the farm. Amberson even accused Eddy of yelling at the members on one occasion during a particularly tense meeting, "If you can't do what you are told to do then goodbye, brother, go on down the road!" If Delta failed, insisted Amberson, it was not "because of the antagonism of the planter aristocracy but because of the inexperience and the dishonesty of such men as Franklin and Eddy." Amberson's accusations revealed serious disagreements among Delta's leadership and proved a reflection of Delta's gradual downward spiral. Amberson's fears of financial dishonesty grew when Sam Franklin suddenly, and with little consultation, purchased a new tract of land—known as Providence Plantation—on behalf of the trustees.[35]

Although Eddy and the other trustees hoped that Delta Cooperative Farm would be the flagship of multiple cooperative endeavors in the rural South, no real opportunities to purchase more land presented themselves in the first eighteen months at Delta. Then, in late 1937, Sam Franklin found 2,800 acres of land with a working dairy in Holmes County, on the edge of the Mississippi Delta. Franklin, without consulting the Board of Trustees, took steps to purchase the land and the dairy. The land struck Franklin as ideal for beginning another cooperative. Although the Board of Trustees quickly approved the purchase of the Providence tract in January 1938, Amberson abstained from voting on the purchase because he objected to blindly following Franklin's suggestions without seeing the land for themselves. Amberson's disdain for Franklin and the other board members continued to grow.

At its hasty founding in 1938, Providence was nearly indistinguishable from the already fraught experiment at Delta Cooperative Farm. The gradual move to Holmes County began in 1938 and lasted four years. The new farm, covering just over four square miles, sat astride the geological boundary of the eastern edge of the Mississippi Delta. About five hundred acres at Providence were lowland and planted in crops. Most of the rest of the land was hilly and mainly covered in oak, pine, and cottonwood trees. Bluffs that signaled the eastern boundary of the Yazoo-Mississippi Delta ran along the western edge of the property. Chicopa Creek, which flooded often, ran through the eastern section and offered a natural source of irrigation along with several sloughs and a natural spring that residents dammed and made into a swimming hole.[36]

The property contained two large outbuildings, a dairy, which would be Providence's main focus in the first years, and the old plantation commissary, which cooperators turned into the Providence Cooperative Store. Because it was a former plantation, the tract housed several sharecropper families. Franklin asked cooperator Wilmer Young to visit each sharecropper, explain the new ownership, describe the cooperative model, and give them the option of staying on as members or finding employment elsewhere. As at Delta three years earlier, some moved and some integrated into the new community at Providence. Sam Franklin and his wife Dorothy made the first move to Providence in June 1938, the same month that electricity from the Rural Electrification Administration reached the farm. Franklin attempted to manage both farms from Providence, maintaining a dwelling at both locations and making weekly visits to Delta. This proved too difficult, and soon operations at Delta were divided awkwardly between Blaine Treadway, a local farmer employed at the cooperative named Albert Day, and Gene Cox. As a local white farmer with perceived racial prejudices, Day was an unpopular choice to run operations in the fields. Treadway, Delta's original assistant director, was asked by Franklin to take over the creamery operations at Providence, despite having no practical experience in this area. Treadway wavered and temporarily chose to remain at Delta.[37]

Continuing a commitment to diversified agriculture, the 1939 crop rotation plan at Providence included cotton, soybeans, corn, small grain and hay, and a cover of clover. Over one hundred acres were used for hogs, and thirty milch cows were put to pasture. The creamery was a new venture for the staff, residents, and volunteers, many of whom now had to make milk deliveries all over the county. With no experienced members who could run a creamery, the endeavor was a source of frustration for Sam Franklin.

The purchase of a new farm put the population at Delta in flux. The number of white farmers at the cooperative dropped dramatically in the late 1930s and early 1940s. There were three reasons for this trend. First, several white farmers complained directly to STFU official H. L. Mitchell that they were "invited" to leave the farm by Sam Franklin and Sherwood Eddy. These whites believed that African American farmers were receiving preferential treatment. In December 1941, white resident Wilburn White, a founding member of Delta Cooperative, wrote to H. L. Mitchell complaining that Franklin reportedly told the entire farm that "he could no longer raise any money on the white families and thought he could on the Negroes." Several white families, especially those who were critical of Franklin, were directly asked to leave by either Franklin or Eddy. As his Christian philosophy evolved, Eddy considered the plight of poor African Americans to be the most pressing issue of his time. In an early publication on Delta Cooperative Farm, Sherwood Eddy stated that "the Negro is doubtless the acid test of America's principle of democracy." Eddy's public speeches reflected his evolving philosophy as well. In public remarks at historically black North Carolina A&T College in 1941, Eddy focused on the troubles of African Americans in general, not sharecroppers specifically.[38]

Second, the onset of World War II meant that whites could now enter the workforce in greater numbers. Many rural white and black southerners migrated to urban centers in the South, North, and West. African Americans wishing to stay in the South found fewer jobs in the war industry than did whites. Many whites joined the military.

Last, the increased mechanization of agriculture meant that Providence could not support as many families as Delta had in the 1930s; Providence simply needed fewer laborers to run farm operations. Delta may have been on the cutting edge of Mississippi race relations or economic reform, but it was not a trailblazer in terms of modernizing the business of agriculture. A large, plantation-sized cooperative with hundreds of workers became obsolete almost as soon as it got under way in the late 1930s; although the cooperative used both mules and tractors, the farm could not keep up with the rate at which the rural South mechanized. The Board of Trustees had hoped that John and Mack Rust's mechanical cotton picker would revolutionize field labor and socialize farming equipment by funneling profits into cooperative communities, but their invention failed to sell and was soon eclipsed by International Harvester.[39]

The Board of Trustees also experienced changes in membership, but not in its oversight of the farm and continued support of Sam Franklin. Sociologist and activist Arthur Raper joined the board in late 1937, and fellow sociologist Charles S. Johnson, president of Fisk University, integrated the board by becoming a trustee in early 1938. Raper and Johnson had published extensively on sharecroppers' circumstances and suggested many avenues of relief. In 1936 they had collaborated on a report that suggested drastic changes to the southern plantation economy, changes that would have given more croppers ownership of the land they worked and thrown government support behind cooperative farming. Raper specifically took note that the Deep South's cotton economy had "its economic background in feudalism and racial background in slavery." It was here, in places like Arkansas and Mississippi, suggested Johnson and Raper, that ownership of large plantations should be divided among croppers. Although the Board of Trustees now more closely reflected the racial makeup of the cooperators with the addition of Johnson, Sam Franklin remained a dominating influence at Delta. Because most of the trustees rarely visited the farm, Franklin continued to be the major source of information for the board. Having few opportunities for interaction with disgruntled cooperators, the trustees did not seek to make changes. The power dynamics Franklin developed early remained in place.[40]

In 1938 and 1939, as cooperators began the slow task of moving to Providence, Amberson's continued alienation and black members' complaints of racial discrimination came to a head. White and black members separately accused Sam Franklin and Sherwood Eddy of discrimination and antiunion sentiment in 1938. The Board of Trustees and the STFU, however, seemed uninterested in exploring the matters until the grievances were brought before a union convention meeting later that year. Several STFU members visiting Delta complained that cooperators were being treated unfairly. In all, these members, supported by an initially indignant H. L. Mitchell, leveled fourteen specific complaints to the union office, the foremost of which called the members "Clients at Will" of the trustees. By this accusation, members meant that their situation was little better than it had been while they toiled under the sharecropping system. The members accused farm management of being heavy-handed, untruthful about financial affairs, and discriminatory in their policies. White and black farmers declared that they were not receiving proper wages and that they had received no "settlement" from legal victories won by the STFU.[41]

Farm residents were also furious over a farm council vote that took place when Sam Franklin began long absences from Delta as he traveled to Providence to prepare the new community. The council voted that Albert Day, the farm's paid white "director of agriculture," be left in charge of agricultural operations instead of the well-liked Blaine Treadway. African American farmers felt that they were being made "slaves" of Day, who was a native of Bolivar County and had professional and personal ties to the area's white planters. After Franklin stood and publicly endorsed Day, the council voted that "Albert Day should be executive at Rochdale over field and garden crops, timber, sawmill, and livestock; that Blaine Treadway should have direct oversight of garment-making, movies, and furniture making and should exercise general supervision and represent the farms to the public." Cooperators felt that Franklin had unfairly swayed the opinion of the council with his endorsement of Day, and left the well-being of the cooperative and its members in the hands of a man almost no one except Franklin trusted. The schism between Franklin and the STFU was palpable when H. L. Mitchell publicly accused Franklin of ignoring the union's role on the farm altogether and of supporting Day, who had growled that he "didn't intend to allow any damned union organization" at Delta. Accusations and ill will threatened to tear the endeavor apart from the inside.[42]

It took the Board of Trustees and the STFU over a year and a half to cobble together an investigating committee to look into the accusations of mistreatment, mismanagement, and racism. Trustees Arthur Raper and John Rust joined STFU National Executive Council members Howard Kester, D. A. Griffin, and J. F. Hynds in announcing that they would hear any public or private grievance while making inquiries into each allegation. Although the committee visited the farm to investigate, there is no record of their meeting one-on-one with the members. A community meeting was held, which Franklin attended, where the committee asked members to stand up and talk about their grievances. None did.

The committee chalked up the grievances to unfortunate misunderstandings and the discontent of a few. Addressing the most serious accusation that members were "Clients at Will" of the Board of Trustees, the committee attributed this to a lack of communication between the members and the trustees. Many cooperators were "unaware of their rights and responsibilities" at Delta, reported the committee, and did not fully understand the communitarian nature of the cooperative effort. The committee drew the same conclusion in investigating undispersed wages, subsidies, and settlements. Although the committee suggested altering the bookkeeping practices at Delta to allow for more transparency, they concluded that it was necessary for monies received from the producers' cooperative or government aid to go directly into the cooperatives' overhead costs. This necessity, the committee posited, "seems to have escaped many of the people."[43]

In all cases of apparent discrimination, the committee found that the contrary seemed to be true. "Negroes," wrote the committee, "were not found to be discriminated against in any manner." To prove this point they highlighted that an African American woman had received the highest wages of any unskilled laborer at the cooperative. The investigating committee suggested that the trustees and managers engage in more transparent and clearer communication about farm operations with its members. To aid in this reform, the committee asked the managers to "employ language generally understood by the people." The language chosen by the committee echoed the condescension of Sam Franklin, who felt that cooperators needed constant supervision in order to work effectively. The only significant redress to any grievances was in clarifying Albert Day's position at Delta and diminishing his role as "executive," essentially leaving the cooperative in Bolivar County in the hands of Blaine Treadway and Gene Cox. In concluding, the committee commended Sam Franklin "and his associates for their devotion to this heart-breaking and difficult problem." Despite the committee's inadequate conclusions, the usually fiery H. L. Mitchell seemed pleased with the report and concluded that the "greatest good that came from the investigation was in opening Raper's and Rust's eyes to the fact that the folks down there ought to be permitted to run the farms with less interference from the outside."[44]

The committee's investigation, however, did not satisfy Amberson or his allies. McDonald and Amberson speculated that the members did not raise their concerns in front of Franklin for fear they would be kicked off the cooperative. McDonald hypothesized that Raper and Rust were not fully committed to the investigation, and "had no place on such a committee under any circumstances that I can conceive of; men do not investigate their own actions impartially." "Griffin and Hynds were the only members of the committee who were really interested in making an investigation," thought McDonald, but "they were wholly lacking in the qualifications that were needed." Finally, McDonald considered Kester "a church politician whose principles are just about as elastic as a rubber band." McDonald chalked up most of the cooperative's problems to Sam Franklin, the Board of Trustees, and the investigating committee, who possessed a "lack of confidence in the ability of the common man to understand, to plan and to execute." Quoting a friend who had briefly volunteered at Delta but left in disgust, McDonald called Franklin's style of leadership "paternalistic feudalism." The majority of the committee approached the cooperators with some of the same misunderstandings as did Franklin. The ideological assumptions of the committee—that ex-sharecroppers were the burden of men like Franklin—hijacked the investigation from the outset. Ultimately, though, McDonald blamed Franklin and Kester for colluding to whitewash the investigation. Amberson took a slightly different tack. Although he was utterly disgusted by Franklin, he believed that Kester influenced the investigation because he wanted to maintain his friendship and financial relationship with trustee Reinhold Niebuhr. Niebuhr had in fact raised funds on behalf of many of Kester's organizations. Despite Amberson's contemptuous understanding of the situation, Kester clung to the hope that the cooperative farm could accomplish its original lofty goals but that the process would be a slow one.[45]

During the long deliberations of the committee, Amberson became too frustrated with his associates to continue his relationship with Delta Cooperative Farm. At a February 1939 meeting of the Board of Trustees, Amberson read aloud his six-page resignation letter, stating that he felt the operations in the fields were "a dictated rather than democratic program." On the issue of Franklin encouraging the farm council to appoint Albert Day as executive, Amberson scoffed that "to claim that the procedure actually used was democracy is to trifle with words. Better by far to say frankly that the Board or the Resident Director will appoint the farm foreman, than to go through this elaborate hocus-pocus of seeming to give the choice to the people while in fact denying it to them." Amberson added that "it was sociological ventriloquism at its dreadful worst." He then devoted the majority of his resignation letter to breaking down the farms' finances to conclude that both endeavors were firmly in the red and that Franklin and Eddy were misleading donors and the members when they stated that both farms were succeeding. Amberson saw the difference in his figures and the official bookkeeping as dishonesty on the part of Franklin and Eddy. But he also viewed the problem as ideological differences. "Never before have I seen with such blinding clarity," declared Amberson, "the essential and irreconcilable conflict over the scientific and ecclesiastical approach to social problems." Competing ideologies, thought Amberson, blinded the trustees to the actual problems at the cooperative. Amberson also perceived that Sam Franklin had blamed him for fomenting the "subterranean rumblings" of dishonesty and racism. Franklin had dismissed the complaints as the results of "instigation from the outside." Amberson concluded that Franklin was essentially calling him an "outside agitator" and "the pattern of plantation thought which he [Franklin] had meant to break, rises up again to grip his own mind." Condemning the board as a whole, Amberson concluded that in "criticizing absentee landlordism, we have ourselves created its most vicious form." Finally, he asked to be immediately removed from all publicity associated with the cooperative farms. The Board of Trustees accepted his resignation without discussion. Amberson wrote a cooperative resident after his resignation, summing up his feelings in blunt terms. "I regret more than I can say that this venture, conceived on so high a plane, should have fallen into the hands of a bunch of dishonest ecclesiastics," Amberson lamented. "I loathe them all."[46]

Amberson's dispute with the trustees, however, did not immediately come to an end. He and Eddy waged a bitter row in the pages of the *Christian Century*, each refuting the other's claims and both sounding defensive and shrill. Amberson proved quite adept at convincing others of misdeeds at Delta Cooperative. J. P. Warbasse, the president of the Cooperative League of the USA, sided with Amberson. "Too many people serving on boards and committees are putting up with all sorts of humbug, ballyhoo, and chicanery because they do not know what their organizations are doing," Warbasse commiserated with Amberson. "A host of noble names are serving as window dressing for the exploitation of tawdry wares," concluded Warbasse. Amberson was persuasive in his case against Eddy, Franklin, and the Board of Trustees. But even without Amberson's gift of persuasion, many of his accusations were correct. By 1940, the cooperative effort was still not a true cooperative, and members did not own the land or their labor outright because Sam Franklin and other trustees did not believe that the members were ready to run the farm's operations without supervision. Despite the discord, operations pushed forward and Eddy continued to raise money for the endeavor as though the cooperative was flourishing. Writing of Eddy, Amberson declared that "this colossal fraud brazens his way onward in spite of his own dishonesty." "It is enough," Amberson concluded, "to make the angels weep."[47]

Delta Cooperative Farm experienced a dramatic decline after 1939. Even though the *Washington Post* recently wrote a long, glowing article about Delta as a "revelation of the shape of things to come in the New South," the Eddy-Amberson dispute fueled speculation that Delta was failing in its stated goals. Staff and members left in droves. Some, like A. James McDonald, Amberson's ally, were asked by the Board of Trustees to vacate the cooperative because, according to the board, they did not align themselves with the mission of the endeavor. Original Delta cooperator James Moody wrote William Amberson in November 1940 fully dejected about recent events on the farm. "We have come about to the end of our road as a cooperative," lamented Moody. "The trustees was to be here the 15 of this month but mr Franklin went to New York instead. Mr Franklin has been telling us that the charter has been changed claims we will never be anything but tenents [sic]. Remember I have a copy of the old charter and the only way they could alter the charter was before the people became members of the farm, and if I am not right I would like you to tell me how they could change it without their consent. Am well aware that the trustees has taken everything in their hands. The council is only a figurehead. The great blow out we had there by the union was a whitewash for Franklin. I never heard anyting [sic] more about [it] after they left the farm. I guess I will have to leave the farm this fall." Within a month, James Moody and his brother, Carl, had packed up their families and left Delta for Flint, Michigan, where they hoped to find industrial work. STFU president J. R. Butler received word from Art Landes, a white union member, in June 1941 that "only a few of the clients are attempting to farm cooperatively" but that the cooperative store seemed to be "succeeding very well." Landes wrote H. L. Mitchell the next month to inform him that because only three residents, including Landes, had been attending the sporadic STFU meetings at Delta, they decided to dissolve the local altogether. He reported that the local possessed "between 4 and

5 dolars [*sic*] in cash" and no other assets. By the next spring, Landes and his wife Margaret had moved from Delta, and the cooperative retained only tenuous ties to the STFU through a few residents.[48]

From 1938 until 1942, all operations gradually moved to Providence Cooperative Farm in Holmes County. Over that period, Delta was divided up by the board and sold to various private landowners, businesses, and the state of Mississippi, which coveted the land because of its proximity to the Mississippi River. In December 1942, the final acres were sold to a local landowner for $36,400 in cash. Only one of the original Arkansas refugee families lived at Delta in 1942 when it closed. Cooperators simply packed up and left Bolivar County. Many made their way to Providence along with Gene Cox and his family, but most, like Blaine and Dorothy Treadway, frustrated and weary from their experiences, chose to make their lives elsewhere. For Treadway, his dissolution with the farm had mounted for some time. William Amberson had publicly advocated that Treadway replace Franklin as Delta's manager as early as 1937. This amounted to a colossal hassle for Treadway, who now had to defend himself against Franklin's accusations that he was gunning for Franklin's job. Treadway wrote Amberson to complain and reveal that he was casting about for other employment. "Among other things he asked if I wanted to take his responsibilities over," Treadway wrote of Franklin. "I told him then that he misjudged me if he thought that our differences arose over that." The Treadways returned to Memphis, where Blaine worked two part-time jobs in the main office of the STFU—where he was named acting secretary for a short period—and in the evenings at the Memphis *Press-Scimitar* as a printer.[49]

Poor soil, harsh weather, blinded ideologues, racism, and classism combined to defeat Delta Cooperative Farm. Additionally, some of the same types of personality clashes that doomed the STFU also haunted Delta. Minutes of the Cooperative Council meeting in 1939 show that discussions were plagued by disagreements, personal vendettas, and indecisions. Reflecting years later on Delta's closing, Arthur Raper declared that "such an undertaking elicited the interest of people with a bold faith in the common man, and the belief that they themselves should help these dispossessed people if they could. The result was the coming together of well-meaning people trying to do an almost impossible thing. They were strongly individualistic, articulate, and motivated by high moral courage. So they held marked differences of opinion, carried on searching discussions, and even then sometimes no consensus was reached." The ever blunt William Amberson put it more succinctly when considering what he believed was Sherwood Eddy's potentially dishonest fund-raising and naïve faith that the effort would succeed. "Led by such a man," he spat, "the farm was bound to fail."[50]

Soil quality and poor crop yields were also factors that contributed to Delta's failure. The region's mix of poor buckshot soil and erratic flood/drought cycles contributed as much to its doom as any other factor. As previously stated, when agricultural practices were tough, and financial hardships arose, latent racial and class antagonisms bubbled to the surface, exacerbating an already dire situation. The land at Providence, many miles from the Mississippi River levee system, was more predictable, but by the early 1940s, members were moving away from full-scale cooperative farming anyway, and the survival of the endeavor did not depend solely on agricultural production.

Yet Delta Cooperative Farm brought Americans' attention to race, labor, and economic discrimination and exploitation in the Deep South. Although Delta mitigated the pain of enduring poverty, it did not solve the problems created by plantation agriculture and white supremacy. The men and women at Providence Farm, soon under the new leadership of Gene Cox, would have to carry out what Sherwood Eddy, Sam Franklin, William Amberson, and scores of sharecropping families began at Delta. "Much can be pushed forward; much may have to be changed; the whole must be deepened," wrote cooperative member Mildred Young upon Delta's closing. "The great thing is that life has stirred in the dark seed and growth is occurring."[51]

CHAPTER 4

The Concrete Needs of the Thousands among Us

Returning from a conference in Raleigh, North Carolina, in March 1943, Sam Franklin felt energized by the like-minded conferees and stirring speakers. The conference was convened by his old friend, Howard Kester, and sponsored by the Fellowship of Southern Churchmen, an interdenominational and interracial group of liberal laity and clergy from the South who worked toward ameliorating the region's many social problems. Kester titled the conference "Christianity, Democracy, and the Healing of the South." It was just the kind of work that the residents at Delta and Providence had attempted for the past seven years. At Kester's invitation, Franklin had been a featured speaker at the conference. Returning to Providence, Franklin thought about how to implement healing in his own small community.[1]

The trip to Providence was long. Franklin traveled by bus from Raleigh to Meridian, Mississippi, where he then took a train to Jackson. In Mississippi's capital, he boarded another bus and rode sixty miles north to the small crossroads town of Tchula, Mississippi. From downtown Tchula, he hitchhiked the remaining seven miles out to the farm. The lengthy journey gave Franklin time to reflect on Kester's conference, but it also provided him ample opportunity to observe the racial customs of public transportation in the South and overhear southerners' conversations about race relations. At the conference, Franklin had taken part in discussions with like-minded activists, many of whom were southerners, who viewed Jim Crow as an impediment to "healing the South." As he returned to Providence Farm, he saw and heard white southerners of a different mind, who were determined to maintain Jim Crow at great cost. "As I traveled in Mississippi, I not only saw new evidence of almost sadistic inhumanity in the needless humiliations imposed on Negroes in bus travel," Franklin lamented, "but also heard one middle class white woman telling another that she had been warned to go armed at all times as the Negroes were soon going to 'rise.'"[2]

What Sam Franklin witnessed in his travels was a South in transition and on the verge of crisis. World War II had made race relations more elastic, forcing many Americans to confront the realities that fighting fascism overseas would be an empty gesture to black veterans who returned home to Jim Crow. Meanwhile, African Americans increasingly drew on local organizing networks to agitate for equal rights. Yet for others, the late 1930s and early 1940s increased fears of black advancement in all areas of American society. The continued calls for racial integration, both socially and economically, among returning veterans and the black press led to defiant entrenchment on the part of many white southerners. Even moderate liberals warned of moving too fast too soon in the direction of racial equality. Sociologist Howard W. Odum's 1943 book *Race and Rumors of Race* cautioned how white supremacists would resort to violence to maintain Jim Crow. The South was not yet ready, he concluded, for sweeping changes in race relations.[3]

Additionally, the steady emigration of sharecroppers to industrial areas, which was fueled by the pull of wartime employment and the mechanization of agriculture, contributed to a tense racial atmosphere across the rural South. Thousands of African Americans joined the Great Migration and moved from the rural South to new homes in the urban North and West. Panicked planters begrudgingly turned to other populations to supplement the dwindling black population. On several Delta plantations, Mexican Americans, through the Bracero Program, and German POWs joined African Americans in the fields. World War II and the planter aristocracy had unintentionally made cotton chopping a culturally diverse affair in the 1940s. Preferring to maintain a native labor force while continuing to deny African Americans political participation, white southern conservatives employed their own brand of a Double Victory campaign. They championed white supremacy and protection from federal intervention. Southern whites who were invested in Old South economics and race relations were anxious about the encroachment of the federal government, the slow decay of one-party politics, and overt affronts to segregation. The South, as they had known it in the 1930s, crumbled all around them. The challenges to white supremacy wrought by the New Deal order and World War II struck many white southerners with alarm, especially in Mississippi Delta locales like Holmes County, where blacks outnumbered whites by more than three to one.[4]

Black initiatives at Providence were an outgrowth of what was taking place around the South in the late 1930s and early 1940s. Sociologist and Providence trustee Charles Spurgeon Johnson accurately declared in 1944 what many blacks had felt for years: that "the great majority of southern Negroes are becoming dissatisfied . . . and want a change." Another sociologist, Samuel Adams, surveyed the Mississippi Delta during World War II and found significant race pride among African Americans, a conclusion that was a perplexing revelation to many of their white neighbors. In Coahoma County, just a few miles from where Delta Cooperative Farm had operated, blacks staged a strike to protest planters' attempts to decrease their cotton picking wages.[5]

Many whites blamed black veterans for recent racial anxieties. On the floor of the U.S. Senate, Mississippi senator James O. Eastland fanned the flames of racial animosity by falsely claiming that black soldiers in Europe had abandoned their posts and systematically raped European women at gunpoint. It was a political ploy meant to win over Mississippi's votes. White racists viewed returning black veterans as threats to their economic hegemony and personal safety. The U.S. military trained African Americans for a variety of professional tasks and instructed them in firearm proficiency, making black veterans seem doubly dangerous to white racists. As Johnson and fellow sociologist Odum pointed out in the early 1940s, many whites feared a "Negro insurrection." Fantastic rumors, one of which included an army of ice-pick-wielding blacks attacking whites during Defense Department–imposed nighttime blackouts, ran rampant throughout the South. Rumors of "Eleanor Clubs" told of black sharecroppers and servants plotting bloody uprisings against white employers. The types of rumors that Odum and Johnson documented were nearly identical to the conversations Sam Franklin overheard while returning to Providence Farm from North Carolina in the spring of 1943.[6]

The early 1940s constituted the most transformative moment of modification for the cooperative communalist effort in Mississippi. Changes occurred as a result of two major overlapping developments. Increased willingness by blacks to embrace a self-directed, self-help approach to activism and the entrance of the United States into World War II played out in rich detail at the farm as managers and staff scaled back the cooperative model, most whites left the farm, and residents concentrated their efforts on black human rights. The interracial cooperation that had been the crux of earlier efforts at Delta Cooperative Farm was feasible because black and white sharecroppers had experienced the nadir of American opportunity in the 1930s. Together, the sharecropping class was at the bottom of the socioeconomic hierarchy that American capitalism and plantation agriculture had created before World War II. Farm trustee Charles Spurgeon Johnson observed that the fight against fascism in World War II had made increased numbers of Americans realize that blacks and whites were "fellow citizens in the world community." "More and more we are realizing that in world community, in national community, or in local community," Johnson declared, "we shall build soundly only when all citizens participate." The Atlantic Charter and World War II patriotic rhetoric seemed to codify human rights and gave international credence to the efforts at Providence. Johnson's outlook for cooperative race relations was positive. Yet the position that patriotism would overcome racial difference was short-lived.[7]

The war changed relationships between whites and blacks in ways that Johnson did not anticipate. The war industry opened opportunities for white ex-croppers in Mississippi in ways that it did not for blacks. No longer were the rural poor, black and white, in their economic struggle together. Black-centered initiatives at Providence were reactions to the improved economic circumstances World War II offered most whites, but not many blacks. Now, evolving race relations and new approaches by African Americans and their allies to lay claim to civil and economic rights, indeed a broad swath of human rights, permeated nearly every interaction at Providence.

With so many material and financial resources pouring into the war effort, little was left for those who did not find jobs in war industries or join the military. Donations for endeavors like Providence simply dried up. Victory taxes and rationing, two ways civilians ostensibly aided the war effort by economic means, hurt rural southerners' pocketbooks. For Sam Franklin, a man who made roughly $250 per month, his monthly victory tax was $12.40, 5 percent of his total monthly earnings. With outside financial resources declining and whites deserting the farm, Providence residents turned to black self-help initiatives to redress their own poverty.[8]

The notion of black self-help, what contemporary activists called black uplift, had its antecedents in the Reconstruction-era freedmen attempting to seek out freedom for themselves and the late nineteenth-century ideas of Booker T. Washington. Freedmen explored black self-help by buying land, organizing denominational churches, becoming politically active, and pursuing formal education. Thriving all-black communities like Mound Bayou, Mississippi, founded in the 1880s, embodied the strivings for black autonomy and uplift. But like the reality of post-freedom life for many former slaves, Washington's version of black uplift relied heavily on the patronage of paternalist whites. The idea of black uplift was further adapted in turn-of-the-century northern black communities and among middle- and upper-class blacks who constituted W. E. B. Du Bois's "talented tenth." Taking their cues from wealthy blacks, many 1920s middle-class civic organizations, such as the YMCA, began to get involved with similar uplift initiatives. "Through Christian education, edifying lectures, courses on hygiene, and camping and recreation programs," explains one historian, "the Y would transform simple country women into upstanding, respectable urban citizens." His time with the YMCA influenced Sherwood Eddy to promote similar self-help initiatives at Delta and Providence.[9]

In the 1940s, rural African Americans embraced the idea of uplift shorn of its Victorian cultural assumptions. Instead of the talented tenth elevating the race, ex-croppers at Providence were doing it for themselves from the bottom up, much like their freedmen ancestors had done in the wake of emancipation. This sort of autonomous self-help occurred because of the growing popularity of citizenship politics among African Americans. Blacks founded civic organizations and voter leagues in southern communities in the 1930s that grew in number in the 1940s. These black-directed organizations modified human rights work. "The emergence of these new organizational forms and new leadership," according to political scientist Kimberley Johnson, "marked a decisive shift away from the interracialism and elitism of the earlier period of black political life." Residents at Providence turned to increasingly localized, civic-minded activism beginning in the 1940s. Coupled with increased mechanization during World War II and white plantation owners' diminished influence over black work, black political and labor activism at Providence—as throughout the South—changed significantly.[10]

Beginning gradually with the establishment of Providence Farm, and taking shape throughout most of the 1940s, residents made the transition away from earlier goals of cooperative production, a socialized economy, and interracial cooperation. As the number of whites in the community drastically decreased, and as outsiders questioned the viability of a large-scale cooperative farm, Providence residents slowly implemented new tactics that focused particularly on barriers to economic freedom, adequate education, and proper health care for African Americans in the rural South. Farm residents worked toward black self-help with aid from profit made by the cooperative store and the dairy, increased access to health care through the cooperative health center and traveling summer health clinics, and improved educational opportunities for children and adults through a variety of courses conducted year round at Providence. Yet the changes did not suit everyone. Finding Providence no longer addressed his needs, longtime resident Koss Kimberlin, a white socialist who initially ran the creamery at the new farm, left to pursue other work opportunities. Like so many other white families, nearly 80 percent in fact, the Kimberlins found work in industrial areas. Not yet fully integrated into the industrial workforce, the majority of black ex-croppers, like original Delta Cooperative member Jim Billington who made the move to Providence in 1942, remained at the farm.[11]

The Board of Trustees also experienced change in 1941, almost two years after the resignation of William Amberson. Joining Reinhold Niebuhr, Sherwood Eddy, Sam Franklin, John Rust, Arthur Raper, and Charles S. Johnson were Reverend Emory Luccock of the First Presbyterian Church in Evanston, Illinois, and Frederick Douglass (F. D.) Patterson, the president of the Tuskegee Institute and the founder of the United Negro College Fund in 1943. This Board of Trustees proved to be a stabilizing force throughout the subsequent evolution of Providence and remained unchanged for the rest of the decade.

Although World War II began for the United States in earnest in December 1941, the effects of the war did not come to Providence until the fall of 1942. By some measures, the summer of 1942 was an invigorating time to be at Providence. The farm's staff, volunteers, and residents held their highest attended summer health clinics and youth summer camps that year, while formal and religious education programs continued to draw students from all over the county. From late 1942 until the end of the decade, however, Providence had to evolve with the rapid changes occurring in the rural South and develop new strategies for alleviating poverty and race prejudice in the region.

Holmes County was a different place, geographically and socially, than Bolivar County. The soil was rocky and ill-suited to grow cotton. The surrounding community was also different than any near Delta. The town of Tchula, seven miles down Mississippi Highway 49 from Providence, had a population of one thousand inhabitants, far bigger than the hamlets around Delta Cooperative. Tchula was a typical crossroads town in rural Mississippi in the late 1930s and early 1940s. Situated on two blocks, downtown Tchula contained Clark's Drug Store, Joe Maggio's Groceries, a dime store, a whites-only coffee shop, the Presbyterian, Methodist, and Baptist churches for whites, the Rose Hill Baptist and Mount Zion churches for blacks, a hardware store, a bank, a jail, a two-story white school, and the water tower that rose high above the cotton fields surrounding the town in every direction. Although white neighbors had been skeptical of Delta, they were geographically scattered and unorganized. Tchula offered Providence farmers an outlet for their goods, but its tight-knit white community would become more apprehensive about Providence with the rising civil rights movement and reemergence of anticommunism. An inescapable similarity linked both Bolivar and Holmes counties, however. White supremacy ruled. Holmes had witnessed three lynchings in the first thirty years of the twentieth century—about the state average in Mississippi—while Bolivar had been the site of eight lynchings—second highest in the state. In 1940, Bolivar and Holmes counties were both 75 percent African American, yet whites firmly controlled all politics and nearly all economics.[12]

The new location precipitated changes, minor at first, that demonstrated cooperators' willingness to adapt their original goals. Given the challenges that the new farm presented, the "sense of the mission of our enterprise began to change," reported Sam Franklin. "It was directed to the concrete needs of the thousands among us, victimized by racial prejudice and by economic injustice. We asked ourselves how we could make our little Farm community a center for social change in the whole locale," he continued. The result was a focus on the surrounding black community through economic advancement, medical care, and education.[13]

The new residents and emerging leadership at Providence Farm had bold visions for the future of blacks in a portion of Mississippi where three-fourths of the residents were black in the 1940s and 1950s, but less than 13 percent of the total farmland was owned by African Americans. For black Holmes Countians, adequate health care, economic security, and educational opportunities were nearly nonexistent. They could have moved almost anywhere in the country and had better access to these three necessities. But beginning in the early 1940s, Providence Cooperative Farm offered practical strategies to begin to meet their needs.[14]

The only aspect of Providence's new structure in the first years of the 1940s not wholly aimed at economic uplift or health care was the Providence Cooperative Association. The brainchild of Sam Franklin, the cooperative association began in 1943 as "the formulation of long range community-wide objectives." The objectives were aimed at "physical, economic, educational, and religious" uplift of the surrounding community and included "100% of the community in church, 75% in Sunday School, and Bible reading and prayer in every home." Aside from the maintenance of the spiritual health of the community, the association strove "to get half of our children of high school age into high school." It targeted "those families within a radius of six miles of this farm, most of whom are Negroes who are day laborers, tenant farmers, or owners of small tracts of eroded land." Franklin thought it was "interesting and challenging to be able to have a part in the gradual transformation of a community through the practical application of the teachings of Christ. It is a community that emphasizes the number 1 economic problem in America as the President's Commission has termed the South," he continued, "and which reveals the starkest need along every line from the physical to the spiritual."[15]

Importantly, the first president of the Providence Cooperative Association was Robert Granderson, a black farmer from rural Holmes County and member at Providence Farm. Granderson "had suffered from the arrogant discrimination which deprived black people of political rights and made education in the segregated schools little more than a gesture." Despite these hardships, he "had grown to middle age with dignity and an independent spirit, with a deep

Christian faith and a strong concern for social well being." Granderson steered the association and the farm in important directions throughout the 1940s by reaching out to the surrounding black community, offering them financial, spiritual, and community-oriented support.[16]

Although many of the staff and volunteers at Providence in the 1940s were no longer dyed-in-the-wool Christian Socialists, the teaching of social justice on the farm now had a long history that would continue into the next decade. Granderson oversaw the Educational Institute for Negroes held each December at Providence. Beginning in 1941 and recurring throughout the decade, the institute consisted of instruction in agricultural practices and handicrafts, Bible lessons, and advanced courses that prepared black youth for college. Signifying the importance of social justice to black pupils, one teacher offered "classes in Isaiah and found my listeners very responsive as we talked of the prophet's ideals of justice." One educational institute culminated in a Christmas service "with a colored Madonna," reported one teacher, "which was very beautiful."[17]

The classes offered at the Educational Institute for Negros reflected the farm's new commitment to black self-help and human rights. Beginning with the first institute, some of the most influential black leaders of the era came to Providence to instruct black residents of the Mississippi Delta. Instructors included the longtime farm ally Howard Kester, civil rights activist and educator Juanita Jackson, who had organized a march in Annapolis to repeal Maryland's Jim Crow laws, and Dr. Jacob Reddix, who was then president of the Jackson Training College for African American students and who had organized a successful African American cooperative in Gary, Indiana, called the Consumers' Cooperative Trading Company. Other instructors came from the surrounding black churches and a dozen colleges and institutions including Tougaloo College, Jackson College, the Saints Industrial School in Lexington, and the Farm Security Administration. Course titles included "Church Work," "The Art of Cooking and Homemaking," "Cooperative Organization," and "Toward a More Healthy Community." In order to attract a large audience, attendance was free.[18]

The Cooperative Association quickly became the main focus of farm activities and bolstered the farm's reputation among local blacks. The popularity of the Cooperative Association marked a shift in the community's goals. Franklin noticed that, beginning in the early 1940s, Providence had "an increasing range of influence in this impoverished community of Negro farmers and sharecroppers. At this time when it is so necessary that we realize at home the ideals for which we are fighting abroad," Franklin declared. "I think there are few causes which will yield better returns in aiding worthy people to help themselves than this community-wide program that we are carrying on." "To appreciate what it meant one has to think of it against the background of ignorance, preventable disease, abject poverty, denial of elementary civil rights, and confused and distorted religious thinking which characterizes most of the Negro life of this section," Franklin wrote a friend in 1943. "We feel the Providence Farm is strategically located here in a county where three-fourths of the population is colored and where nearly all of the moral issues arising out of the sharecropping and tenant system are found in an acute form. It is a satisfaction to us that though our progress has been very slow we now have mobilized many of our neighbors within several miles of the farm to make a constructive attack upon the evil condition under which they have been living."[19]

Franklin's views that African Americans in the Delta had "confused and distorted religious thinking" once again betrayed his paternalistic tendencies as a lifelong missionary to cultures he deemed unsophisticated. Soon, however, under less dogmatic leadership, the educational institutes fostered black-centered guidance and increased the prominence of black teachers and community members.

Among the top concerns of staff and volunteers at Providence was the medical care of the rural population in the county. The sisters of Alpha Kappa Alpha Sorority, INC (AKA). had initiated their traveling health clinics in 1935 at Mound Bayou, moved to Delta Cooperative Farm in 1936, and then initiated another temporary traveling clinic at Providence in 1939. Before the clinic opened at Providence, dental care had been nearly nonexistent in that part of Mississippi. No black dentist had maintained a practice in the county, and most residents had never had access to dental care. The closest white dentist was in Lexington, nearly twenty miles from Providence, and he offered only limited service to black patients. Instead of being able to wait in the large waiting room with whites, black patients had to sit in the stairwell leading up to his second-story office. Because of the hardship of traveling great distances to see a dentist and the demeaning way blacks were treated when they arrived, over 90 percent of the AKA's patients had never visited a dentist. Even a decade later, there were only thirty-three black dentists in the entire state of Mississippi.[20]

Throughout the summer clinic's existence, AKA sorority sisters teamed with the medical staff at both farms, which consisted mainly of Dr. David Minter and white nurses Lindsey Hail Cox and Dorothy Binns Treadway, before she and Blaine left in 1939. Minter and Lindsey Cox had traveled once a week to Providence beginning in 1939, but maintained their permanent clinic at Delta Cooperative. So when the AKA sisters came to Providence in the summers between 1939 and 1942, it was the best chance for many poor Holmes Countians to receive satisfactory health care.[21]

Health conditions among many rural blacks and whites in the Mississippi

Delta were grim. One patient history of a regular attendee at the Providence clinic noted that "J. R." lived on a plantation with a family of five. "House in very bad condition. No screens, no toilet. Works at least 13 hours per day. Average breakfast—eggs, butter, molasses, biscuits. Dinner—a vegetable, milk, bread. No supper." Like J. R., most sharecroppers lived on milk, molasses, vegetables, and cornbread. To address malnourishment, which caused ubiquitous cases of pellagra, rickets, and a host of other maladies, the clinic brought sorority sisters trained as nutritionists to demonstrate "methods of combining foods with a large vitamin content to 'stretch' or increase" the nutrition of each meal.[22]

Offering all manner of medical services, from dental care to contraception, Minter and the AKA sisters provided the African Americans of Holmes County with dependable health care and treatment for the first time in their lives. "When we heard about you all coming," reported a black sharecropper to the clinic staff, "we just ran outside and thanked God. We have been praying for someone to be sent in His name," she continued, "to speak for his poor laboring people."[23]

The AKA health clinic reached the most rural Mississippians in the summers of 1941 and 1942. During those summers alone, the clinics aided nearly six thousand patients in Holmes County. Providence Farm served as the headquarters for the clinic, housing the sorority sisters while some of the farm's residents cooked for the clinic staff. Because of the year-round health care Minter offered, using Providence as a base allowed the sorority to learn about the health histories of patients that they would see only during the summer months. The clinic staff and the residents at Providence grew close over those summers. Sam Franklin and Ida L. Jackson, an AKA soror and Mississippi native who worked at the sorority headquarters in Oakland, California, and who was the cofounder and director of the health clinics, kept up a correspondence throughout 1942 and early 1943. The relationship between the cooperative and the sorority developed to the extent that Sherwood Eddy secured a $1,500 annual donation from the AKA beginning in 1943 in exchange for a promise that the sorority could use Providence as its headquarters for subsequent summer clinics. Eddy also spoke with the sorority about having a representative serve on the farm's Board of Trustees, granting the African American sorority the privilege of appointing the first woman to serve on the board. This plan, however, never materialized.[24]

The cooperative's health care activism peaked in 1942. Dr. Minter treated over ten thousand patients—one in four Holmes County residents—at Providence, both black and white. In only a one-month period, the AKA summer health clinic saw 10 percent of the county's black population. As the summer of

1943 approached, Providence Farm and the AKA were planning another successful summer clinic.[25]

Delta Cooperative Farm was finally sold on January 2, 1943, for $33,600 to a private land owner. The previous month, Gene Cox had worked tirelessly to liquidate Delta's assets and move the last remaining families, including his own, to Providence. By early January, Delta founding families the Billingtons, the Hendersons, the Morgans, and the Erwins joined the Franklins, the Coxes, the Minters (who had set up a permanent clinic at Providence in 1942), and ten other families at Providence to carry on their experiment in cooperative work and communal living.[26]

The profit from the sale of Delta Cooperative enabled Providence to "proceed with a certain degree of economic security and stability." The Cooperative Farms, Inc. could pay off all debts related to Delta and close the mortgage on Providence Farm outright. The biggest debt was to board member Sherwood Eddy, who had fronted the $15,000 down payment on the Providence purchase in 1938. Eddy had received $1,000 toward the repayment of that debt, and the Cooperative Farms, Inc. paid him the remaining $14,000 after Delta's sale. A Holmes County attorney living in Lexington named Pat Barrett, who would ironically play a pivotal role in the eventual demise of the cooperative experiment, prepared the deed for Providence Cooperative Farm and officially transferred the ownership of the tract from Sherwood Eddy to Cooperative Farms, Inc.[27]

In owning two properties in Mississippi from January 1938 until January 1943, the Cooperative Farms, Inc. had stretched already scarce human, material, and financial resources to the limit. The introduction of a creamery at Providence had residents scrambling to learn how to operate it. Although Franklin urged Eddy to buy the creamery on behalf of the farm, he would later call it the source "for some of the most traumatic experiences of my years with the Farms." The purchase of the creamery meant that staff and residents at the farm had to deliver milk all over the county. While they barely kept up this schedule for several years, it soon became clear to Franklin that this purchase had been ill-advised.[28]

Operating the creamery and processing milk at Providence had proved too much to handle for any of the regular residents who migrated over from Delta Farm. Because no dairy operator held the position for longer than a few months, the responsibility often fell to Sam Franklin and some of the female staff and volunteers. Tending to the milch cows and the dairy was nearly round-the-clock work, with residents often milking after dark and rising at three thirty in the morning for the first milking of the day. Franklin admitted that his "hair grew gray over such matters as bacteria counts, leaking compressors, and lost milk bottles." In 1943, exactly one week after the Cooperative Farms, Inc. finalized the sale of Delta Cooperative, they also sold the rights to the creamery to Mann Smith, "an enterprising Negro who has a business of his own and who will in all probability be able to meet these notes without difficulty." Once the creamery was sold, instead of pasteurizing the milk themselves, Providence obtained a contract with a creamery in Greenwood where they shipped their raw milk. The end product went to a military base in Mississippi. In April 1943, with more staff freed from the milk delivery schedule to work exclusively at the dairy, Franklin reported that the farm was producing one hundred gallons per day of raw milk.[29]

The sales of Delta Farm and the creamery were only part of larger transformations taking place within the cooperative endeavor. Beginning in 1942 and lasting into the next year, Cooperative Farms, Inc. drastically downsized their responsibilities and activities. The most obvious change for residents was the population decrease that began when some cooperators elected not to make the move from Delta to Providence and crested in late 1942 and early 1943 when the effects of America's entrance into World War II finally reached Holmes County, Mississippi.

As of the spring of 1943, there were seventeen families at Providence. Ten of these families were African American, including former Delta Cooperative farmers such as Jim Billington and his family. "Most of the white people from Providence had gone into war work as was natural," explained Sam Franklin, "and some of those from Rochdale have gone into industry or have chosen to remain in Bolivar County." The compulsory draft and war industries beckoned. For many rural southerners who had experienced hard lives in the fields, the war was an opportunity to escape the ever-present threshold of poverty. The missionary and medical experiences of some of the staff at Providence made them attractive to the armed forces.[30]

Many of the volunteers who passed through Providence were idealistic young men who felt strongly about the war—either as pacifists who refused to fight or as antifascists who were anxious for the United States to enter the fray. Charles Merrill, a Harvard-educated volunteer and son of the founder of Merrill-Lynch & Co., arrived in the summer of 1941 and planned to take up long-term residence on the farm. Despite his tony upbringing, Merrill had become committed to cooperative modes of labor and living as well as black education (he would go on to found Commonwealth School in Boston in 1957). When he arrived, it was clear to Sam Franklin that Merrill was "inwardly raging at the fascism which was devouring Europe" but was able to direct his energies into cooperative farming at Providence. On December 7, 1941, the young Merrill, surrounded by other volunteers and residents, listened to news coverage of the bombing of Pearl Harbor by Japanese forces on the radio in the Providence Community Center. Within days he had enlisted in the Canadian Army, not waiting for the U.S. Army to mobilize, becoming the first person from Providence to leave the farm because of World War II.[31]

The suddenness of Merrill's departure signaled the first of many changes at Providence. The first permanent staff member to leave the cooperative effort because of the war was Dr. David Minter. Minter had assumed that one military branch or another would draft him and commission him as a medical officer. To his wife, Sue, he privately predicted that his experience treating malaria in the Mississippi Delta would make him a prime candidate for military service in the Pacific Theater. The Minters did not want to leave the farm, nor was Dr. Minter particularly interested in serving in the military. Although he had a medical degree from the University of Pennsylvania, which ensured him at least the possibility of operating a lucrative practice anywhere in the United States, Minter felt called to come south and serve an underprivileged population in the Mississippi Delta. He knew he was the only doctor on whom many Holmes Countians could rely. Driven more by his Hippocratic oath and his Christian faith than any ideological dogma, Minter treated all patients equally and had an integrated instead of the customary segregated waiting room. Simply put, he did not want to give up his practice for a stint in the military. Providence was his home and there was important work to be done there. The Minters' attachment to the farm was deep and personal; after all, David and Sue had met and married at Delta Cooperative in 1938.[32]

As the war set in, Minter went about his medical practice and hoped that the draft board would overlook him. In 1942, however, he was notified by the Army Air Corps that he would be drafted and, pending a review, commissioned as a medical officer. After the AKA summer health clinic in 1942, Minter left for service in the Pacific Theater, treating soldiers for malaria. Sue Minter moved back to Indiana to live with her parents.[33]

Dr. Minter's entrance into military service dealt an immediate blow to the farm because he had been the only doctor at both locations for the past four years. He left at the height of his practice as word continued to spread among the rural poor that he was a capable doctor who treated all patients, regardless of color or class, with the same kind and humorous bedside manner. "Our work is quite unspectacular," Sam Franklin revealed to a friend in early 1943, "especially since we have lost our doctor to the Air Corps and our medical program is much curtailed."[34]

In the immediate wake of Dr. Minter's departure for the Air Corps, Franklin had scrambled to keep the health care initiatives of the farm intact. Lindsey Hail Cox resigned as farm nurse in December 1942, feeling that she could not run the clinic by herself and needing to take care of her newly adopted infant daughter, Carol. With Minter gone and Cox resigned, Franklin pursued the services of a black doctor to come to the farm.

Franklin had made contact with Clarence M. Wigfall, an African American medical student who was interning in the spring of 1943 at the Kate B. Reynolds Hospital in Winston-Salem, North Carolina. Wigfall was born and raised in rural Georgia. His parents were small business owners and his mother had worked for a district office of the largest black-owned company in America, North Carolina Mutual Insurance Company. He was a "Southerner by birth, training and choice," and, on paper, was just the kind of doctor Franklin was looking for to fill Minter's vacancy at Providence. Wigfall seemed progressive in his ideas about race relations, but understood that the endeavor at Providence necessitated moderate actions by the staff so that the enterprise would not provoke white violence. In his letter of application, Wigfall quoted Booker T. Washington's Atlanta Exposition speech, stating that he agreed with Washington's assessment of economic unity and social segregation. Wigfall was also respectful to "the white man," he assured Franklin, "so long as there are no overt threats to my safety."[35]

Like many black doctors in the urban South, Wigfall worked in a segregated hospital managed by white administrators. Kate B. Reynolds Hospital was the "colored branch" of City Memorial Hospital in Winston-Salem. Although most of the doctors and nurses were African American, many of the administrators were white, including the superintendent. At first, Franklin received glowing letters of recommendation from former professors and administrators on Wigfall's behalf. Then, the superintendent of Reynolds Hospital sent Franklin a letter declining to recommend Wigfall, dismissing him as "lazy" and resentful of authority. Wigfall may have anticipated this turn of events when he wrote Franklin that "a reference is no better than the man who gives it, favorable or otherwise." Franklin immediately wrote Edward L. Turner, the president of Meharry Medical College in Nashville, Tennessee, where Wigfall had obtained his medical degree. Turner confided in Franklin that the white superintendent at Kate B. Reynolds hospital was a man of questionable character who harbored racial prejudice. Turner concluded that the superintendent was upset at his black intern staff and had retaliated by writing negative letters on their behalf. After hearing this perspective, Franklin moved forward with attempting to secure a salary for Dr. Wigfall.[36]

The challenge of securing a doctor had occupied much of Franklin's months at Providence since Minter left in 1942. He kept assuring Wigfall that a salary would be in place as soon as the doctor arrived. At the same time, however, Franklin was communicating with Sherwood Eddy and Ida L. Jackson of the

AKA, asking for donations toward the doctor's salary. Neither Eddy nor the AKA could secure the money, but before word could be relayed to Wigfall, the doctor removed himself from consideration. With Minter's military draft and a paucity of funds, the farm was without a practicing medical doctor for the foreseeable future.

The draft claimed other members of the farms, too. Sam Checkver, an ardent socialist, pacifist, labor organizer, and cooperative store manager at both Delta and Providence, ran afoul of Selective Service in 1942, only months after leaving Providence. Checkver was born in Russia to a Jewish family that had immigrated to the United States shortly after his birth. Graduating magna cum laude from Harvard, Checkver attended Harvard Law School in the 1920s and served on the editorial board of the *Harvard Law Review*. After arriving at Delta in 1938 and even after he moved to Providence in 1940, Checkver often found his radical positions in opposition to Sam Franklin's leadership and theology. Much like A. James MacDonald, a socialist at Delta who had reported back to William Amberson and found every possible opportunity to argue with or chide Franklin, Checkver's socialist convictions and confrontational nature often led to heated, public disagreements with Franklin.[37]

Mostly, Checkver took issue with how labor operated at Providence, and he secretly reorganized a Southern Tenant Farmers' Union (STFU) local in early 1940. Other Providence residents, however, were not persuaded by his organizing. The only cooperative member other than Checkver who attended the meetings was original Delta cooperator and white ex-sharecropper Wilburn White. The remaining twenty members were black sharecroppers from neighboring plantations. That only one other resident attended these meetings demonstrated a shift away from labor-focused reform at Providence. Ties to the STFU had dwindled since Providence scaled down agricultural initiatives and focused more on the dairy and cooperative store. Sam Franklin soon learned of Checkver's STFU meetings and wrote a concerned letter to Eddy detailing the situation. "They have been meeting surreptiously [*sic*] in a vacant house three miles from the farm," Franklin informed. "Now we who are from the South, know that it is about three times more dangerous for Sam to be doing this than anybody else. When it leaks out, as it inevitably will, that a Russian Jew from New York is holding clandestine meetings with Negroes in Mississippi organizing them into a union, there is likely to be trouble of a very serious sort." Franklin's private letter to Eddy underscored the murderous reality of the situation in the Mississippi Delta. Franklin was right that Checkver's ethnicity and northern accent would make him an easy target for white supremacists looking to punish anyone challenging the status quo. Checkver's activities were especially serious since it involved the black labor force. Franklin's letter also made clear that, as long as he was in charge, Providence was looking for only the "right" kind of social activist. Being a dogmatic non-Christian did not ingratiate Checkver to the farm's severe director.[38]

Franklin knew, however, that Checkver's undeniable abilities as the cooperative store manager had increased the store's profits and members' dividends. "With immense business ability he built up the stock in" the Providence store, Franklin asserted, "helped to draw in scores of members from the disadvantaged Negroes around us, and raised the level of the store's earnings to a high figure." Nevertheless, he convinced Eddy to personally ask Checkver to leave the farm in early 1942, saying that it was perhaps best if Checkver found a situation more fitting of his "radical" views. Unbeknownst to Franklin or Eddy, a warrant had been issued for Checkver's arrest on charges of draft evasion. After leaving Providence, Checkver bought land in Celo, North Carolina, a communal village where conscientious objectors, including some previous volunteers at Delta and Providence, had settled. Within a few months of leaving the farm, however, Checkver was arrested for avoiding Selective Service and imprisoned at a federal work camp in California.[39]

In addition to changing the racial makeup of the cooperative, America's entrance into World War II also meant women began to outnumber men in the farms' workforce. Women took over doing much of the work that had been previously reserved for men. Before the war, women primarily performed three jobs at the cooperatives: nurse, teacher, and homemaking-related tasks like sewing and cooking. The war pushed the farm to downsize much of its operations, although the dairy, the cooperative store, and all agricultural work continued. Much of this work fell to Gene Cox and Sam Franklin, but they, even with the aid of other cooperators, could not handle all the manual labor and attend to their administrative duties. Franklin had to rely on the female staff and volunteers to cover at the dairy and occasionally drive the milk truck full of raw milk to Greenwood. Necessity led to unfamiliar and unprecedented practices such as having a woman operate a large delivery truck off of the farm.

Dorothy Franklin took on much of the farm responsibilities in early 1943. The staff shortage reached almost crisis proportions in that year, and when her husband was convalesced with an abscessed tooth, Dorothy stepped in to run the farm in all but name. Sam spent much of his time off the farm, seeking treatment in Lexington and Jackson. Besides her duties as a mother, Sunday school teacher, and unofficial one-woman hostess for frequent overnight visitors to the farm, Dorothy took on more than her share of farm tasks.

In addition to suffering constant pain with his abscessed tooth, Franklin was distracted from his duties as farm director for another reason. He had spent many months considering the wars in Europe and Asia and wondering where God was leading him. Were his abilities best employed at Providence, or did his experiences as a missionary in Japan—during which time he became fluent in Japanese—make him valuable to the war effort? At first, Franklin decided to inquire with the Navy about the possibility of a commission. He figured that he would let the Navy make the decision for him. On February 8, 1943, Franklin received a one-line letter from the Navy saying that his request to be commissioned into the Navy as a chaplain was denied. He guessed it may have been because of his associations with the socialist farms or because local people around Tchula, skeptical of the farms' presence, may have painted him negatively when the Navy sent representatives to inquire about him. Four days after receiving the Navy's rejection, Franklin wrote a cousin in Georgia that he and Dorothy were relieved "to have the matter settled and to know that I can now continue with a clear conscience in the work here. Dorothy and I are celebrating," he continued, "by enlarging the garden."[40]

Franklin's willingness to take the Navy's refusal as the final word on the matter did not last long. In March, Franklin revealed to Eddy that he had appealed the Navy's rejection of his commission as a chaplain. The Navy denied him a second time, but then shortly after sent him a message that he needed to submit his papers for reconsideration. Taking time away from the farm, Franklin hand-delivered his request papers to the regional Office of Officer Procurement in New Orleans to ask about his rejections. "There I learned that the original rejection had been because mu [sic] work was not regarded as being properly that of a minister," Franklin wrote Eddy. The officer in charge "indicated some knowledge of the project, asked me about Mitchell and the S.T.F.U.," he continued, "and revealed that some of the prejudice against our experiment had quite considerably colored the decision of his office."[41]

Eddy begged Franklin to reconsider his decision to pursue a military commission. Instead of giving in and returning to the farm, Franklin took a trip to Atlanta to meet with the Army about a chaplain's commission. Providence once again was in the hands of his wife and Gene Cox. Franklin admitted to Eddy that he went to Atlanta to meet with the Army because he was a "hard loser." The dogged pursuit of a commission, however, reveals more than simple personality traits. The Franklins had an affinity for Japan they could not dismiss, and Sam considered the war a way to get back to Asia. Additionally, despite strong convictions as a social Christian, he was not a conscientious objector. He argued with many college-aged Quaker volunteers at Delta and Providence about the dictatorships in Asia and Europe and bitterly disagreed with their pacifist views that America should stay out of the world's affairs. Finally, Franklin's eagerness to be a wartime chaplain meant that he was beginning to acknowledge that the potential for success at Providence was limited.[42]

Franklin's friends and associates did not see the endeavor at Providence in this limited way. Eddy wrote him almost daily requesting updated news of his plans and asking him to put the needs of Providence before his own desires to return to Asia. Ida L. Jackson, who had befriended Franklin as the AKA director of the clinics at Providence, wrote him in May 1943 after hearing from Eddy that he might leave the Delta for military service. "Conditions are so tense everywhere now, and Negro-White relations are always strained in Mississippi that I really hate to think of facing the situation in Holmes County with you away," Jackson wrote. "Your presence was not only the moving force and inspiration for us, but you offered a certain amount of protection against the 'evil forces emanating from the great White world.' Soooo, I hope Uncle preferred to leave you there to do a job that is in my way of thinking just as essential." Jackson's letter revealed her fear about the future of Providence and the AKA health clinics, and expressed a belief that what Franklin was doing in the Mississippi Delta was making a positive difference in race relations. Within a few days of opening Jackson's letter, however, Franklin received word from the Navy that they would finally commission him as a chaplain. In mid-May 1943, the man who was most responsible for the establishment and direction of Delta and Providence cooperative farms, and the only manager either farm had known, shipped off to naval boot camp in Williamsburg, Virginia.[43]

Although there was continuity in some of the farm's programs after 1943, Franklin's departure was the pivotal moment in Providence Farm's saga. Despite his best efforts, Franklin often hindered the democratic spirit he wanted to foster. Franklin frequently made decisions unilaterally or wrote Sherwood Eddy to gain the advice of the trustees. With Franklin gone, decisions were more frequently made by farm residents. The only obvious choice to take over as director was Gene Cox. Although Eddy pleaded with Cox to keep him informed of the farm's inner workings, Cox found it almost painful to take the time to write letters. Franklin had inundated Eddy with a surfeit of letters each week as resident director. Cox, as a quiet leader who would rather "climb on the tractor and work all day to escape the writing of a single letter," oversaw the transition to a much more democratic atmosphere on the farm than Franklin had been able to accomplish. As a result, Providence residents found an increased level of autonomy they had previously lacked with Franklin at the helm.[44]

Franklin recommended to Eddy that Cox lead Providence "until I return." He hoped that the military commission would be a brief interruption. Eddy had a clearer understanding of international affairs and knew that Franklin could be away for several years. Armed with this assumption, Eddy did not think Cox was the best person to take over as manager at Providence farm for the long term. Eddy wrote Franklin in 1943, explaining why he did not think Cox could handle the responsibilities of the job. "From my point of view," Eddy explained, "he must have two qualifications, both of which you have: first, spiritual consecration, and vision, and purpose; and second, practicality—a man who could make a farm a success and not a terrible money losing liability. Gene for instance could do the second, but not the first." Despite Eddy's misgivings about Cox's dedication to the cooperative's goals, the endeavor at Providence had to move forward as seamlessly as possible. Only a month before leaving, Franklin described himself as "persona non grata with most of the farmers in this section." He wrote to trustee Arthur Raper that he did "not participate in much of the small talk about crops, labor, etc. that goes on in the barber shop, pool room, etc. of Tchula and other small towns." Cox, in contrast, did not come across as severe or as ideologically driven as Franklin and had the potential to bridge some of the divides that existed between the farm and the surrounding community.[45]

When Franklin left, various plans for Providence collapsed. A plan to relocate Japanese American internees, for instance, fell through. During 1942 and 1943, two eighth-graders at Providence, Barbara Jean Erwin and Otto Morgan Jr., became pen pals with Japanese American students interned at the Tule Lake Relocation Center in Newell, California, after President Roosevelt signed Executive Order 9066, which decreed the evacuation of all Japanese Americans on the West Coast. Spurred by the students' epistolary relationship, Franklin had struck up a correspondence with managers at the Tule Lake Center and began talks to have several interned Japanese American families interested in cooperative farming transferred to Providence Farm as members. This idea grew out of Franklin's continued interest in Japanese culture and no doubt also revealed his concern for interned Japanese Americans. The Tule Lake Center had gained notoriety for housing families who had supposedly refused to declare allegiance to the United States.[46]

Franklin's desire to use Japanese American labor was not an original idea, however. Planters in Arkansas and Mississippi petitioned the state of Arkansas to allow the internees of two Japanese American internment camps to work on their plantations to help solve the labor shortage caused by the war. While some German and Italian POWs were allowed to do this sort of work, fearing the complication of how introducing a nonnative "race" into Jim Crow's rigid system might upset racial customs, the relocated Japanese Americans were not allowed to work on plantations. The Japanese relocation idea blossomed only weeks before Franklin left for military service, after which correspondence stopped and no interned families were relocated to Providence.[47]

When Franklin left the farm, the deal to bring a replacement doctor to

Providence was still unresolved. Gene Cox took up the correspondence, but did not hear from the doctor for several weeks. In the end, Wigfall perceived the absence of reliable funding and declined the invitation to set up a practice at Providence. Around the same time that Wigfall wrote Cox to tell him he was not coming to the Delta, the AKA wrote to inform Cox that money for the doctor's salary could not be secured.[48]

Providence was dealt another serious blow to its human rights activism from the AKA sorority in late summer 1943. Ida L. Jackson wrote Cox to say the sorority was unable to secure volunteers and funding for the Mississippi health clinics and was forced to cancel them for the year. Jackson related that many sorors with medical training or experience as nurses, which was virtually the entire volunteer staff for the health clinics, had been pulled into the war effort. Additionally, securing travel for the volunteers and their medical supplies had always been a challenge, but in 1943 it proved completely impossible. Because of fuel rationing, the federal government issued a request to all organizations not to travel unless absolutely necessary.[49]

As a result of Dr. Minter's absence and the AKA halting their trips south, between 1943 and 1945 Providence Cooperative Farm had no health clinic. Repeated attempts to entice black nurses and doctors to the area proved unsuccessful. The loss of the health clinic severely hindered the work residents at Providence hoped to accomplish. Many patients had previously learned of farm activities through their visits to the clinic. In this fashion, the clinic represented significant community outreach. The lack of a clinic also hurt the area's black population. In the preceding years, rural blacks in Holmes County had received excellent health care from Minter and the AKA summer clinics. With Minter away in uniform and wartime rationing restricting travel, ailing African Americans had to once again rely on folk medicine or white doctors who did not always treat them with dignity or appropriate care.

Despite these setbacks, and in the absence of Franklin and other whites who had dominated the farm's affairs, African Americans built a strong community at Providence. They made the choice to stay because they saw Providence as their best chance to obtain material stability, physical security, and human dignity. Residents had also come to view Providence as their home where they had sunk roots. Still, hardships remained. Residents at Providence faced the winter of 1943, like so many seasons before, with uncertainty about the future of their endeavor and their own lives. The Board of Trustees, including Sherwood Eddy, was still committed to the mission of the farm, but with Sam Franklin's departure, the endeavor had lost a visionary and a man who, in spite of his flaws, simply got things done. With no medical clinic, dwindling population, new leadership, and questionable crop yields, Cox and the remaining

African Americans were forced to either come together or abandon the farm altogether.

Everywhere farm residents looked, their world was changing. The war dominated conversation and media coverage and preoccupied the nation. Only four white families and nine black families remained at Providence in the fall of 1943. To many casual observers, the experiment at Providence now seemed a curiosity at best. Ralph Cessna, central news editor for the *Christian Science Monitor*, wrote to Providence in 1943 to inquire about writing an informational piece on Providence. Cessna typed up a draft of the story, but for months the article languished while he tried and failed to fit it into an issue. According to Cessna, the delay was because "the thing lacks vital news interest." If Cessna's estimation was correct, it was an indication that the public's fascination with the curious and laudable cooperative project in the Mississippi Delta had run its course. Donors who had previously supported the effort at Providence now put their energies and finances into the war effort. Additionally, board member Charles Johnson had noticed that news outlets during the early 1940s dwelled on negative stories about black/white relations. Johnson had written to the farm in 1943 that "there are many developments in the relations existing between white and Negro peoples in the United States that point in the direction of an intelligent and satisfying human relationship between racial groups." He added, however, that "these seldom come to the attention of the public. The tragic, the bizarre, the sensationally troublesome items," he concluded, "are the more usual focus of our interest and, so, of our attention."[50]

Despite outside ambivalence, the residents at Providence made the most of their circumstances. By late 1943, Providence Farm was organized into four spheres: the Producers' Cooperative, the Extension Farm, the Cooperative Store, and the Providence Cooperative Association. The Producers' Cooperative handled the dairy and beef herd and operated on the same Rochdale Cooperative model that drove the farm at Delta Cooperative. All profits from the production and sale of raw milk and beef went into overhead costs and member dividends.[51]

The Extension Farm, a small tract of land worked by residents and renters, was a new endeavor for Providence, mainly because the land used for farming was far smaller than that used at Delta Cooperative Farm. Yield from the Extension Farm was sold at the Cooperative Store. The crops from the Extension Farm were subpar in 1943, and Gene Cox sought to boost the farming potential of Providence for 1944. Cox wrote to Eddy that he had "secured four large families to farm on the place next year. They have moved in and with the other families on the farm," he reported, "we should have sufficient labor to farm next year." But as the population at Providence dwindled, Cox gradually phased out the extension aspect of the cooperative.[52]

The Cooperative Store operated similarly to the store at Delta. Members of the store gained a dividend from all profits. The major change to the store was that white volunteers and staff no longer exclusively ran the register. By late 1942, all former employees at the store had left Providence. New store staffers were recruited from ex-sharecropping families. Gene Cox convinced Lilly Little, an African American teenager who lived with her family at Providence, to run the counter. Little had no experience working a register, but Cox trained her and within days she was operating the store. By 1943, the Providence cooperative store had all African American clerks who served both white and black customers. In addition to Little, Robert and Hattie Granderson and Fannye Booker ran the register and stocked shelves. Finally, the Cooperative Association was a new concept that Franklin had developed and that came to fruition under Cox's leadership. The Cooperative Association's purpose was arranging and systematizing community outreach. Through this initiative, Providence consolidated outreach programs in education, economic development, and religious guidance.[53]

The sale of Delta Cooperative Farm and sales from the cooperative store kept Providence and its residents afloat during the war years. The store became the social and economic center of Providence as it had been at Delta previously. In an unpublished memoir, Sam Franklin remembered how the cooperative store had replaced old, inequitable places of business in the plantation South. "Customers from the hills and some of the plantations flocked to the 'Co-op' where blacks were treated without discrimination and where the profits that once went to the owner of the commissary were returned to members in proportion to their purchases," wrote Franklin. "Saturday was the peak business day of the week. Black and white were relaxed and ready to linger around the stove in winter or under the shade of the surrounding oaks in the summer. Soon after we came, we established a reading room and library in one of the two small back rooms of the store building. The store was the natural connecting link between the Farm and the larger community, helping us to understand the needs, physical, economic, educational, and spiritual, of the people by whom we were surrounded." The cooperative store was the most successful economic venture the farm pursued. Selling dry goods and some farming tools and housing a small café, the store served as the lifeblood of the surrounding black community for nearly twenty years. The co-op store was much like any other crossroads store of its time, serving both black and white customers. The big difference, of course, was that dividends from the store were divided among Providence residents instead of going solely to a merchant. By the end of 1943, the store made $15,000 in revenue, reportedly $500 better than sales a year earlier.[54]

By the mid-1940s, Cox was nearly fed up with the producers' cooperative and its failure to be consistently self-sustaining. "I have the feeling that collectives can succeed only where there is a large degree of regimentation," concluded Cox, "and I cannot see the farmers in this country accepting very much of it." Even Sherwood Eddy conceded that "there is not a natural tendency for the average man to work as hard for a cooperative or a collective as he would on his own where he gets all the fruits of his labor." Thus Cox implemented a modified producers' cooperative for those who wished to participate and encouraged the cultivation of personal plots.[55]

The population continued to drop at Providence. Both the Erwins and one branch of the Hendersons, original residents at Delta Cooperative Farm, left Providence in January 1944. Following the trend of whites moving out of the rural South and away from farming as a profession, Jess Erwin and John Henderson "were not interested in farming" any longer and took work down the road in Tchula at a mechanic's garage.[56]

Even with several new families who were willing to farm, Cox knew that to rely on financial returns from the dairy and the store could result in serious economic jeopardy. "Many of our families left the farm and went to the city for defense work," Cox somberly reported. "The result is that we are limiting our program here until the others return from their present duties." Instead of sitting idly by, waiting for former residents to return, Cox had all families at Providence filed with the Farm Security Administration for the 1944 fiscal year. He did so as a precaution in case the farm could not support itself. If it came to that, Cox hoped that Providence could be taken over by the FSA and transformed into a resettlement community like those created by the federal government elsewhere in the South, including Mileston, only a short distance from Providence.[57]

The FSA never took control of Providence because Cox's efforts kept the farm economically viable. Cox, whose first job at Delta in 1936 had been as the farm's accountant, was able to see beyond the limits that Sam Franklin's ideology had placed on the endeavor. Cox negotiated deals that leased over a thousand acres of Providence's original tract to the Texas-based Atlantic Refining Company and the Mississippi-based Magnolia Oil Company, both of which sunk oil wells on the land. In all, the oil companies paid Providence $2,000 per year for drilling rights. The profits from these deals went directly to the Cooperative Farms, Inc. Eddy wrote Cox in 1945 that all income from the leasing of land to the oil companies should be for the "wide benefit of the sharecroppers of Holmes County and the South. The idea all along," Eddy continued, "has been that members and people on the Farms should make all that was possible from the annual income of the farming operations, but that the capital account and the future of the farms was to be held by the Directors to carry out our original purpose to serve the sharecroppers of the South."[58]

Eddy's vision that capital gained from ventures like leasing the land go to the Cooperative Farms, Inc. instead of directly to the ex-croppers, underscored his ten-year desire to leave his mark on the South. But Eddy was vague on exactly what he meant by "to serve the sharecroppers of the South." Was Providence not accomplishing this, even if on a limited scale? Eddy's refusal to allow the cooperative members to receive all profits and his vague statements were the same kind of obfuscations that had infuriated William Amberson and caused him to leave the Board of Trustees. Ostensibly, though, whatever income came from leasing the land went toward overhead costs for the Producers' Cooperative, the Extension Farm, the store, and the outreach programs at Providence.[59]

Perhaps no resident, other than Gene Cox, proved more important to the new goals of Providence Farm than Fannye Booker. The guidance of Booker, an African American woman and Holmes County native, signaled a major shift in how residents of the farm viewed the purpose of their endeavor. Booker spearheaded the education initiatives, worked in the health clinic and cooperative store, and helped found a credit union. Through these projects, Providence Farm exemplified the coalescing civil rights movement taking shape in the rural South, as African Americans relied on local community initiatives to push for equal access to public resources. Still, farm residents initiated a host of activities that moved beyond the boundaries of early civil rights activism that might more adeptly be described as the pursuit of human rights. Booker, as much as Gene Cox, influenced the farm's path in its last decade and a half. Providence was a different place under the leadership of Booker and Cox.

Fannye Thomas Booker was born in the small community of Sweet Water, near Lexington, Mississippi, in 1906. Booker had been orphaned as a child and taken in by Joe and Cornelius Thomas, a black couple who owned and farmed 360 acres. Sweet Water was home to African American subsistence farmers, some of whom were landowners, instilling in Booker from a young age a sense that landownership and self-improvement were essential elements in African American progress. Unlike most rural black Mississippians, Booker completed high school and was able to attend classes at Jackson State College and Mississippi Industrial College, a Colored Methodist Episcopal–affiliated school in Holly Springs. After college she married William Shank Booker. They had no children.[60]

Booker moved to the Tchula area in 1944 to become a county school teacher. She soon took an interest in the black self-help initiatives at Providence, especially those that focused on education. To supplement her meager county teaching salary, she initially worked part-time at Providence Cooperative Farm as a summer school instructor. In 1944, at Cox's invitation, Booker attended an integrated labor union meeting of the National Agricultural Workers Union as a delegate from Providence. Not long after returning from the union gathering, Booker was fired from her county teaching job. Although no cause was given, she and Cox assumed it was because word had spread among whites in Tchula that Booker was involved with black self-help and labor agitation. Her firing caused anger among the residents at Providence. Ironically, however, it meant that Booker could now devote her full attention to her activities at the farm. She first took a position at the cooperative store working the register and stocking shelves. In this capacity she came into contact with hundreds of black families and became a "student of living conditions in Holmes County." As a result, Fannye Booker fully embraced the interracial, democratic, and cooperative principles of Providence Farm. More than many residents, black or white, Booker grasped the radical potential of the farm. She equated the economic and educational efforts to emancipation. "Well it's like when the Yankees came through," she told an interviewer before her death. "They was tired of people living in slavery and they was trying to let you come out on your own. And they was doing that to show you that you could make profits for yourself. You could—you didn't have to be the underdog all the time. You could work for yourself and save for yourself. You were being taught, you see."[61]

Booker took it upon herself to increase the educational opportunities for blacks in Holmes County. Despite statewide efforts to equalize segregated education in the 1940s, black schools were vastly underfunded compared to white schools. Like elsewhere in the South, black students in Mississippi were the recipients of a second-class education. In Holmes County, in the school year 1947–1948, 7,108 black students attended school compared to 1,441 white students. Although this number accounted for nearly all the school-aged black and white children in the county, access to education was far from equal. In the same year, Holmes County spent an average of $12 per black pupil versus $44 per white pupil. The county spent $28.67 on transportation for white students, while not a penny was spent on transporting their black counterparts to school. Average annual salaries for black teachers were approximately $480, while annual salaries for white teachers reached nearly $1,500. Between 1890 and 1937, statewide salaries for black teachers had in effect stayed the same. They rose only marginally in the 1940s. In short, black children in the county badly needed Fannye Booker's school at Providence. Cox described the dismal situation before Booker arrived. "Our county has a total population of about 45,000 of which over 36,000 are Negroes," Cox explained. "The schools in the rural areas of the county run for not more than six months per year. We have no four year high-schools for Negro youth in the rural sections, and the county furnishes no bus services for Negro youth in our county. The children who plan to go to high-school must room in one of the towns where they can attend high-school, and this is difficult for the majority because of expenses involved."[62]

Providence provided Booker space and resources to transform the education of local blacks. Soon after moving to Providence, Booker expanded the summer school program to include high school lessons. All year through her school lessons and summer camps, local youth came to the farm for Booker's instruction. In the spring of 1945, Booker ran a school for African American children in the Providence Community Building. Booker's school opened after county schools for black pupils closed—usually six weeks before they closed for white students—and picked up again in the fall six weeks before the customary opening of black schools. Forty students attended Booker's classes that session. Booker also began supplemental summer courses for African American students who had fallen behind in their schoolwork in the county schools. The farm charged attendance fees, but many impoverished parents bartered in exchange for their children to attend Booker's courses.[63]

Among black youth, Booker's summer camps were as popular as her classroom courses. Cox reported that thirty-two girls boarded for the summer camp in 1947. Although Booker had decided that a shorthanded staff meant they could accommodate only girls, several parents dropped off three boys for the camp. Booker made arrangements for them to stay. An additional thirty girls were day campers. Activities at Booker's camps consisted of "recreation, Bible study, classes in handicraft and elementary education, and a bus trip to Jackson." Booker recruited female students from Mississippi's black colleges to serve as camp staff. Because they were not from Holmes County, the staff had little concern that they would jeopardize their careers, as had Booker, by being involved with Providence.[64]

Booker and Cox also played an important administrative role in another significant aspect of the Providence Cooperative Association, the establishment of a credit union. One of the most entrenched barriers to economic freedom African Americans faced in the Jim Crow South was their inability to obtain fair loans from banks and "furnish," or credit, from their employers. Even though Providence was the center of important health and education initiatives, the establishment of a credit union was perhaps the most radical project undertaken by members of the Providence Cooperative Association.

Since the founding of Delta Cooperative Farm, establishing a credit union had been a long-term goal of the endeavor. "I have recently heard of colored men of the locality being called to Lexington and being threatened with having their 'furnish' cut off if they had anything to do with us," Sam Franklin reported in the early 1940s. "One of the men who participated in this intimidation was said to be a banker," Franklin continued, "a leading citizen of the county." Local white racists who did not like the presence of social activists in their county used the threat of refusing credit to intimidate African Americans who attended meetings at Providence or patronized the cooperative store. The Board of Trustees, Franklin, and Gene Cox gradually worked toward gathering "resources sufficient to extend credit to anyone who is denied it through the ordinary agencies because of prejudice against us." The Great Depression also helped promote support for cooperative credit unions. As banks lost deposits and failed, Americans saw credit unions as a safer alternative. Deepening unemployment and staggering poverty facilitated creative solutions to the credit problem. As a result, disaffected Americans began a credit union movement as thousands of credit unions blossomed in every state by the mid-1930s.[65]

In the early 1940s, Gene Cox, on behalf of the Providence Cooperative Association, applied for and received authorization from the federal government to start the Providence Cooperative Federal Credit Union, one of only three dozen credit unions in Mississippi at the time. The Providence Cooperative Federal Credit Union was another way that the Cooperative Association hoped to break down the strong hold of the plantation that gripped some rural blacks, while providing them with fair and affordable loan rates. Cox assumed the position of treasurer of the Credit Union and Fannye Booker served as its first president, making it perhaps the only credit union in the state with an integrated administration and a female president. By the end of the 1940s, the credit union had one hundred six members from Providence and the surrounding area and paid dues to the Credit Union National Association (CUNA). Cox joined the board of directors of the Mississippi Credit Union League, which had seventy-five members by the mid-1950s, and often represented all of Mississippi's credit unions at CUNA annual meetings. Membership in the Providence Cooperative Federal Credit Union rose steadily each year until the mid-1950s.[66]

Residents at Providence made significant strides to overcome hardships and move forward with their lives despite their lack of resources and the upheaval of World War II. In 1945, it seemed clear that Sam Franklin would not return to Providence, electing to stay on as a missionary in Japan at the conclusion of the war. He would, however, remain a member of the Board of Trustees for the next ten years. Sherwood Eddy wrote to Cox that "if you are left to carry on alone, I would favor increasing your salary, asking you to carry the books, the store, and the Farm." At the same time, Eddy hinted at a profound and far-reaching reorganization of the farm. Eddy first mentioned to Cox that he favored selling individual plots at Providence to the "ten families now on the Farm" and "persons in Holmes County thoroughly reliable." These discussions, however, did not mean an end to the cooperative; both Eddy and Cox had plans to restart a medical clinic as soon as a doctor could be secured at war's end. Importantly, however, this conversation signaled the first time that the trustees seriously considered selling the land to the cooperative members, as was the original plan at Delta in 1936. For the time being, however, Cooperative Farms, Inc. maintained ownership of the land at Providence.[67]

In early summer 1945, David Minter, now a recently retired lieutenant colonel in the U.S. Army Air Force, returned to Providence with his family and resumed the medical clinic he had left three years earlier. Minter steadily rebuilt his patient base, Lindsey Hail Cox rejoined the clinic as nurse, and the clinic once again flourished as it had before he was drafted into military service. By the end of the year, Dr. Minter and Cox were treating between thirty and fifty patients per day in the clinic and on house calls. Eventually, Minter built the clinic into a state-of-the-art center with a fluoroscope, an x-ray imaging machine, and a cardiograph machine, all donated by the sisters of AKA.[68]

While the postwar years were celebratory for residents at Providence, as some residents and staff returned and black-led initiatives continued, the late 1940s produced new sets of challenges for a radical social experiment in the Mississippi Delta. Fearing that blacks, communists, and the federal government would soon impose their agendas on the nation, many white Mississippians, like other southerners, closed ranks after World War II. In 1944, when the U.S. Supreme Court struck down the all-white primary in *Smith v. Allwright*, Mississippi's politicians ramped up their rants against the federal government and intimidation of potential black voters. Mississippi senator James O. Eastland assured crowds that the feds would soon "Harlemize the country." In 1946, Mississippi's other senator, Theodore G. Bilbo, openly encouraged all white Mississippians to intimidate, harass, and threaten any black person who dared vote in that year's election. In 1948, Mississippi governor Fielding Wright became the vice presidential nominee on the States' Rights Democratic Party ticket. The Dixiecrats, as they were better known, mostly represented the economic, political, and social views of southern planters. In the election, the Dixiecrats won every county in Mississippi with around 90 percent of the statewide vote, but carried only three additional states—all in the South. No wonder that the planter interest carried Mississippi, even in counties where blacks numerically dominated whites. Approximately one percent of adult African Americans were registered to vote that year.[69]

Flying under the radar so as not to be detected by white supremacists was a difficult task for Providence Farm in the late 1940s. That maneuver of invisibility was made harder when the endeavor was beholden to outside financial support for success. The national support that Delta Cooperative Farm had enjoyed in its early years sagged dramatically for Providence. Cox was not the fund-raiser that Franklin had been, and Sherwood Eddy, approaching his eighties, was eager to hand off the financial burden of the farm to another organization. Eddy's own finances were suffering along with his health, and he hoped that a group with ample financial resources could replace him as trustee and benefactor. Eddy suggested that the Church of the Brethren—a Christian denomination known for their stance on peace and nonhierarchical, egalitarian membership—take over the charge of Providence, a proposal Cox adamantly opposed. Cox felt that the Brethren's lack of experience in race relations in the South would run them afoul of Mississippians already leery of the farm. The Brethren, thought Cox, were too forceful in their approach to race relations and would demand too much from Providence and its residents. Certain that the Brethren would bring unwelcome press coverage from the Mississippi media, Cox warned Eddy that a local newspaper editorial included a scathing review of cooperatives in the South. "At this time there is great talk about the Negroes getting power in this section," the editorial warned. "If anything hurries the day when the Negro takes a big hand in our financial and political affairs, it will be through the Co-op movement." Given the negative publicity, Eddy eventually agreed with Cox that the Brethren were not the best choice to take over administering Providence.[70]

On New Year's Eve 1947, Cox, Minter, and Eddy met to discuss the future of Providence Cooperative Farm. Eddy declared that if the farm kept operating at its present budget, the enterprise would be broke within two years. Donations had shrunk to a mere $1,000 per year while the farm operation cost over $6,000 annually. Eddy seemed completely flummoxed. But Cox and Minter asked Eddy to remain on the Board of Trustees while proposing two ideas. The first was that Cox and Fannye Booker would reduce their salaries to ease the financial strain on the board. Cox was making $2,400 per year, Booker $900. Cox desperately wanted Booker to receive a raise, so that her salary would be commensurate with the best-paid white teachers in the county. But because Providence faced financial ruin, both Cox and Booker agreed to salary reductions.[71]

The second proposal was that, if necessary, the Cooperative Farms, Inc. would be liquidated and Minter, Cox, and others on the farm would take over as directors and trustees. A foundation that Cox had formed called the Delta Foundation, Inc., which was a nonprofit organization originally chartered to buy discounted war supplies for use at Providence, would take over ownership of the farms. Eddy agreed to the first idea and stated that the second idea was a good one but that liquidating the Board of Trustees was unnecessary at the moment.[72]

Two years later, however, that moment had come. From 1941 to 1949, the trustees had remained unchanged. Reinhold Niebuhr, Sherwood Eddy, John Rust, Arthur Raper, Charles S. Johnson, Emory Luccock, and F. D. Patterson all served on the board for nearly a decade. In January 1950, however, the Cooperative Farms, Inc. was liquidated by the Board of Trustees and the Delta Foundation, Inc. took over control of the farms. Johnson, Rust, Luccock, and Patterson all let their terms expire. Niebuhr, Eddy, Franklin, and Raper remained affiliated with the foundation, but took drastically reduced roles. Those added to the new Board of Trustees under the Delta Foundation, Inc. were Gene Cox, who replaced Niebuhr as president, Lindsey Hail Cox, who replaced Eddy as secretary-treasurer, David R. Minter, who replaced Franklin as vice president, Sue Minter, and Louise Gates Eddy, Sherwood Eddy's wife. The majority of the trustees now lived at Providence and their financial actions were no longer subject to approval by a distant board, freeing them, for the first time, to make all financial and operational decisions as they saw fit.

The 1940s brought major transformations to Providence. World War II solidified a modification of interracial practices that had already begun in the late 1930s through black self-help endeavors. Providence saw drastic changes to the farm population and its operational structure, but the residents and staff handled those challenges by adapting their original goals and embarking on new ventures in black uplift. When Gene Cox took over the day-to-day management at Providence, the community became more egalitarian in nature. While the residents at Providence kept their commitment to a broad spectrum of human rights goals, they were no longer beholden to Sam Franklin's Christian Socialist doctrine and micromanaging. Cox's laissez-faire leadership, by contrast, lacked dogma but contained plenty of conviction. Under his management, the community was less often in the news, but continued a more localized revolution on the small postage stamp of soil in the Mississippi Delta. The summer camps, the education initiatives, access to health care, the credit union, and the routine respect with which blacks and whites treated each other at Providence thrived by decade's end. The entire decade of the 1940s could be summed up by an African American farm resident who fell into conversation with Sam Franklin one evening in 1942 before the director had shipped off to war. "In the course of general conversation last night one of the older Negroes said quite spontaneously and naturally, 'I never heard of democracy until the last four years when this farm started.'" More so than during its heady beginnings, Providence Farm was now beginning to live up to its democratic and egalitarian ideals.[73]

The 1940s marked a new period for Providence Farm. The staff and residents now had an increased degree of autonomy and were not beholden to the ideologies of thoughtful men of faith, who nevertheless had little practical knowledge of the day-to-day realities of operating a social experiment in the Jim Crow–era Mississippi Delta. Black self-help would continue to be the major focus at Providence, albeit with an increased level of autonomy within the community. The race-baiting tactics of the late 1940s by state and local politicians would not abate in the coming decade. In fact, they would worsen. The 1950s brought a new set of challenges as the battles over Jim Crow and communism reached a boiling point in the already roiling Mississippi Delta.

CHAPTER 5

Preventing Another Emmett Till

On a hot evening in late September 1955, Gene Cox and Dr. David Minter were called to a community meeting in the Tchula High School auditorium, seven miles from their homes at Providence Farm. Five hundred of their neighbors, many of whom leaned against walls, filled the room to capacity. Temperatures in Tchula registered in the low eighties that night, and the auditorium, packed with people, was uncomfortably humid. Learning of the meeting only hours before, Cox and Minter were not sure what to make of their summons to the high school auditorium. They had known most of the people in the room for at least fifteen years, but were now called before them to defend their very livelihood. By the conclusion of the three-hour meeting, five hundred people—half of all Tchula residents—had voted, in a near unanimous showing of hands, that Cox and Minter should leave Holmes County. Attendees at the meeting, which had been called by members of the White Citizens' Council, accused the two men of being communists, preaching racial equality, and breaking Mississippi's segregation laws. As Cox and Minter left the meeting, a white neighbor loudly offered an alternative solution to their leaving the county: he thought the two men should be lynched. The lives of the families at Providence Farm would never be the same.[1]

Since moving to the area in the late 1930s, Providence Farm and its residents had been under the constant scrutiny of surrounding white communities. Although Cox and Minter had improved the public image of the farm among skeptical whites after Sam Franklin left in the 1940s, local and national events transpired to lead whites in Holmes County to demand that Cox and Minter abandon Providence Farm and leave the county.

Holmes County had become a hub of white backlash to the civil rights movement since Cox, Minter, and the ex-sharecropping families first arrived there in the late 1930s and early 1940s. Racial and political upheaval rallied many whites to the cause of what historians have called "massive resistance," the organized effort to "legally" resist racial integration, federal intrusion, and black civil rights more generally. The willingness of hard-core segregationists to use political and economic pressure as well as violence in defense of Jim Crow shaped the 1950s. By the time white Holmes Countians gathered at Tchula High School to condemn Cox, Minter, and Providence Farm, civil rights activists and the federal government had challenged white racial privilege and de jure segregation in well-publicized campaigns. The eviction meeting in Tchula occurred less than a year and a half after the *Brown v. Board* decision directed public schools across the country to desegregate and only days after the accused white murderers of fourteen-year-old Emmett Till were acquitted. In the aftermath of *Brown v. Board* and the Till murder, many white racists hardened their resolve to maintain segregation and white supremacy. The coalescing of white racists into a massive resistance movement made it much harder for civil rights activists to accomplish their work of racial amelioration and black self-help. Although work continued at Providence, resistance by outsiders, particularly in the nearby town of Tchula, became more severe and unrelenting. Whites in Holmes County who wanted to maintain segregation and racial discrimination had to look no further than Providence Farm to locate agitators and race traitors.

In this age of anxiety, nearly any event, from the most personal to the most public, could elicit swift and severe punishment. Anxieties over race relations were only part of the social landscape of the Mississippi Delta in the early 1950s. A Red Scare had swept across America beginning in 1950 when Joseph McCarthy, a little-known senator from Wisconsin, gave a speech in Wheeling, West Virginia, claiming that he knew the names of communists working within the federal government. Hysteria spread quickly as McCarthy accused respected institutions, from Protestant clergy to the U.S. Army, of supporting communist subversives. Even some of the more progressive-minded Holmes County residents, like newspaper editor Hazel Brannon Smith, fully supported McCarthy's mission. In 1954, Smith wrote a paean to McCarthy in her weekly column, "Through Hazel Eyes." "McCarthy, in my opinion, is doing a vitally important and necessary job in ferreting out Communists in our government," Smith told her readers. "In any job this big where there are powerful entrenched interests someone is bound to get hurt—as we have said before. If a few innocent people get hurt it is to be regretted—but understandable. In war a lot of people get hurt, a lot of innocent people, too. And don't forget this

is war." For many Americans who were invested in maintaining racial segregation, civil rights activists spread the red menace to American soil.[2]

Southerners believed that their home region was "the last bastion of
American-ness," as one historian phrased it, in a country that they felt was increasingly given over to radicals. This belief was thrown into sharp relief when,
in the wake of World War II, the Soviet Union had shrouded Eastern Europe
in an "iron curtain." Many of the nation's staunchest Cold Warriors, like Mississippi senator James O. Eastland, were southerners who viewed themselves
as inheriting a cross-generational antipathy for tyrannical government. Eastland's grandfathers had, as they saw it, thrown off the yoke of dictatorial car-
petbaggers during Reconstruction. Now, Eastland would defend the world
against the spread of communism. In the 1950s, through the Senate Internal
Security Subcommittee (SISS), Eastland brought McCarthyism to the South
and used "federally mandated anticommunism to enforce racial conformity."
As another historian of the southern Red Scare has documented, an exasperated SISS witness exclaimed, "'just as Joseph McCarthy saw a Red behind every government door, Eastland saw a Red behind every black.'" To even suggest
"egalitarianism" was to side with the United States' sworn enemy. As such, the
South's antiradical tradition funneled into a focus on combating communism,
labor organizing, and integration in the 1940s and 1950s. While many southern
anticommunists were indeed committed to the cause, the main goal of using
red-baiting tactics was to chip away at the advancements of black civil rights.
The wedding of anticommunism and anti-integrationism left many civil rights
organizations such as the NAACP and the Urban League scrambling to avoid
public relations disasters as red baiters accused them of communist ties. The
damage done to left-leaning organizations and civil rights groups was severe. A
culture of fear continued as Americans felt compelled to be suspicious of their
own neighbors.[3]

In 1954, Eastland ran on three promises—weeding out communists, upholding segregation, and supporting Mississippi farmers. Eastland's intense
anticommunism dated to his post–World War II tour of Europe. When he returned home, he vowed to protect his country from the creep of communism
and to maintain racial segregation. For Eastland, and many southerners of
his political persuasion, the Cold War acted as an entrenching force. At every
turn, Eastland and his segregationist colleagues fought any federal initiative to
trigger racial change, accusing even the mere suggestion of racial equality as
communism itself. While many Americans began to see international attention to America's racial caste system as an embarrassment and contradictory to
its aims in the Cold War, Eastland saw blacks as the inferior, undemocratic underclass that could easily be swayed by the overtures of communism. Holmes

County residents who favored segregation and deplored communism were also swept up by the tide of anticommunism. Rural Mississippians loved Eastland as much for his unwavering support for agricultural price controls as for his stances on communism and segregation. Eastland won Holmes County in 1954 by a count of 1,745 to 382. Only 22 people in Tchula voted against the incumbent senator. In March 1955, circuit judge Tom Brady—who would later be appointed to Mississippi's Supreme Court at the height of the civil rights movement—spoke to a packed Tchula High School auditorium, calling the attack on segregation an "all-out war." Brady began his remarks by referencing the Bible when he traced the "development of the human race" and the "divisions of the various tribes." Brady stressed the "Biblical basis for racial purity" and blamed leftists for defying the word of God by supporting the desegregation of public schools. "The question of segregation today is only a small segment in the plan to destroy Christianity and the world," Brady told the Tchula crowd, "and the Socialists and the Communists" were leading the charge. Brady assured his audience that communists and socialists had "brain-washed" many teachers and preachers into thinking that Jesus wanted "one world." He concluded the evening by declaring that "it is the preservation of our Christian civilization that we are dedicated," then added, "don't forget to pray to God every night." Brady was introduced to the Tchula crowd that evening by World War II veteran Robert B. Patterson from Indianola, Mississippi. Two months later, Patterson would put Brady's words into action and organize the first White Citizens' Council.[4]

Rumors, insinuation, and inflammatory rhetoric by anticommunists and anti-integrationists—and their political uses of violence and threats of violence—led to the closing of Providence Farm in the 1950s. As historians of the civil rights movement have masterfully demonstrated, white racists used intimidation and violence—like the kind that residents at Providence endured in 1955 and 1956—in times of social change and upheaval to control the psyches and bodies of African Americans. But violent threats were not the only tactics used by segregationists. Accusing racial progressives of communist ties was a politically expedient way for segregationists to discredit their adversaries. In an era when local law enforcement and politicians winked at hostility against blacks and their white allies—or openly engaged in it—intimidation and violence operated as political capital for hard-core segregationists. At Providence, residents found themselves the targets of incendiary accusations and threats.[5]

Providence Farm had also changed since ex-sharecroppers first arrived in 1938. Although the community at Providence persisted, it did not have much in common with its predecessor. Delta Cooperative Farm had been a radical interracial experiment to save sharecroppers. The identity of the residents as ex-croppers was important to Delta's goals and international appeal as an experiment in cooperative communalism. Providence in the 1950s, however, was something different. The identities and occupations of the residents were less important now that Providence focused mostly on human rights outreach. Most of the residents who called Providence home were more than a decade removed from their sharecropping days. The farm also had fewer residents in the 1950s than at any time in either cooperative's history. The key members of the community were engaged in initiatives that mainly served people living off the farm. Dr. Minter and Lindsey Hail Cox continued to operate the clinic, while Fannye Booker ran the summer camps and black school. Only Gene Cox and a few resident families continued to grow cotton and other staple crops to supplement the farm's meager earnings. Minter's clinic and Booker's camps and schools were now the crux of the farm's identity. Farming was rendered nearly irrelevant. Providence was now more like a small community focused on good works than a radical cooperative challenging the South's power structures.

Unlike Sam Franklin's hectic life as director of Delta Cooperative Farm, the Coxes and the Minters led lives that resembled many Americans experiencing post–World War II prosperity. Both families took vacations to popular destinations like the Great Smoky Mountains and Devil's Den State Park in nearby Arkansas. The Cox and Minter children enjoyed birthday parties at the farm, often attended by their Tchula classmates, where Gene Cox treated them to "moving pictures" from the farm's projector. Cox's daughters had sleepovers with their friends while Lindsey Cox cooked a themed "ethnic" dinner for the girls and their friends. Both families took the time to write to the local newspaper about their vacations, parties, and day trips to bigger cities like Jackson. Less is known about the other families living at Providence. They did not write to the white-owned local newspaper about their lives, and their occupations became less important to farm activities. Although many area blacks who were involved with uplift initiatives at Providence later helped lead the charge for voting rights in Holmes County, the lives of residents in the early 1950s merely faded into the background of farm activities.[6]

The letters that Cox left behind reveal that some of the residents were not involved with the outreach programs. Even though he cared deeply about the individuals on the farm, Cox mostly wrote about the deeds of the outreach programs rather than the day-to-day lives of the residents at Providence. The silence of these residents conveys the image of a community in decline. The issues the farm tackled in the 1930s and 1940s were in the vanguard of human rights work in the Mississippi Delta. By the 1950s, however, Providence's outreach programs were circumspect and ill-defined when compared to some of the more dynamic challenges to Jim Crow that swept the country.

After the consolidation of ownership under the Delta Foundation, Inc. in 1950, Providence puttered along. In addition to the summer camps, school, and medical clinic, membership in the Providence Cooperative Federal Credit Union crested with around two hundred members annually from 1950 and 1955. In 1955, Cox attended the Credit Union National Association annual meeting, where he represented all ninety-five credit unions in Mississippi. The community building at Providence hosted a smattering of union meetings, the Providence Woman's Club, church services, evening forums, educational films, and association meetings—all of which remained integrated but were attended mostly by area blacks. The films often drew the biggest crowds, with an average of fifty-five viewers showing up each night in the early 1950s.[7]

Because the cooperative was still not self-sustaining, Cox occasionally had to solicit donations. In 1952, the John Rust Foundation, Inc., headed by the farm's former trustee, donated one thousand dollars toward the farm's educational and health programs. Rust wrote to Cox that "we have read your charter and by-laws and are impressed with the activities of your Foundation in conducting educational and health activities among people who otherwise would have little, if any, opportunity to avail themselves of these services." To lessen the foundation's financial problems Cox lived on a meager income. Beginning in 1950, he received fifty dollars a month from Sherwood Eddy. Eddy increased the amount to seventy-five dollars in 1952. The monies Cox received from Eddy, along with Lindsey Cox's modest salary from the medical clinic, constituted the Cox family's entire income.[8]

For farm residents, life in the rural South did not get easier in the 1950s. Heavy rains and a boll weevil infestation ravaged cotton throughout Holmes County in 1949 and 1950, putting farmers a month behind their usual planting schedule and resulting in several years of poor yields. On some Holmes County farms, extension agents counted as many as 1,250 weevils per acre, slightly above the average for farming counties from Georgia to Texas. The rains that fell on the Mississippi Delta led to emergency conditions at Providence. Chicopa Creek periodically flooded the property, saturating fields, threatening livestock and homes, and cutting Providence off from the main roads in Holmes County. White children missed school, and their neighbors could not shop at the community store or visit the community's clinic. As soon as the rains stopped, however, a severe drought set in that lasted throughout the mid-1950s. In 1954, Holmes was one of fifty counties in the state to be declared a disaster area by the secretary of agriculture. Holmes County farmers applied for relief in droves.[9]

Because losses in cotton production devastated farmers, Gene Cox pushed for relief in crop diversification and cooperatives. Holmes County farmers needed to "plant orchards and raise cattle," Cox instructed, "not depend so much on cotton." He also hoped that local farmers would "join the Providence Credit Union, and through it buy and sell in bulk." Cox confided in the trustees that "for a number of years we have realized the futility of the small farmers of our community placing primary emphasis on cotton as a cash crop. On the other hand," Cox tempered, "we know that any attempt to shift the farm pattern requires considerable capital, initiative and technical experience." Even though Providence possessed some of the capital needed to make the shift away from cash crops, Cox had to use what little money the farm had on the unexpected setbacks that often occurred on a farm, especially in a region as unforgiving as the Mississippi Delta. In 1950, the farm lost five milch cows and a colt "due to stealing, dogs, drowning, and rattle-snake bites." Cox considered the animals' deaths "a financial loss greater than we have suffered in the past 7 years combined."[10]

The number of patrons at the cooperative store also fell in the early 1950s. Cox attributed the decline to competition from the influx of chain stores in the county, such as the popular Jitney Jungle in downtown Tchula. That the farm's store operated on a strictly cash basis added to its difficulties. The miserable crop production in the county as a result of the boll weevil and natural disasters also left neighbors with less money to spend. Cox and Fannye Booker often discussed closing the cooperative store, but working at the store was Booker's only income, aside from what Sherwood Eddy could raise for her teacher salary and from summer camp fees.[11]

Booker's summer camps, now called Camp Springs after the popular swimming hole at Providence, continued to be one of the farm's more successful pursuits and brought scores of "Negro young people" to Providence. Activities offered at Camp Springs included "religious education, health, weaving, handcraft, home economics and recreation." In 1950, registration cost seven dollars per child, and all children had to come with the majority of their food to last them a month. Some African Americans who had been campers in the 1940s returned in the 1950s as college-aged staffers, carrying out Booker's program of black self-help.[12]

Even while Providence Farm continued to offer Holmes County African Americans some uplifting opportunities, race relations remained treacherous in Mississippi. White racial hostility in the county worsened significantly in early 1954. Over the span of a year and a half, four racially charged events contributed to mounting suspicion of and antagonism toward the community at Providence. Murders, manhunts, shootings, and a court decision turned suspicious Holmes Countians against Providence like never before. Still, opponents of Providence needed an excuse to turn public opinion against the farm and its residents. That moment came in the form of a flirtatious comment from an African American teenager.

Curtis Freeman, a nineteen-year-old African American, was riding in the back of a pickup truck with three black teenagers on the morning of September 26, 1955. Only three days had passed since the acquittal of Roy Bryant and J. W. Milam, the two white men accused of murdering Emmett Till, a fourteen-year-old African American from Chicago spending the summer in Mississippi. The news was still fresh to all Mississippians. That morning, the conservative *Jackson Clarion-Ledger* had reported that Mose Wright, Till's relative who had bravely pointed out Till's murderers in the courtroom, had fled to the North because he "sold out" his white neighbors. As the truck carrying Freeman passed a school bus stop along Highway 49, Mary Ellen Henderson, the ten-year-old daughter of Jim and Shirley Henderson, was waiting to catch her bus to school in Tchula. The white Hendersons lived on Providence Farm and had been among the original residents at Delta Cooperative Farm in 1936. Shirley Henderson's father, James H. Moody, had been a committed socialist and follower of Norman Thomas. Jim Henderson's father, also named Jim, was a member of the interracial Southern Tenant Farmers' Union in the 1930s and had stood guard with a shotgun while his belongings were loaded into a truck by union volunteers and shipped to Delta Cooperative Farm. When Sam Franklin traveled the Arkansas Delta in 1936 looking for families who were in perilous conditions and who would make ideal cooperators in an interracial community, he chose the Moodys and the Hendersons among the first dozen families. Shirley Moody and the younger Jim Henderson met at Delta Farm in 1936 and quickly married in the first ceremony performed at the cooperative. Throughout their stay at Delta and Providence, the Hendersons and the Moodys prospered and displayed an eagerness to engage in the interracial endeavors of the farm. Still, their lives were not without tragedy. Jim and Shirley were pregnant often, losing several children in childbirth or at young ages. In 1945, their young son Donald was hit by a car and killed. Jim Henderson's father died unexpectedly in 1952. The remaining Hendersons relied on welfare from the federal government and on the kindness of their black and white neighbors at Providence to get by. Yet when a black teenager apparently flirted with Jim and Shirley's daughter, Mary Ellen, the limits of interracial cooperation at Providence surfaced.[13]

As Mary Ellen Henderson waited with other children at the bus stop, the truck motored by and Freeman yelled out, "Hey sugar, you look good to me," in Henderson's direction. Henderson assumed the flirtatious statement had been meant for her, and began crying. Why Freeman's comment upset Henderson, a girl who had grown up with black neighbors all her life and who lived on a farm that was dedicated to black self-help, is unclear. Maybe it was the fact that she was white and he was black that most upset her. Or maybe it was the unwanted flirtation of an older boy that caused her reaction. Either way, what happened in the next few hours proved to be the undoing of Providence Farm and its nearly twenty-year promotion of African American–centered human rights activism.[14]

When Henderson boarded the school bus, the driver noticed she was upset and asked her what was wrong. The driver in turn reported the incident to the Tchula school principal, who immediately called Holmes County sheriff Richard Byrd. Byrd quickly "apprehended" Freeman and his three teenaged companions. Freeman knew Sheriff Byrd. Everyone did. Freeman understood that the sheriff had a reputation for kicking blacks around and that rumors implicated him in the murder of his own deputy. Freeman probably knew about Emmett Till's fate too and hoped he would not meet the same end. Byrd called county attorney and Citizens' Council member Pat Barrett, who was already skeptical of the practices at Providence. Byrd, Barrett, and a few others—all members of the Holmes County Citizens Council—questioned the four black teenagers for hours. Freeman swore that he was speaking to someone else at the bus stop, an African American girl whose nickname was "Sugar" and with whom he had a friendly relationship. Byrd and Barrett did not believe him, or did not care. They told Freeman that it did not matter who he was speaking to, but that he uttered the phrase within earshot of Henderson, a white girl. The sheriff charged Freeman with the "unlawful use of vulgar and obscene language" in the company of a white woman. Several weeks later, a Holmes County court sentenced Freeman to six months of hard labor on the county farm.[15]

In another context or another decade, the incident with Freeman and Henderson might not have had much impact on Providence Farm or its residents. If the incident had happened even two years prior, it might not have resulted in jail time for Freeman or eventually led to Providence's closing. But by the fall of 1955, several events had altered the terrain of race relations and hardened the resolve of many white segregationists in Holmes County. Headlines screamed of Mississippi atrocities. In December 1955, the editors of the black newspaper the *Pittsburgh Courier* published a full-page open letter to President Eisenhower asking him to send U.S. soldiers into Mississippi to protect black citizens. One example the letter used as evidence of unconstitutional actions was the attempted expulsion of Cox and Minter from Holmes County. As a result of increased federal and media pressure, white racists hunkered down.

Holmes County, in particular, became an epicenter of racial tensions in the mid-1950s.[16]

The first incident that intensified white hostility in Holmes County occurred in January 1954 and also involved the specter of interracial sex. Eddie Noel, a twenty-eight-year-old African American World War II veteran who lived in rural Holmes County, approximately ten miles from Providence, shot and killed Willie Ramon Dickard, a white roadhouse owner and part-time moonshiner who may have been having an affair with Noel's wife, Lu Ethel Noel. Lu Ethel was a waitress at the roadhouse, and when Eddie came to the bar to confront the two, Dickard beat him up and threw him out of the front door. Noel retreated to his vehicle and grabbed his .22 caliber rifle. While white and black customers looked on, Noel shot Dickard in front of his establishment. For the onlookers, it was the first time many of them had seen a black man retaliate against a white man, much less kill one.[17]

Noel fled into the countryside. Over the next nineteen days, Holmes County waited in fear as manhunts and shootouts became common occurrences. Over five hundred men turned out from all over Mississippi to participate in the hunting of Noel. Several times he narrowly escaped capture, managing to kill a well-respected Holmes County deputy as well as a World War II veteran who had cornered Noel with a Luger the veteran had retrieved from a dead German soldier. The Luger misfired. Noel's .22 did not. Noel also severely injured three others, nearly killing them all. As the manhunt continued, Noel gained an almost mythical status among both black and white Holmes County residents. Three times Noel was cornered, and three times he escaped by shooting his way out, operating his bolt-action .22, local African Americans remembered, with the precision and efficiency of a highly trained soldier. The whites who tracked him—trained law enforcement officers, hunters, and World War II veterans—concluded that Noel was the living embodiment of what they had feared when black veterans first returned from World War II. Not only were blacks agitating for increased rights, they were armed and trained by the U.S. Army. In the same breath that whites condemned Noel as a "crazy nigger," they were awestruck by his marksmanship. Some feared that Noel's murderous rampage would spark an all-out race war in Holmes County. In the end, however, the posse never caught him nor was he lynched, a fate that met hundreds of Mississippi's black men in the early twentieth century. In late January, cold and hungry, Noel surrendered without incident. Noel was tried, found legally insane, and sentenced to a medical ward for detention.[18]

The Noel incident propelled Holmes County sheriff Richard Byrd, the officer who would arrest Curtis Freeman for the bus stop incident the next year, into the media spotlight. At the time of the manhunt, Byrd had been in office for only two years but had already garnered a reputation for breaking the law more than upholding it. Because of the Noel incident, however, Byrd's questionable character came to light even more. First, Holmes Countians widely understood that Byrd orchestrated one of the largest manhunts in Mississippi history so that if it failed, the blame would not fall on his shoulders alone. Second, rumors circulated that he had murdered his own deputy during a shootout with Noel and then blamed it on "that little nigger." The deputy had been the former Holmes County sheriff and had a reputation as a fearless protector of law and order, specifically targeting bootleggers in the county. Byrd, however, was rumored to be taking money from the very same bootleggers in exchange for their protection from legal prosecution. There exists no preponderance of evidence to support the claim that Byrd murdered his own deputy. The fact that the rumor existed at all and was widely believed, however, underscores that Byrd's previous behavior had led many to deem him as the kind of sheriff who was capable of such a crime.[19]

Sheriff Byrd's reputation became the focus of journalist Hazel Brannon Smith's editorials in her newspaper, the *Lexington Advertiser*. Her columns were unpopular among many conservative whites because Smith was progressive—by 1950s Mississippi measures—on the issue of race relations. Smith wanted to blame someone for the killing sprees and thought it was too simple to blame only Noel. The Noel incident, she concluded, illuminated deeper issues in Holmes County that needed to be addressed. First, she took aim at moonshine and excoriated officials, namely Sheriff Byrd, who allowed it to circulate throughout the county unregulated. Then Smith devoted column after column to Byrd's miscarriages of justice, gaining her both friends and enemies. The columns seemed only to fuel Byrd's hot temper and frustration with the manhunt. He assaulted Noel's friends and family and threatened them with murder if they did not turn Noel over to him.[20]

After Noel surrendered, tensions eased temporarily in Holmes County, although Smith's editorial attacks on Byrd continued. If the incidents with Noel had been the only racially charged events in Holmes County before Curtis Freeman whistled toward that bus stop, he might have not been pursued by local law enforcement. But racial antagonisms in that part of Mississippi were just beginning to boil over. In May 1954, the U.S. Supreme Court handed down the *Brown v. Board of Education of Topeka, Kansas* decision, ruling that public school segregation was unconstitutional. As news spread, tensions rose again in Holmes County. Less than two months after the Supreme Court's verdict, Robert Patterson formed the first White Citizens' Council in Indianola, Mississippi. Patterson's group targeted "respectable" white individuals, mainly middle-class professionals and business owners, who could block desegregation and the civil rights movement by political and economic means. Only days after Patterson convened the first Citizens' Council, a second was chartered in Lexington, Mississippi—making Holmes County an epicenter for the fight against black civil rights.[21]

After the Supreme Court decision, Gene Cox noticed that "tensions, rumors and suspicions have been multiplied" about Providence Farm. What Cox called a "smear campaign" against the community included a rumor that either he or David Minter had been arrested by the Federal Bureau of Investigation "as a Red spy." A friend informed Cox in September 1954 that he had been approached by a private investigator in Jackson who had been hired to look into Cox's subversive activities. "It appears that all the rumors of the past 18 years," surmised Cox, "are being remembered and put back into circulation. For twenty years" Cox and other residents at Delta and Providence farms "had been talking to educators and business people in Mississippi," Cox admitted, "trying to get better schools for Negroes." When the Supreme Court issued its decision in the *Brown* case, Cox knew that "extreme segregationists" in Holmes County would target Providence. Citizens' Council members, some of the leading businessmen and politicians in Holmes County, spread rumors about Providence's racial policies and ties to communism. Cox and Minter called on other friends in high places around Mississippi to write letters to Holmes County officials and state legislators to assure them that Providence harbored no communists. They looked to Lexington attorney Pat Barrett for council. Barrett had drawn up the deed to Providence Farm in 1943, had personally handed it to Sam Franklin, and had known Cox for over a decade. To the dismay of the cooperators, Barrett publicly called Cox's motives into question, insinuating that Cox was a communist dupe. "It is very difficult to prove you are not a Communist," a frustrated Cox stated, "when people are not aware of just what constitutes communism."[22]

Making matters worse for farm residents, over the Fourth of July weekend in 1954, Sheriff Byrd again sparked controversy after he was involved in an incident that ended with a black man being shot in the thigh and David Minter as the attending physician. Around eleven o'clock on the night of July 3, Sheriff Byrd and three other lawmen were driving down Highway 49 near Tchula's outskirts in a patrol car. As the law enforcement officers passed Henry Randle, Isaiah Carlton, and Missouri Hunter—African American men in their late twenties—Byrd thought he heard one of them let out a loud "whoop." Byrd had roughed up Holmes County blacks for lesser offenses and told the officer driving to turn around and head back to the three men. When Byrd got out, he approached the twenty-seven-year-old Randle and asked why he and his friends had made the "whooping" noise. Randle replied that "it wouldn't none of him that whooped." Byrd then struck Randle across the head with his black jack. Byrd told the men to "get goin," while Randle and his two companions turned to run.[23]

What happened next was where Byrd's and Randle's stories diverged. Randle claimed he heard four rapid shots, one of which hit him in the back of the left thigh and passed through the other side of his leg. As he stumbled in agony, he looked over his shoulder to see Byrd's pistol pointed in his direction. In later court testimony, Byrd said that he did not draw his weapon, but that one of the other officers "fired a .44-calibre pistol in the air three times in an effort to disperse the crowd of Negroes." Isaac Randle, Henry Randle's father, first took his wounded son to a doctor in Tchula but could not find the physician at home. Next, they drove out to Providence, only two miles from the Randle home, and awoke Dr. Minter around midnight. Minter later testified that he treated Randle's wounds, noticed a "goose egg" on the side of his forehead that he assumed was from the sheriff's black jack, and smelled no alcohol on Randle's breath.[24]

Word of the shooting spread quickly, and Hazel Brannon Smith once again accused Sheriff Byrd of unlawful activities in her newspaper editorials. Smith insinuated that Byrd and his companions were out for a good time that Saturday night and had accosted another half-dozen men. This time, Byrd countered with a libel lawsuit—totaling $57,500 in damages—against Smith. Smith responded in her column that "we don't know whether to be flattered at being sued for so much—or surprised that the Sheriff places the value of his reputation at so little." Perhaps to escape being the center of attention in the Byrd incident, only days after the shooting, Minter packed up his family and spent a weeklong vacation at Cumberland Falls State Park in Kentucky.[25]

Being the first white person to hear a direct account of Randle's story, Minter was a chief witness in the libel court case. As the trial drew near, Minter became the target of a smear campaign and rumor mill. In an attempt to discredit him, "there were many rumors spread all over the county that I was a Communist," Minter remembered later, "that I was heading a spy ring and holding secret meetings, that I was distributing communist literature." Building on the pretrial accusations, the defense only had to impugn Minter with the white jury by accusing him of "communist interracial activities" and simply asking if he lived "in a community called Providence." Apparently, the mere mention of Providence carried enough weight to discredit Minter. In a moment of exasperation, Gene Cox wrote FBI director J. Edgar Hoover in the hopes that he would clear the air of the rumors leveled against him and Minter. Cox also could not resist admonishing Hoover for what he felt were the director's irresponsible comments about "Red doctors regularly dish[ing] out communist propaganda." Cox worried that these statements had worsened the atmosphere surrounding Minter.[26]

The initial result of the civil suit was a victory for Byrd. The court ordered Hazel Brannon Smith to pay the sheriff $10,000 in restitution. Smith appealed to a higher court, and the decision was eventually overturned. Still, the case had damaged Minter's reputation in Holmes County and heightened suspicions about the purpose of Providence.[27]

The downward spiral continued in late March 1955, when Minter was asked by the First Presbyterian Church of Tchula, where he was a deacon and had been teaching Sunday school classes for seven years, not to return as a teacher in light of the allegations against him. One year earlier, the Tchula church defied the General Assembly of the Presbyterian Church of the United States, which had resolved that legal segregation was un-Christian and that their congregations would be desegregated. The elders of the Tchula church issued a statement saying the congregation would "pledge ourselves to retain segregation under the guidance of the Holy Spirit and for the glory of God." The unanimous pledge by the elders continued that "non-segregation would destroy not only the peace of the church but also the purity of its message established in the Word."[28]

The Tchula congregation was like thousands of other white churches around the South after *Brown v. Board*. For them, Christian theology clearly taught that miscegenation and more casual integration were cosmologically forbidden. It was God's will that segregation was necessary for peaceful coexistence between the races. Despite the congregation's racial views not aligning with his own, Minter stayed on because of his devotion to his Sunday school students. Minter and his wife, Sue, had been involved with the youth at First Presbyterian for several years, taking a group of young high-school-aged congregants to the Presbyterian Youth Rally in Jackson once a year. For several years Sue had been the chairman of Christian education at the church and, along with Lindsey Cox, was an active member of the Women of the Church, who sponsored fund-raising and membership drives. The congregation's view of the Minters was not improved when Sue Minter was compelled during a service to defend her views on teaching communism in college classrooms. When pressed about her beliefs in front of the congregation, she answered that college educators ought to be able to teach their students the differences between communism and other philosophies. That she condoned the discussion of communism at all angered parishioners.[29]

David Minter was devastated by his excommunication. "To this son of a Presbyterian minister and brother of two missionaries," remembered one friend, "this dismissal came as a very great shock." The Minters were not without sympathizers in the congregation, however. Lindsey Hail Cox, who also taught Sunday school at the church, resigned her position in protest. Two sisters, former Sunday school students in Minter's class, wrote the doctor and expressed their sorrow at the situation and anger at "this injustice that has been done you. The Christian-like manner in which you have reacted to this situation," the girls continued, "has convinced us even more of your true faith and Christian devotion." Despite several letters of support and the girls' impression that Minter was taking his dismissal with quiet dignity, the action of his church deeply hurt Minter and his family.[30]

The accusations by Sheriff Byrd and the reaction by the Minters' congregation proved that race baiting and red baiting would be the tactics white racists would use against racial moderates and progressives in Holmes County. The ways these two tactics came together in Holmes County after Curtis Freeman's incident at the bus stop were clear evidence that they would be used with impunity. Since before the United States became formally involved in World War II, the accusation of communism had been used to defy any challenge to Jim Crow. Even as early as the mid-1930s, Sam Franklin and Sherwood Eddy worried that their Christian Socialist views on race would lead white Mississippians to brand them as communists. Oscar Johnston, manager of the Delta Pine and Land Company, had done just that in a 1937 meeting of the President's Commission on Farm Tenancy. The commission invited both Franklin and Johnston to speak at the hearings. After Franklin spoke, Johnston devoted the beginning of his testimony to denouncing the cooperative's initiatives as "communistic." In 1937, however, having no nearby community of white business leaders to support his anticommunist claims, Johnston was merely tilting at windmills. Conversely, in the mid-1950s, the relationship between residents at Providence and the conservative white community was already too tenuous for Cox, Minter, Booker, and the other farm residents to weather a frontal assault by anticommunists in the wake of the bus stop incident.[31]

For months, news of federal challenges to segregation and the threat of communism dominated the press in Holmes County. Editorials debated whether Mississippi's schools would ever desegregate. Gene Cox wrote a friend in September 1954 that racial tensions were high. "I imagine you are aware of what is happening here in connection with the segregation question," he wrote. "Two Negro teachers have lost their jobs in Holmes county. One after she had been shot by a prominent farmer and business man of Lexington. On the front page of one of the Jackson papers last Friday appeared this statement: 'One said, "a few killings" would be the best thing for the state just before the people vote on a proposed constitutional amendment empowering the legislature to abolish public schools." Cox concluded wryly that it was "such a nice place to be living just now."[32]

In December 1954, Mississippi held a special election spurred by the U.S. Supreme Court's decision on school desegregation. By a wide margin, voting Mississippians gave the state legislature the power to abolish public schools if deemed necessary to uphold segregation. Holmes County voted for the amendment 2,393 to 70. A single voter in Tchula voted against the proposal. Publicly, politicians who supported the measure touted it as in the best interests of all Mississippians. Segregationists also pointed to recent "improvements" in Mississippi's black schools and argued that separate could be equal. Still, in 1954, white Holmes County teachers made an average of $320 per month, while black teachers made an average of only $175 per month.[33]

In August 1955, the murder of Emmett Till further plunged the state into turmoil. The teenager's apparent "wolf-whistle" at a white woman enraged Roy Bryant and J. W. Milam, the woman's husband and his half brother, so much that they beat the fourteen-year-old teenager, shot him, and then tied his body to a cotton gin fan and threw him into that Tallahatchie River. Several days later, Till's body was fished from the muddy river.[34]

Mississippians, black and white, were apprehensive about what was happening in their state. African Americans and their white allies saw a child murdered and his white killers go free. Pro-segregationist whites felt that their way of life, their time-honored racial privilege, was being severely challenged by "outside agitators" and "race traitors." Given all the events of the past months— Noel's rampage and subsequent manhunt, Sheriff Byrd's frustration with Hazel Brannon Smith, communist accusations against David Minter, the *Brown v. Board* decision, and Emmett Till's murder—Curtis Freeman could not have picked a worse moment to flirt at a bus stop.

During Curtis Freeman's interrogation, Sheriff Byrd and Holmes County attorney Pat Barrett asked Freeman and his friends questions about Providence Farm. All the boys had spent time there. The boys' parents shopped at the cooperative store, patronized the credit union, came to the educational and religious institutes, and were patients at the medical clinic. Byrd and Barrett used the four teenagers as scapegoats to outflank Gene Cox and David Minter, men with whom they had serious disagreements ever since Minter was Henry Randle's attending doctor and the chief defense witness in Byrd's libel lawsuit against Hazel Brannon Smith. In the interviews with the four teenagers, most of the questions were about the goings-on at Providence Cooperative Farm. Did Mr. Cox talk about integration? Did Dr. Minter encourage blacks to register to vote? Did interracial swimming occur at the swimming hole? The boys answered variously, but most said they did not know what went on at the farm. After intense questioning, the sheriff concluded that those in charge at Providence had broken Mississippi state laws by promoting integration—he especially dwelled on the swimming hole where whites and blacks supposedly recreated together—and for being communists. The fight to integrate public swimming began long before *Brown v. Board*, and the backlash by white opponents was often violent. For white segregationists across the country, segregated swimming pools were as sacred as segregated schools for their spurious connection to interracial sex. Upon the conclusion of the interrogations, the sheriff and attorney called an emergency community meeting for the following evening on September 27.[35]

Gene Cox and David Minter were among the last to receive word about the meeting. Reverend Marsh Calloway, a white Presbyterian minister from nearby Durant, Mississippi, who had struck up a friendship with both Minter and Cox over the years, heard about the meeting and immediately drove out to Providence to inform them and their families. Several hours before the meeting, incoming state representative J. P. Love called Minter and brusquely told him to be at that night's gathering. Cox assumed that the meeting was more of the same accusations they had been hearing for years, and he and Minter decided to attend in order to defend themselves in person. Neither man had any idea that their fates at Providence would be sealed that night.[36]

Cox and Minter were shocked when they arrived at the auditorium. Around five hundred people, half the population of Tchula, showed up to hear the recorded "confession" of the four black teenagers and to listen to Cox and Minter defend themselves. The meeting was convened by retiring Mississippi legislator Edwin White of Lexington and his recently elected replacement, J. P. Love, who was an influential member of the Tchula Citizens' Council. Attorney Pat Barrett and Sheriff Richard Byrd joined White and Love on stage to lead the meeting.[37]

All of the meeting's conveners were well-known in their communities and were either violent racists, in the case of Sheriff Byrd, or prominent Citizens' Council members who pledged at every turn to uphold segregation. Edwin White was a Lexington attorney by trade, but had represented Holmes County for two terms in the state legislature. Among Mississippi's elected white supremacists, White was an especially stanch ideologue. Particularly preoccupied with interracial sex, White had supported eugenics and railed against all forms of integration. "I feel that due to the modern liberal teachings in our Churches and in our colleges," White believed that "a great majority of our people are either unaware of, or overlook, the ethnological truth that unless we observe strict segregation it will be only a matter of time until the white and Negro race in the South will become a mixed race." In the last months of his term, White had been deeply disturbed by both the Eddie Noel incident and the U.S. Supreme Court decision to strike down segregation in public schools. To guard against more "crazy niggers" with guns, White proposed that the state legislature pass a law requiring the registration of all firearms and ammunition. In his testimony, White alluded to the rising number of blacks who were purchasing guns and expressed alarm. The proposed bill died in the Senate. After the *Brown* decision, White was a vocal proponent of giving the legislature the power to abolish the public school system in Mississippi. White was fond of quoting the Bible's passages that, to him, prohibited "racial amalgamation." He called the *Brown* decision "sinful, unholy, and unworthy of obedience." "There is only one thing in the whole situation which the white man asks for," White assured his supporters, "and this is the privilege of his children, and his children's children continuing to be white people." By the time of the mass meeting at the Tchula auditorium, White was serving out his last months as a state representative. He continued to be active in the Holmes County Democratic Party, however. As chairman in 1956, he strongly supported "pro-segregation" candidates and helped push through a resolution that Holmes County delegates at the state and national conventions would vote only for candidates supported by the Citizens' Council. Cox and Minter sat horrified at the mass meeting as White "fanned the emotions of the crowd with Hitler-like, fascist oration."[38]

Representative-elect J. P. Love and incumbent county attorney Pat Barrett also took well-known stances in defiance of the Supreme Court's *Brown* decision. Love, the head of the Tchula Citizens' Council, announced his candidacy by proclaiming he would uphold "the framework of existing Southern traditions and principles." One of Love's first acts in the legislature was to introduce a bill that would "permit county boards of supervisors to make unrestricted donations of public funds to the pro-segregation Citizens' Councils." Barrett was not as veiled as Love had been in his reelection announcement. In a letter to the *Lexington Advertiser*, Barrett clearly told Holmes Countians where he stood on the issue of school segregation. "With reference to the tragic and deplorable situation caused by the shameful decision of our Supreme Court," Barrett declared, "I do not believe it is necessary for me to remind my many friends throughout the County that I shall continue individually and as your County Attorney to strive unceasingly and unendingly to preserve our Southern way of life; and I believe my training and experience will be a valuable asset to this office during the critical period we are facing." That Holmes County politicians were quick to take up the mantle of the Citizens' Council was not uncommon. All five candidates for governor of Mississippi in 1955 made campaign promises to support the "southern way of life" and the pro-segregationist stance of the Citizens' Councils.[39]

The gathering convened by White, Love, Barrett, and Byrd began with the minister from the Tchula Methodist Church giving an invocation. Byrd then played the "confession" of the four black teenagers. On the tape, the boys were repeatedly asked what went on at Providence, and most of them answered that they did not know, even though they had attended religious and educational meetings at the farm. David Minter remembered thinking that "either they were not answering questions completely truthfully or that we had done a damn poor job of education of people for what we were trying to really do in the community in the way of health education, better farming methods, etc." Cox and Minter were then "subjected to a barrage of questions" from the conveners and attendees. The two men attempted to answer accusations that they had broken the law but instead were shouted down by more accusations of communism and integration. Upon being pressed about his opinions on school segregation, Cox finally replied that he believed segregation to be "unchristian." An angry crowd member yelled back that "this isn't a Christian meeting."[40]

Only three men spoke up in defiance of the crowd. A Tchula banker suddenly stood up and left the meeting, stating, as he made for the exit, that he did not want to be a part of what was happening to Cox and Minter. A local planter named Samuel J. "Bobo" Foose, from a prominent Tchula family, made a long speech in which he spoke glowingly of Minter as a doctor and "good Christian." "I may not have a friend in Holmes County tomorrow," declared Foose, "but I want to go home and sleep with a clear conscience tonight." After he spoke, Foose left the meeting as well. Marsh Calloway, the Presbyterian minister who accompanied Cox and Minter to the meeting, spoke for the embattled men and questioned both the legality and morality of the mass meeting. A chorus of boos cascaded down on Calloway. Sitting in the back of the meeting, and unbeknownst to Cox and Minter, was crusading newspaper woman Hazel Brannon Smith. In her next editorial, she wrote of the meeting that "the Rev. Mr. Callaway conducted himself with dignity and honor as befitting a brave man." Even so, two months later, Calloway slinked away from Holmes County, having been told by his Durant congregation—in a vote of forty-three to two—that they did not agree with his support of Cox and Minter and no longer wanted his spiritual guidance.[41]

Finally, Representative Love concluded that Cox and Minter may not be card-carrying members of the Communist Party, but that they were "following the Communist line," which was a distinction without a difference to nearly everyone in attendance. Love then called for a vote to ask Cox and Minter to leave the county. The vote for them to leave their homes of almost two decades was nearly unanimous. Only Cox, Minter, Calloway, and a local blacksmith who believed he needed to pray about the situation before he gave his decision voted in favor of allowing the men and their families to stay. The rest, perhaps swayed by their own convictions of white supremacy and anticommunism or convinced by hearing their county leaders call Cox's and Minter's actions into question, agreed that the men should leave "for the good of Holmes County."[42]

As they left the meeting, shocked and sullen, Cox and Minter walked out of the school behind Tchula resident Jeffery "T. J." Bogue. The elderly Bogue was a well-known member of the Tchula community whose life was not unlike those of other well-to-do white Tchula residents. Bogue's wife was an active member of the Tchula Baptist Church. They had successful children, one of whom was the superintendent of a consolidated school system in Mississippi. Bogue had grandchildren whom he lavished with gifts and extravagant birthday parties. Exactly a year before the mass meeting at the Tchula High School, Bogue received the awful news that a granddaughter, who lived in Greenwood, had contracted polio. Had his granddaughter lived in Tchula, she might have been treated by Dr. Minter. Had they gone to the same church, Minter and Cox might have personally comforted Bogue and prayed with him about his granddaughter's illness. But T. J. Bogue was not the sort of man who associated with Providence residents. As Bogue filed out in front of Cox and Minter and approached three of his friends, he said in a loud voice, "What we need for these S.O.B.s is a couple of grass ropes." Cox and Minter kept walking, trying not to react to the threat of lynching their neighbor had just uttered. "I really think they would have killed us," Minter later reflected, "except for the school-children." "Just about the time the vote was being taken on telling us to leave the state," Minter remembered, "the [football] game ended and there were kids all over the schoolyard."[43]

Attorney Pat Barrett, who was a key member of the witch hunt against Providence, told a reporter after the meeting that "there is nothing personal" about the accusations leveled at Cox and Minter, and then added that "my best friend is a Negro." Further reflecting on his friendship with blacks, and perhaps hoping for some absolution in the matter, Barrett concluded that it was best for the county if Cox and Minter left because "we don't want a lot of good Niggers getting killed." J. P. Love echoed this sentiment when he told a reporter that "we don't want a Sumner here," referring to the media frenzy around the Emmett Till case. Barrett, who had known Gene Cox for nearly twenty years, visited the farm to encourage the Coxes and Minters to leave quietly and quickly. Cox simply and tersely told Barrett how his daughter came home from school one day upset about the possibility of leaving her childhood friends if they were forced to move. Cox had struck a nerve with the attorney, and Barrett left without saying anything further. Later that night, Barrett called Cox, and although he did not apologize, he said he "had been sitting with his own daughter on his knee and he just couldn't make Gene leave." J. P. Love, who had used Dr. Minter as his family physician for several years, also partially regretted the mass meeting and said Minter "is well liked personally in the community and a real fine doctor."[44]

Edwin White, however, was unrepentant. Speaking of Providence, White bellowed that "some people believe what they want to believe. But what those nigger boys said was enough for us people who have suspected what was going on for 20 years. We know the minds of these Negroes are being poisoned down there," White added. The retiring politician pursued the residents of the farm vociferously after the mass meeting. White bluntly told a reporter that Cox and Minter were "practicing social equality out there. We won't have that," he added pointedly. White later claimed, contrary to the evidence on the tape-recorded interviews, that the four black teenagers questioned had told him that "all white girls are whores." The specter of miscegenation loomed large over the entire incident, from the first remark made by Freeman to his conviction for uttering vulgarities in the company of a white woman and Byrd's and Barrett's questions about interracial swimming at Providence. Several years later, Love remarked to an investigator for the Mississippi Sovereignty Commission that he once observed Cox dancing with Fannye Booker in the cooperative store. Love did not have to say any more on the subject—the insinuation was that Cox had transgressed racial and sexual mores. For White, Love, Byrd, and Barrett to insinuate that the activities at Providence would inevitably lead to interracial sex was to roll out an argument white southerners had used to defend informal and formal racial segregation since the end of the Civil War. The argument that segregation guarded against miscegenation was as much political capital for segregationists as was their use of intimidation and violence.[45]

The night of the meeting, Sue Minter and Lindsey Hail Cox stayed home with their children, "shivering with fear" for the safety of their families. When their husbands arrived home to recount their ordeal, Lindsey went to her Bible for guidance and found it in Isaiah 8. She took strength in the call to "Say to those who are of a fearful heart, 'Be strong, fear not!'" She hoped, as the passage continued, that her adversaries' blind eyes would be opened and deaf ears unstopped by God's love, or his vengeance. The next morning, Sue and Lindsey gathered their children on the front porch of the Coxes' home to speak with them about what had happened the night before. Both women fully expected their children to be the targets of taunts or violence in school after the meeting. "Looking out over the beautiful view" of Providence Farm, the mothers prayed with their children to find strength in their faith. Lindsey Cox read aloud from Romans 8:38–39: "For I am convinced that neither death nor life, neither angels nor demons, neither the present nor the future, nor any powers, neither height nor depth, nor anything else in all creation, will be able to separate us from the love of God that is in Christ Jesus our Lord." The Coxes and Minters were relieved when their children came home to report no incidents at school.[46]

After the mass meeting in Tchula, the Citizens' Council began a boycott of the cooperative store while the Holmes County Sheriff's Department, with the unofficial aid of armed Klansmen, "guarded" the only road leading into and out of the farm for ten nights. Lindsey Cox wrote a friend that she did not think what the sheriff was doing could be called "protection" and revealed that she felt much safer when the law enforcement officers ended the blockade. A local white minister stopped by David Minter's home unannounced one afternoon to say that he thought it best if the Coxes and Minters left the county. The minister scoffed at the black human rights efforts Providence residents worked toward for over a decade. Besides, the minister remarked, what was the use of calling a black woman "Mrs." when everyone knew black people were never actually married? Minter resisted the urge to physically throw the minister out of his home and, as politely as he could, asked him to leave.[47]

Cox and Minter attempted to alert their allies to their dangerous situation. Cox called his friend and longtime labor organizer H. L. Mitchell, who was used to dealing with threats to his safety and livelihood. Upon hearing Cox's account of the meeting, Mitchell was outraged and called the U.S. Justice Department for help. Apparently Mitchell's phone call precipitated a small inquiry by the FBI into the incidents involving Providence. Mitchell insisted on undertaking a letter-writing campaign to spread the word about the injustices against Providence. Cox rebuffed Mitchell's advice and asked him to remain calm, preferring to "keep this quiet and attempt to work it out on the local level." Still, fearing for his safety and the well-being of his family, Cox wrote Mitchell three days after the mass meeting at the Tchula High School, detailing T. J. Bogue's lynching threat and making it clear that if "anything serious should happen to us here," Bogue and his friends could be responsible. Cox instructed Mitchell to open the letter only if he should be attacked or killed. Mitchell did as he was instructed, returning the unopened letter to Cox some twenty years later. David and Sue Minter discussed the safety of their children and Dr. Minter's aging mother who had come to live with them on the farm. Throughout the accusations of communism against her son and threats to their lives, "Mother Minter" had met the sentiments with "good Presbyterian righteous indignation," which had kept both David and Sue in high spirits. After David and Sue's own pastor remarked to the Minters that they could "not get mother Minter out of the house if it were burned," however, they decided that it would be best for her safety if she moved in with relatives in Texas.[48]

Providence residents were encouraged by old allies who showed their support—some wrote letters while others made the journey to the farm. Sam and Dorothy Franklin were the first old friends and members of the farm to visit after the mass meeting. Franklin appealed directly to Pat Barrett, whom Franklin had known for many years. He asked Barrett to hold another meeting to express "confidence in the Coxes and the Minters." Barrett refused. A. James McDonald, the idealistic volunteer who had butted heads with Sam Franklin at Delta Cooperative, also came in September and visited again in April 1956. The ever-fiery McDonald told Gene Cox that "I'd like to see you show the blankety-blanks that you can stay." Providence residents were probably relieved when McDonald left, however, because of his actual ties to the Communist Party.[49]

In October 1955, like-minded leftists and journalists flocked to the farm. Alice and Howard Kester paid a visit, as did journalist and future Pulitzer Prize winner David Halberstam, who visited on a research trip that would yield his first foray into exposé journalism. Another journalist who had already made a name for himself, Hodding Carter, invited the Coxes and the Minters to his lake house near Greenville, Mississippi, for the weekend as a respite from the pressures mounting in Holmes County. Carter and Hazel Brannon Smith took up the defense of Cox and Minter in their newspapers. Carter wrote an open letter to Holmes County residents in which he lamented that if Cox and Minter leave, "something will leave Holmes County with them, something very precious and American, something for which a great many Holmes County citizens apparently don't give a damn. That something," continued Carter, "is the spirit of the Bill of Rights."[50]

Despite support from longtime friends around the country, friends in Holmes County who were willing to support residents at Providence, however, were few. One month after the meeting, Lindsey Cox wrote letters to everyone in Holmes County who had stood up for her family during the mass meeting or sent the Coxes and Minters letters of support since. She wrote only six. "Few others have voiced their faith in us," wrote the Coxes and Minters in a joint letter to friends in 1955. "Above these small voices," the letter continued, "is this frightening SILENCE."[51]

Nerves began to fray at the farm after the phone lines were deliberately cut. Residents began to fear impending vigilante violence and reached out to anyone who might help. Hazel Brannon Smith accompanied Cox and Minter on a visit to the office of the Mississippi governor-elect James P. Coleman to ask for help in resolving the situation. Smith had publicly supported Coleman in her column and believed him to be an honest and fair man. Coleman was a moderate by Mississippi standards but won the gubernatorial race by promising to uphold racial segregation, a tactic that proved even more effective than the histrionic race-baiting of politicians like Edwin White. The future governor and Pat Barrett were also associates and fellow Rotarians, and Barrett had invited Coleman to speak at several civic events in Holmes County in the early 1950s. Cox, Minter, and Smith met with Coleman for nearly two hours, and Cox left with an "understanding that Mr. Coleman made some contacts in an attempt to have some of the heat taken off our backs." Before concluding the meeting, Cox sought Coleman's council. "What shall we do if the threats continue?" Cox asked Coleman. The governor-elect turned away from his guests and stared thoughtfully out of the large window behind his desk. After a long pause, Coleman told Cox and Minter how, as a judge and prosecuting attorney, he had sent many people to the state penitentiary. Some of those sentenced had promised to kill him upon their release. Coleman was reminded of those threats "often times, when working alone late at night." Finally he returned his attention to Cox and pointedly said, "You can't run from it." The meeting with the governor-elect, however, yielded no reprieve from the intimidation in Holmes County.[52]

Another Mississippi ally, Will Campbell, who was director of religious life at the University of Mississippi at the time, came to Providence with a friend to size up the situation for himself. As progressive on the issue of race as anyone at Providence, Campbell considered racism a sin and later devoted his career to social justice activism. As he entered the farm, law enforcement officers stopped Campbell and took down his license plate number. Upon his return to the university, the dean called Campbell into his office and asked what his business had been in Holmes County. Apparently, local law enforcement ran Campbell's tags and notified the university to further intimidate individuals sympathetic to Providence Farm.[53]

Although they had become the focus of racists, most Providence residents hoped the whole ordeal would blow over. Determined not to be intimidated, residents at the farm attempted to go on living their lives as best they could. Trying to keep a normal schedule, David Minter went into Tchula every day "to buy gas at the local station, stop and have a cup of coffee," and patronize the bank, drug store, and post office just so things appeared normal and to give everyone the impression that he and his family planned to stay at Providence. In November, Sue Minter threw a big birthday party for her nine-year-old daughter, Susan, with several children from Tchula attending. In December, Gene Cox wrote to Sherwood and Louise Eddy that "things are much quieter here in Holmes County just now—on the surface, at least." "Everyone is preparing for Christmas as in former years," he continued, "however, we are not having a public Christmas program as we have in the past."[54]

The calm façade did not last. The Coxes and Minters wrote a joint Christmas letter to friends and supporters of Providence in 1955. The weariness of each family was palpable, even on paper. They wrote of threatening and intimidating phone calls in the middle of the night, callers snarling, "When are you Communists going to leave?" Worried for their children, parents experienced many sleepless nights and deteriorating health. A friend of Lindsey Cox's wrote Sue Minter expressing concern that Cox "has been quite ill. Probably accumulated anxieties just wrought her insides to an unendurable pitch of inflammation." The Coxes and Minters were disappointed that few members of their churches had written them expressing their support. Most troubling, though, was that Cox and Minter felt they had endangered their friends, particularly the black residents at Providence. Cox attempted to secure some protection for them and instructed Fay Bennett, the executive secretary of the National Sharecroppers Fund, to contact the Mississippi secretary of the NAACP on their behalf. "I believe his name is Evers," Cox wrote.[55]

Even after the blockade ended, Minter's medical clinic, the coopertive store, and the credit union suffered mightily throughout the end of 1955 and 1956. The blockade had turned away many of Minter's patients who had come to the farm by foot, mule, horseback, or tractor. Countless patients were stopped from receiving medical care. Intimidation continued, and Minter's patient numbers fell off drastically. Minter blamed the Holmes County Citizens' Council and their influence among whites and intimidation of blacks. "Most planters [had] stopped sending patients to me," remembered Minter. "There were a few exceptions, but there was evidently a concerted effort on the part of the council members to boycott me. . . . One former patient [a white man] confided to me while drinking that he would have been to see me but that the council had told [people] to stay away. . . . It is hard to say if the council would have bothered us if the Sheriff had not laid the groundwork, although eventually there would have been something done because our opposition to them (not open but just the fact that we did not join)." Minter's practice experienced the same fate that other civil rights supporters experienced at the hands of the Citizens' Councils. First suggested at a council meeting in Sunflower County, Mississippi, boycotts were a common way for segregationists to effectively fight civil rights while claiming the mantle of respectability. "Economic pressure," as the Citizens' Council often termed it, put scores of blacks and their supporters out of work or out of business.[56]

Still, a few friends and patients trickled in and out of the clinic. One black farmer who had visited Minter's health clinic for several years accompanied his wife on a visit to Providence. The man walked in the front door holding his wife's arm in one hand and a rifle in the other. He reached the farm without incident, but swore to Minter that if anyone had tried to stop them, he would have shot his way through to keep the appointment. Another patient heard about Minter's trouble and came to Providence just so that he could pay an outstanding debt of eleven dollars because the man thought Minter might need some "traveling money."[57]

As Providence's funds dwindled, the campaign of intimidation from the surrounding community escalated. United States Fidelity and Guaranty Company, through which Minter insured his practice, received word that arsonists could lay siege to the clinic at any moment. With no warning, the company promptly cancelled the coverage. A reporter who was sympathetic to Providence later found that the Holmes County insurance agent was a member of the local Citizens' Council. Minter was exasperated and losing money. When a visitor asked Minter why he was considering closing the clinic, Minter simply answered, "you can't practice medicine without patients."[58]

The cooperative store took a financial hit too, with sales dropping from over $12,000 in 1955 to only $3,000 in 1957. The African American families at Providence, including the Bookers and Robert Granderson, tried to keep up the store and return it to its heyday as the center of the community. Their efforts met with little success. The decline of the store was an example of the long-lasting effects of the intimidation meted out to blacks in 1956. From that year forward, many stayed away from Providence Farm.[59]

In late 1955, Gene Cox and Fannye Booker initiated the liquidation of the Providence Cooperative Federal Credit Union. At the time, the credit union had over $9,000 in unpaid loans. As part of the campaign against the cooperative, plantation owners lied to their black employees and told them that they did not have to repay loans the credit union provided. Some black credit union members who lived off the farm were warned by whites to stay away and concluded that visiting Providence would put their lives in danger. In January 1956, the credit union stopped offering loans and only took deposits on an emergency basis. It was clear to Cox that he would have to close the credit union but could not completely repay all deposits because of the unpaid loans. For several years, Cox had been the national director of the Credit Union National Association. He called on his professional relationships through CUNA and wrote over thirty letters to credit unions all over the country, hoping to receive some financial support in order to pay his members their full deposits. Cox wrote of the treatment they had received from their neighbors and pleaded for financial assistance. One sympathetic manager at a credit union in Minnesota sent Cox $100 and exclaimed, "I can hardly believe that the state of Mississippi can still be in the confines of the United States of America." But only one other check, for $20, came from his credit union colleagues. Cox finally cancelled the credit union's charter in late 1957 when he distributed a total of nearly $4,000 among the last eighty members, many signing their reimbursement checks with a simple "X" to mark their endorsement.[60]

From 1955 to 1957, the population at Providence dwindled as residents belatedly joined the flood of southern blacks migrating out of the region. For Cox, Minter, and Booker, vacating residents were signs that segregationists were winning. The three felt "responsible for these families" and attempted to help them relocate. Checks from the credit union were mailed to addresses in Mississippi, Louisiana, Virginia, Illinois, Michigan, Arizona, and California. By the cooperative's final days, only a few families remained in the employ of the Delta Foundation, Inc. They performed maintenance on the farm and worked at the cooperative store. The rest sought new homes. Shirley Henderson, with her children, including Mary Ellen, the girl whose distress had been the catalyst for the cooperative's demise, moved to Edwards, Mississippi, in hopes of finding work at the Mt. Beulah Institute—an educational center associated with Tougaloo College. Several of the black families who moved to Delta Cooperative Farm in its first spring of 1936 were just now giving up on the cooperative effort. Nute Hulsey and his family moved to Roseville, California. The Billingtons moved to Cleveland, Ohio. The Whitneys relocated to Indianapolis, Indiana. Like thousands of other black families, the Hulseys, Billingtons, and Whitneys found housing in new and affordable communities, leaving their rural lives—and the Cotton Belt—behind them.[61]

By mid-1956, depleted incomes, downscaled programs, and continued intimidation finally forced the Cox and Minter families to seriously consider an end to their stays at Providence. "On June 1st I will have completed my first 20 years in Mississippi," Gene Cox wrote Sherwood and Louise Eddy. "I am not certain that there is another 20 left," he admitted, then added, "it has been a wonderful experience and I am thankful that Sherwood directed me to Mississippi."[62]

Finally, in late July 1956, citing drastically decreased income and having no insurance to operate a medical practice, Dr. Minter officially closed the clinic and joined the exodus, packing up their belongings and moving to Tucson, Arizona. Minter had treated patients in the clinic up until the very last night he lived at Providence. Cox wrote a friend of the "sad day in this community when he closed the Clinic for the last day." Less than one month later, Gene and Lindsey Cox moved with their daughters to a suburb in Tennessee called

Whitehaven, the name of which the Coxes found ironic. Whitehaven, near Memphis, "seemed impossible to us after the beauty and peace of Providence," Lindsey Cox wrote not long after moving.[63]

Delta Cooperative Farm and Providence Farm had struggled with near-constant internal turmoil for twenty years. Yet none of the self-inflicted wounds had been fatal. Mississippi's power structure, embodied by the Citizens' Council and the Ku Klux Klan, had been a far more lethal enemy. When the Minter and Cox families left Providence in the summer of 1956, it seemed as though the racists had won. And perhaps they had won this battle. The men and women who had called Providence home, however, continued their previous human rights activism, some as Mississippi dissidents, while some continued to work within the state. Because of their experiences at Providence Farm, Minter, Cox, and Booker would continue their broad approach to human rights during and after the 1950s and 1960s civil rights movement and Holmes County would soon become a beacon of far-reaching and successful civil rights activism.

Epilogue

The summer of 1956 marked the end of Providence Farm. For the past twenty years, the residents at Delta and Providence had heard the rumors of violence and sometimes even felt the hot sting of face-to-face threats. Since that September morning in 1955, however, when Curtis Freeman yelled toward a bus stop from the back of a pickup truck, the threats had become increasingly pointed and more frequent. Anonymous callers had uttered vile and menacing things about the children who lived at Providence. One visitor, with a deceptively calm, matter-of-fact grin, insinuated that the elderly who lived on the farm were at risk if an arsonist started a fire. It was probably best, the man continued, if everyone at Providence just left now before anything unfortunate happened. Most did leave, scattering a community of committed human rights workers across the country.

Even though they no longer had Providence—as it had existed in the 1940s—as a base of operations, David Minter, Gene Cox, Fannye Booker, and other former residents continued the work started at the farm. A few people, including Fannye Booker, stayed for some years longer while most, like the Hendersons, Minters, and Coxes, left. The day after Dr. David Minter packed up his family, locked up the clinic, and drove toward Arizona, Gene Cox wrote a friend of the righteous work Minter had done in Mississippi. "As I told some of the folks here," Cox wrote with vindication, "he will be remembered a hundred years after the local bigwigs are all dead and gone." In Tucson, Minter set up a medical and dental clinic for migratory farmworkers and continued his service to human rights. In 1969, Minter was honored by his Tucson community for "significant achievement in patient care and health services." A Holmes County newspaper picked up the story and ran an article on Minter, complete with a large picture of the doctor. The newspaper gushed that Minter was "still remembered with love and affection by hundreds of friends and patients in the county." In a bewildering display of revisionism, the article listed among Minter's many medical and community service honors that "in September of 1955 he was honored at Recognition Night of the Holmes County Community Council." His old friend, Gene Cox, cut out a copy of the article and wrote in the margin, "white citizens' council." The "Recognition Night" the article mentioned was, in fact, the night that hundreds of Minter's neighbors voted him out of the county and T. J. Bogue had threatened to lynch him.[1]

Others, of course, remembered Minter more accurately. In the early 1970s, black Holmes County residents wrote to Gene Cox, who had kept up his ties to the area, requesting Dr. Minter's address. In a steady hand that belied the near illiteracy of the writer, one letter read, "Mr. Cox so many people here want DRMinter address to see can we get him back here we don't have us doctor here at all." Cox acquiesced and Minter was inundated with letters from former patients who hoped to convince him to return. "Please come," wrote Eva Booker. "Every one that ever knew you and came to you sick, wants you back." The only quality medical care most black residents had access to was the traveling and temporary AKA summer clinics that Fannye Booker and Gene Cox had worked hard to have return to Holmes County in the 1960s. Dr. Minter, however, having started a successful clinic for migrant workers in Arizona, felt he was needed in the Southwest. He did not return to Mississippi.[2]

After leaving Providence, the Cox family settled in Tennessee. In Memphis, Gene Cox took two full-time positions as secretary-treasurer of the Agricultural and Allied Workers Union of the AFL-CIO and director of the Rural Development Program for the Division of Home Missions of the National Council of Churches. Even from Whitehaven, he continued his activism in Mississippi. For many years, Cox returned to visit friends and on business with the National Council of Churches. In 1959, it appeared that Cox might return to Mississippi full-time as a staffer at a new Christian vocation school for black youth in Neshoba County. Already harassed by white segregationists, the school's founders decided it was best not to further cultivate the relationship with Cox. Into the 1960s, however, he visited former Delta and Providence resident Shirley Henderson and her children at Mt. Beulah Institute twice a year. Through connections she had made at Delta Cooperative Farm in the 1930s, Lindsey Hail Cox continued to volunteer at the Western State Mental Hospital in Bolivar County for nearly forty years after leaving Mississippi. Old friends from Providence wrote the Coxes yearly. In 1966, Viola Billington, one of the first black residents at Delta Farm, who also made the move to Providence, wrote the Coxes from Cleveland, Mississippi, to update them on her life. Addressing Lindsey Hail Cox directly, the letter gushed that "my daughter, the one you delivered, has made a fine marriage and is now expecting her first child in June."[3]

About four years after Cox left the farm, he became the target of investigations and a "significant amount of attention" by the clandestine Mississippi Sovereignty Commission, organized by the state legislature in the mid-1950s to ward off the encroachment of federal desegregation policies and civil rights legislation. His frequent trips to Mississippi had raised the suspicions of commission member and state senator from Holmes County Wilburn Hooker. At Hooker's insistence, the commission sent an investigator to tail Cox's 1948 Packard as he traveled around the state. Cox quickly figured out that his activities in Mississippi were being closely followed and decided to turn the tables on the investigator charged with keeping tabs on him. While stopped in Holly Springs, Mississippi, for lunch at a cafe, Cox approached the investigator who had seated himself on the other side of the dining room. The man in the employ of the Sovereignty Commission was Tom Scarbrough, whom Cox had briefly met while still living at Providence. Scarbrough had been sheriff of Chickasaw County, Mississippi, in the 1940s and head of the Mississippi State Highway Patrol in the 1950s. He was appointed to the commission in 1960, and trailing Cox was one of his first assignments. Judging from his commission reports, many of his interviewees found him intimidating. Scarbrough had a robust opinion of himself and viewed his work as defending Mississippi's moral compass. "Holmes County has a very strong and active Citizens' Council and in my opinion is composed of the best citizens of the County," Scarbrough once reported to the commission. "To my thinking," he continued, "Holmes County is in good shape today because of the efforts put forth by these good citizens to see that the County was not taken over by do-gooders and integrationists."[4]

When he asked Cox what he was doing in Holly Springs, Cox matched wits with the glib Scarbrough. "I would assume you would know what I'm doing," Cox brusquely replied. Trying to get more information out of his target, Scarbrough brought up civil rights. Cox told Scarbrough that he supported some of the groups that were working toward civil rights in Mississippi. Scarbrough was disgusted that "his thinking has gotten no better since I saw him last." Cox then admonished the commission for inquiring about his activities when they should be "checking on the Ku Klux Klan."[5]

Although in front of Scarbrough he showed only restrained enmity, in private Cox seethed that the state of Mississippi would stoop to the level of spying. Even ten years after confronting the investigator in Holly Springs, Cox agonized over the insinuation that he had done anything that warranted being the subject of a clandestine commission. In the early 1970s, he began compiling a report to "convince the historians as to how utterly silly some of the work of the Commission really was." When he wrote Will Campbell in an attempt to correct some of the inconsistencies he found in the commission papers, Campbell wrote back that he did "not worry about the Sovereignty Commission checking on any of my activities as I have One far more permanent and authoritative checking also—the Lord Christ Himself." Cox, however, did not share Campbell's dismissively eschatological reaction and, for the rest of his life, harbored anger for the Sovereignty Commission's investigation.[6]

After 1956, Fannye Booker stayed on the farm and attempted to maintain community education initiatives and her summer camp. "Well-placed, subtle suggestions" of reprisal by whites if African Americans continued to frequent the farm kept many students and campers away. Still, Booker was defiant. "If I had been doing something wrong, then I would have had a right to run," she told a journalist decades after Providence closed. "But I wasn't and I didn't." She managed to organize a reunion of former Providence residents in 1966 and continued to offer summer camps for increasingly fewer youth into the 1970s. For the rest of her life, Booker stayed in Holmes County and became involved with promoting black-owned and -operated businesses, including a string of "community pride grocery stores," a home for the elderly, and a museum celebrating black achievements in Holmes County. Visitors were greeted at the door to the Booker-Thomas Museum by a large cast-iron bell that used to call her to and from the cotton fields when she was a girl. She also became intensely involved with the groundbreaking Holmes County Head Start Program from 1964 to 1979 and with voter registration drives after the Voting Rights Act passed in 1965.[7]

In the 1967 election, the first in Holmes County after the landmark 1965 legislation, Booker supported a black Holmes County teacher named Robert G. Clark for a seat in the state legislature. A native of Holmes County, Clark held a master's degree in sociology from Michigan State University and had been working toward a doctorate before deciding to return to Holmes County. The Mississippi Freedom Democratic Party (MFDP), founded in Sunflower County in 1964, had set up a chapter in Holmes County in 1966. Booker became an avid member of the MFDP and canvassed door-to-door on their behalf. By midsummer 1967, the MFDP had a slate of twelve black candidates running for office in Holmes County, including the popular Clark. Rather than competing against the white-controlled Democratic candidates, the MFDP-backed slate ran as independents. In what must have seemed like sweet justice for Fannye Booker, Clark defeated incumbent J. P. Love for a seat in the Mississippi House of Representatives. Love had been among the men who had helped lead the eviction of Gene Cox and David Minter from the county twelve years prior. In addition to the personal victory over Love, Booker had helped elect the first African American to the Mississippi legislature since Reconstruction and the highest office won by an African American candidate in the state's 1967 election. Although most Mississippi newspapers buried Clark's election or ignored it altogether, the New York Times ran a story lauding the "breakthrough for the state's slowly emerging Negro political forces." With Clarke's election—and subsequent reelection in 1971, again over J. P. Love—the quest for black human rights continued in Holmes County.[8]

Booker also continued to tend the cooperative store on a limited basis after 1956. Like it had done with Gene Cox, the Mississippi Sovereignty Commission briefly targeted Booker. The same investigator Cox had confronted in Holly Springs visited the cooperative store and inquired about Booker, Cox, and Providence, attempting to gain information for the commission. In his official reports, Scarbrough condescendingly referred to Booker as "above the average negro in intelligence." Booker did not trust the man and answered his questions with curt responses. After 1967, Booker kept the store open only one hour each day before finally closing it for good in the early 1970s. The store, however, was only a small part of Booker's involvement with the black community in Holmes County. In 1970, she helped organize a rally attended by five hundred people on the lawn of the Tchula High School. It had been over a year since an arsonist had burned the gymnasium to the ground and classes had been indefinitely interrupted. The school had integrated in 1966, but nearly all whites had left to go to private academies, leaving the Tchula High School almost entirely black. Representative Robert Clark, NAACP president Aaron Henry, and MFDP cofounder Fannie Lou Hamer all attended the rally and spoke to the crowd. "We're not going to be violent," Hamer told the crowd, "but we're going to have this school put back here and if we don't have this school put back here, I will start traveling . . . to raise that necessary $300 to get our kids into their private schools." The county soon came forward with the money to rebuild the gymnasium.[9]

Former residents found themselves engaged in the type of soul-searching that often accompanies growing older. As many of Providence's residents approached their twilight years, they attempted to take stock of their lives on the cooperative. In the 1970s, Gene Cox began to organize the papers he saved from his days at Delta and Providence. Cox possessed a paper trail going all the way back to Eddy's and Franklin's first ideas about a relocation farm for evicted Arkansas sharecroppers. Cox thought that an archive might one day be interested in the papers. He contacted some of his old colleagues in the struggle for human rights with the hope that they could help him fill some gaps in the historical record. The occasion allowed Cox and others a chance to reflect on the legacy of Delta and Providence.

Sam Franklin was perhaps most candid about his experiences at the farms. Franklin considered the ventures a "financial failure" but maintained that it was a "human success." His reflection on his own part in the projects was most telling. Perhaps contemplating eternity and seeking some absolution for his heavy-handed leadership, Franklin simply apologized. "I am conscious of having made many mistaken judgments even while trying to do my best," Franklin admitted. "I am also sure that egotism, closed-mindedness and impatience may have complicated the picture. For these 'secret sins,' known to God and usually to others but concealed by the sinner from himself, one can only ask forgiveness from all involved."[10]

H. L. Mitchell, the former Southern Tenant Farmers' Union (STFU) secretary, communicated with Cox about what he should do with his collected papers. Cox was apprehensive about handing all of his papers over to an archive. After his experience with the misinformation spread by the Mississippi Sovereignty Commission, he was justifiably shy about wading into debates over historical events in which he played important roles. "The record is going to speak for itself," Mitchell assured Cox. "No one is going to accept one man's opinion of Sherwood, Sam, you or me. We will be judged by historians on the basis of what we did, or what we tried to do." Then the cantankerous Mitchell reminded Cox that "if someone libels us, we can sue them or our children can do so."[11]

Cox also contacted William Amberson and almost immediately regretted it. Rather than invoke an even-keeled appraisal of the farms, Amberson rekindled some of his accusations against Eddy and Franklin—namely that they had engaged in "dubious or completely dishonest handling of money." The correspondence led Amberson to write to Mitchell to once again complain about the farm. Cox also wrote to Mitchell to object to Amberson's most recent antics. Mitchell again tempered Cox, but remained disappointed by Amberson. "His pursuits of Sherwood beyond the grave," revealed Mitchell, "remind me of Claude Williams who is as bitter about Kester." In the final analysis, though, Mitchell, who had plenty of experience managing loutish personalities while with the STFU, reminded Cox that old wounds should be left alone. "If I were you and Sam, I wouldn't bother," Mitchell told him, referring to Cox's attempts to refute Amberson's recent accusations. "Amberson is old and probably a damn sight crankier than he ever was." After several years of communication, Amberson politely ended his correspondence with Cox. "I cannot embark upon a lengthy correspondence," he wrote in 1973. "I need rest and peace from the problems of the old South."[12]

By the 1990s, Delta Cooperative Farm and Providence Farm began the slow fade from living memory as former residents passed away. In January 1991, Dr. David Minter died of a stroke in Tucson. Will Campbell wrote Minter's widow, Sue, that he "wept when I got the mailing about Dave." "I wish they had taught me some words to say," continued Campbell. "They didn't. Except, 'I'm here if you need me.' And, 'I loved him too.'"[13]

On December 14, 1992, Gene Cox and his wife of fifty-five years, whom he had met at Delta Cooperative Farm in 1936, Lindsey Hail Cox, sat in their Whitehaven living room and chatted, as they did every night. "In the evening while we were talking Gene suddenly slumped over," Lindsey remembered. Gene had suffered a massive stroke. He died five days later. Sam Franklin wrote to Lindsey not long after Gene's death. "He was, I think, more nearly a brother to me during the 56 years since he came to Hillhouse," Franklin said, "than any other living person." At his funeral, the pastor of Cox's church recalled how since leaving college to join Delta Cooperative Farm, Cox had taken "his ministry to the trenches." Cox's old friend and ally since his Providence days, Will Campbell, again eulogized a fallen resident of the cooperative farms. Noting that Cox had helped bring the Kingdom of Heaven to Earth and that he would find familiar surroundings in death, Campbell prayed aloud, "We commend him to that great interracial cooperative, Providence, somewhere up with the wind eternal." Not long after Gene's death, Lindsey Hail Cox wrote a letter to an acquaintance who had asked about Gene's harassment from the Mississippi Sovereignty Commission. Perhaps the lone solace Lindsey could take from Gene's death was that Mississippi racists "can no longer hurt my husband."[14]

In February 1997, Fannye Thomas Booker died in Lexington, Mississippi. Booker's obituary described her as possessing "a long eyesight" for all of the human rights work she accomplished in Holmes County. Hundreds of mourners attended her funeral, including scores of former campers and students she had befriended at Providence.[15]

The Delta Foundation gradually divided the land that once supported the Providence community and sold it to mainly private farm operators. In 1985, a section was sold to the Mississippi Department of Archives and History (MDAH). The MDAH coveted the land not for its historical significance as the home of a community engaged in black human rights activism and defying the state's racial caste system but because the farm contained several ancient Choctaw mounds. Since the MDAH's purchase, the rest of the farm has been owned by a Mississippi-based organization that advocates conservation and environmentally friendly farming practices. The organization, improbably, is named Delta FARM (Farmers Advocating Resource Management). The money that the Delta Foundation made from the sale of Providence Farm went toward an annual scholarship to fund the college education of an African American student from Holmes County. Gene Cox first started the scholarship back in the late 1940s but had trouble finding reliable financial support until the foundation sold Providence.

From 1936 until 1956, Delta Cooperative Farm and Providence Farm provided opportunities for hundreds of destitute rural southerners, particularly African Americans, to pursue avenues for racial and economic equality. A socialized economy, cooperative buying and selling power, and a credit union that offered fair loan rates provided Bolivar and Holmes county residents some economic stability. Health and medical services provided by nurses, doctors, and the Alpha Kappa Alpha Sorority summer health clinics markedly improved the lives of hundreds of rural Mississippians. Educational initiatives in academics, agriculture, and Christianity prepared students for life in a drastically changing South as more southerners moved off the land, attended college, and became involved in the political process.

But even without these measures of success, the simple fact that the cooperative farms existed at all made them extraordinary. Near the end of his life, farm benefactor Sherwood Eddy recalled how he, Sam Franklin, Gene Cox, and hundreds of other residents, volunteers, and staff "had thrilling adventures in fighting lawlessness, race prejudice, and poverty in one of the most backward states in the deep South." Even in Mississippi, a "state sweltering with the heat of injustice and oppression," dedicated farmers at Delta and Providence took part in a twenty-year struggle for labor and civil rights. Although in the end it was segregationist Mississippians who pressured the farms to close, they succeeded in chasing farm residents away only when red baiting and race baiting reached their zenith in the mid-1950s. The farmers' work stood as testimony, as a contemporary *New Republic* journalist noted, that Delta and Providence farms offered proof "of the essential bravery and vitality of human beings that ought always to be remembered."[16]

Aside from those families who were directly affected, however, few people remember Delta and Providence farms. No historical markers commemorate the ground that once supported the farms. For locals, Delta and Providence are puzzling afterthoughts in Bolivar and Holmes County histories, if they are remembered at all. The costs of not remembering Delta and Providence are hard to measure. A clear loss, however, is a narrative of southern history that includes men and women who engaged in what many of their detractors considered radical behavior. The farms existed in a time when the tenets of socialism seemed to be feasible alternatives to capitalism—when living collectively, organizing labor unions, and putting Christian Realism to work in the South were all practical and viable means of reimagining the lives of America's rural poor. Uneducated sharecroppers and idealistic, but practical, Christians and socialists populated the farms. Their daily lives resembled those of many poor farmers in the Jim Crow–era South: they struggled to maintain a farm, support their families, overcome illness, and find joy. In these regards, their actions were mainly practical. But their *idea* was radical—that these two farms would become common throughout the country and change the way Americans approached labor, religion, race relations, and the economy. Perhaps the highest cost of not remembering communities like Delta and Providence is that models for the beloved community are too few. In the present, what we may need is a little conviction and a lot of imagination to realize the beloved community.

The story of the cooperative farms is interwoven with many of the threads that made up twentieth-century leftist and progressive visions for American democracy and human rights. Radical agrarianism, Christian Socialism, cooperative communalism, African American quests for social and economic rights, and cross-racial class consciousness all played important roles in how the farms came into existence and why they persisted, in one form or another, for twenty years. The reasons the farms failed are just as layered and complicated as their beginnings. Like other human rights activists in the vanguard, residents of Delta and Providence weathered violence, economic intimidation, red baiting, race baiting, and clandestine investigations. The farms' internal problems also took measurable tolls. In the end, external attacks and internal cleavages vitiated volunteers', managers', and trustees' efforts to cultivate collective interracial space in the Jim Crow South. For instance, Delta and Providence were managed by whites, some of whom were unwilling, or unready, to check their paternalistic tendencies at the door. Hamstrung by their cultural assumptions, white farm managers and trustees limited interracial communion, even while promoting the farms as racially harmonious. For all the progress made by both farms, the beloved community founded on interracial cooperation had its limits. After all, a white female resident's reaction to a black teenager's flirtatious comment precipitated the endeavor's demise.

Important moments of modification altered the ways residents at Delta and Providence approached their brand of social justice. In the 1930s, a broad alliance opened up space in the agrarian South. The novelty of an egalitarian community wore off, however, as public places were desegregated by federal mandate. By the time the Citizens' Council and the Ku Klux Klan threatened to run Providence residents out of the county, the movement's new generation of leaders had turned their attention elsewhere. Additionally, as the Supreme Court struck down de jure segregation, a community based on social egalitarianism lost much of its significance as a visionary enterprise in the rural South.

By the late 1950s, civil rights activists were accomplishing social equality at a faster clip than the residents at Delta and Providence could hope to realize over their twenty-year existence.

In Providence, the human rights movement had a model for the beloved community—a shared space that promoted diverse approaches to fostering class and racial egalitarianism. The irony is that in the mid-1950s, when Martin Luther King Jr. began speaking publicly about creating the beloved community, Providence Farm officially closed as a cooperative and center for black self-help. Left-leaning activists had long fought for the creation of the beloved community, predating King's speeches in the 1950s. In 1936, the same year the interracial experiment began at Delta Cooperative Farm, the Fellowship of Reconciliation sponsored a series of conferences, workshops, and discussions on "Making the Beloved Community a Reality." Based in the Social Gospel and structured around cross-class and cross-racial cooperation, the beloved community was a vision for an America free of poverty, racism, and war. But by the 1950s, instead of focusing on building communities like Delta or Providence, that vision took the form of desegregating public spaces. Without the support of national organizations and media coverage, isolated rural communities like Providence fell victim to the armies of massive resistance. Sam Franklin, Sherwood Eddy, William Amberson, and others launched Delta Cooperative Farm in a moment of possibility during the New Deal, and ironically, twenty years later, Providence Farm closed during another moment of possibility for African Americans and their allies.[17]

Unlike a similar community that began as a Christian-oriented interracial cooperative and faced racist violence, Koinonia Farm in Georgia, Providence did not dig in and hold on. Koinonia seemed to be the exception and Providence the rule. The frequency of cooperative communalism seriously waned after World War II. In the 1950s, Providence seemed to be an antiquated holdover from the days of the New Deal. For a brief moment in the late 1960s and early 1970s, countercultural communes emerged as back-to-the-land alternatives to a materialist society seemingly tearing itself apart. But these communal movements were diffuse and short lived. Providence Farm signified a specific historical moment.[18]

Delta and Providence were spaces of opportunity for the rural South's poor in the often bleak Jim Crow era. The farms were thresholds between the old and the unexplored—the possible, where boundaries dissolved and historical actors departed into new territory. This liminal space was psychological and physical. In the psychological sense, the farms allowed whites and blacks the liberty to imagine and, to an important extent, realize changes in southern society—changes in social and economic structures that facilitated fuller expressions of their humanity. No longer sharecroppers, cooperators embarked into new, ambiguous territory.[19]

The space at Delta and Providence represented an endless threshold. Cooperators were always on the verge of ushering in new racial and economic orders to rural southern society. Put another way, the ex-sharecroppers seemed to be in a state of perpetual transition. But liminality cannot persist indefinitely. The little upheavals and seemingly minor, day-to-day events that took place at Delta and Providence, and the backlash from outsiders, were the rumblings of the clashes between the plantation mentality of the Old South and the as yet uncharted territory of the modern South. In the end, Providence's failure was a tragic contingency of history, one that Reinhold Niebuhr's Christian Realism might have predicted. The residents, staff, and volunteers were too radical and not radical enough—the farms were ahead of their time and throwbacks to a bygone age.[20]

By the 1950s, Providence was a community in decline. Lacking a clear identity and possessing vague goals, it was no longer the radical endeavor it had been in the 1930s and 1940s. When the soldiers of massive resistance attacked Providence in 1955, the farm did not have a strong network to turn to for support. Still, the farm's initiatives—including the clinic, educational courses, and the credit union—offered Holmes Countians a chance to raise their positions in a rural South that still operated on strict racial and class hierarchies. Of all the reflections on Providence after 1956, perhaps former resident Esther Lou Moody—who had first moved with her parents to Delta Cooperative in 1936—phrased it best. "The kids and I go back over the old days quite often," Moody confided to Lindsey Cox in 1966, "and try to put all the nice things in front of all the heartaches."[21]

NOTES

Introduction

1. "Beloved community" was first coined by philosopher Josiah Royce, but made popular in the twentieth century by Martin Luther King Jr. In King's conception—which has proved most influential—the beloved community was built by those engaged in reconciliation of every type, a community where equality, justice, and peace prevailed.

2. The terms "cooperative communalism" and "communitarian cooperative farms" are used throughout this book as customized terminology to help the reader understand the exact nature of the communities. In addition to being buyers' and producers' cooperatives, Delta and Providence were also close-knit, intentional communities where the residents' fates were bound together. They were members of the cooperatives but also residents of a communitarian endeavor who hoped to dismantle inequality in the Jim Crow South.

3. For parsing out the real Delta from the imagined Delta, see James C. Cobb, *The Most Southern Place on Earth: The Mississippi Delta and the Roots of Regional Identity* (New York: Oxford University Press, 1992); Joseph Crespino, "Mississippi as Metaphor: Civil Rights, the South, and the Nation in the Historical Imagination," in *The Myth of Southern Exceptionalism*, ed. Matthew D. Lassiter and Joseph Crespino (New York: Oxford University Press, 2010), 99–120.

4. For more on the development of sharecropping, see Gavin Wright, *Old South, New South: Revolutions in the Southern Economy since the Civil War* (Baton Rouge: Louisiana State Press, 1996); Pete Daniel, *Breaking the Land: The Transformation of Cotton, Tobacco, and Rice Cultures since 1880* (Urbana: University of Illinois Press, 1985); Pete Daniel, *In the Shadow of Slavery: Peonage in the South, 1901–1969* (Urbana: University of Illinois Press, 1990); Gilbert Fite, *Cotton Fields No More: Southern Agriculture 1865–1980* (Lexington: University Press of Kentucky, 1984). For a succinct and straightforward analysis of the credit system under sharecropping, see Chris Myers Asch, *The Senator and the Sharecropper: The Freedom Struggles of James O. Eastland and Fannie Lou Hamer* (Chapel Hill: University of North Carolina Press, 2008), 68–69.

5. Sara M. Evans and Harry C. Boyte, *Free Spaces: The Sources of Democratic Change in America* (New York: Harper & Row, 1986), 182–202.

6. Victor Witter Turner, *Dramas, Fields, and Metaphors: Symbolic Action in Human Society* (Ithaca, N.Y.: Cornel University Press, 1974), 232.

7. Ibid.

8. Mark Schultz, *The Rural Face of White Supremacy: Beyond Jim Crow* (Urbana: University of Illinois Press, 2005), 7.

9. James W. Silver, *Mississippi: The Closed Society* (New York: Houghton, Brace & World, 1966).

10. John Curl, *For All the People: Uncovering the Hidden History of Cooperation, Coop-*

erative Movements, and Communalism in America (Oakland: PM Press, 2011), 279. The one notable exception that linked many of the tenets that Delta Cooperative Farm would eventually employ was Nashoba in rural Tennessee. Founded by socialist and suffragist Frances Wright in 1825, the community consisted of whites and liberated slaves.

11. For more on interracial political alliances and interracial unionism, see Jane Dailey, *Before Jim Crow: The Politics of Race in Postemancipation Virginia* (Chapel Hill: University of North Carolina Press, 2000); David S. Cecelski and Timothy B. Tyson, eds., *Democracy Betrayed: The Wilmington Race Riot of 1898 and Its Legacy* (Chapel Hill: University of North Carolina, 1998); Daniel Letwin, *The Challenge of Interracial Unionism: Alabama Coal Miners, 1878–1921* (Chapel Hill: University of North Carolina Press, 1998).

12. As New Deal historian Patricia Sullivan observed, "the urgency of the depression combined with the innovative and confident milieu of New Deal Washington" created opportunities for experimentation with social structures. New Dealers saw a twofold opportunity to gain new constituents and make good on the "effort to institutionalize the democratic aspirations of Roosevelt's recovery program by appealing to the expectations of groups long on the margins of southern politics." New Deal progressives encouraged the historically disfranchised to advocate for themselves. For thousands of southern sharecroppers—the very definition of marginalized southerners—that meant joining an interracial labor union and, for scores of destitute families, relocating to a venture in cooperative communalism. Sullivan, *Days of Hope: Race and Democracy in the New Deal Era* (Chapel Hill: University of North Carolina Press, 1996), 42–43; Anthony J. Badger, *New Deal/New South: An Anthony J. Badger Reader* (Fayetteville: University of Arkansas Press, 2007).

13. Edward L. Ayers, *The Promise of a New South: Life after Reconstruction* (New York: Oxford University Press, 1992), 132; Leon Litwack, *Trouble in Mind: Black Southerners in the Age of Jim Crow* (New York: Knopf, 1998); Mark Schultz, *The Rural Face of White Supremacy: Beyond Jim Crow* (Urbana: University of Illinois Press, 2005): Stephen A. Berrey, *The Jim Crow Routine: Everyday Performances of Race, Civil Rights, and Segregation in Mississippi* (Chapel Hill: University of North Carolina Press, 2015), 4. As Berrey has pointed out, "Jim Crow had to be re-created every day." For white supremacists and blacks living under segregation, that involved a host of often complicated performances. Yet the endeavors in Bolivar and Holmes counties contested the ways southerners performed Jim Crow. The aim of the founders of Delta and Providence farms was to encourage interracial cooperation that moved beyond casual interaction and pushed for an egalitarian and shared community in the fields, worship services, and other day-to-day activities, emancipating poor southerners from the shackles of white supremacy.

14. Tracy Elaine K'Meyer, *Interracialism and Christian Community in the Postwar South: The Story of Koinonia Farm* (Charlottesville: University of Virginia Press, 1997), 18–19; Mark Ellis, *Race Harmony and Black Progress: Jack Woofter and the Interracial Cooperation Movement* (Bloomington: Indiana University Press, 2013).

15. Alison Collis Greene, *No Depression in Heaven: The Great Depression, the New Deal, and the Transformation of Religion in the Delta* (New York: Oxford University Press, 2016), 161–193.

16. For the differences among the Social Gospel, Christian Realism, neo-orthodoxy, and Liberation Theology, see Gary Dorrien, *Social Ethics in the Making: Interpreting an American Tradition* (West Sussex: Wiley-Blackwell, 2009).

17. Francoise N. Hamlin, "Collision and Collusion: Local Activism, Local Agency, and Flexible Alliances," in *The Civil Rights Movement in Mississippi*, ed. Ted Ownby (Jackson: University Press of Mississippi, 2013), 35; Francoise N. Hamlin, *Crossroads at Clarksdale: The Black Freedom Struggle in the Mississippi Delta after World War II* (Chapel Hill: University of North Carolina Press, 2012), 2.

18. W. Fitzhugh Brundage, *The Southern Past: A Clash of Race and Memory* (Cambridge, Mass.: Belknap, 2005), 6–8.

19. Earl Lewis, *In Their Own Interests: Race, Class, and Power in Twentieth-Century Norfolk, Virginia* (Berkeley: University of California Press, 1991), 70–88.

20. George B. Ellenberg, *Mule South to Tractor South: Mules, Machines, and the Transformation of the Cotton South* (Tuscaloosa: University of Alabama Press, 2007), 105; Wright, *Old South, New South*, 198–238.

21. Wright, *Old South, New South*, 198–238.

22. For a straightforward discussion of the core–periphery model and its theoretical developments, see Immanuel Wallerstein, *World-Systems Analysis: An Introduction* (Durham, N.C.: Duke University Press, 2004).

23. For works on southern dreamers who fought to widen the scope of democratic inclusion, see Pippa Holloway, ed., *Other Souths: Diversity and Difference in the U.S. South, Reconstruction to the Present* (Athens: University of Georgia Press, 2008); Glenda Elizabeth Gilmore, *Defying Dixie: The Radical Roots of Civil Rights, 1919–1950* (New York: Norton, 2008); Jack Temple Kirby, *The Countercultural South* (Athens: University of Georgia Press, 1995); John Egerton, *Speak Now against the Day: The Generation before the Civil Rights Movement in the South* (Chapel Hill: University of North Carolina Press, 1994); David L. Chappell, *Inside Agitators: White Southerners in the Civil Rights Movement* (Baltimore: Johns Hopkins University Press, 1994); Jacquelyn Dowd Hall, *Revolt against Chivalry: Jessie Daniel Ames and the Women's Campaign against Lynching*, rev. ed. (New York: Columbia University Press, 1993); Robert F. Martin, *Howard Kester and the Struggle for Social Justice in the South, 1904–1977* (Charlottesville: University Press of Virginia, 1991); Robin D. G. Kelley, *Hammer and Hoe: Alabama Communists during the Great Depression* (Chapel Hill: University of North Carolina Press, 1990); Letwin, *Challenge of Interracial Unionism*; Michael K. Honey, *Southern Labor and Black Civil Rights: Organizing Memphis Workers* (Urbana: University of Illinois Press, 1993); Robert Rogers Korstad, *Civil Rights Unionism: Tobacco Workers and the Struggle for Democracy in the Mid-Twentieth-Century South* (Chapel Hill: University of North Carolina Press, 2003); Laurie Boush Green, *Battling the Plantation Mentality: Memphis and the Black Freedom Struggle* (Chapel Hill: University of North Carolina Press, 2007). In *Defying Dixie* Gilmore makes the case for how radical southerners and their northern allies laid the groundwork for the civil rights movement in the half century before the 1950s. Although many of the individuals involved with Delta and Providence tackled economic and racial disparity in different ways than, for example, Frank Porter Graham or Pauli Murray, their mere presence in the South indicates that the radical roots of the civil rights movement ran deep into the southern countryside. Gilmore, *Defying Dixie*, 247–296.

Chapter 1. The Problems of Collective Man

1. Norman Thomas, *The Plight of the Share-Cropper* (New York: League for Industrial Democracy, 1934), 3–14.

2. Ibid., 15–18.

3. Ibid., 20.

4. William R. Amberson, "The New Deal for Share-Croppers," *Nation*, February 1935, 185–187; Gavin Wright, *Old South, New South: Revolutions in the Southern Economy since the Civil War* (Baton Rouge: Louisiana State Press, 1996), 51–80, 97; Thomas, *Plight of the Share-Cropper*, 6; Charles S. Johnson, *Statistical Atlas of Southern Counties: Listing and Analysis of Socio-Economic Indices of 1104 Southern Counties* (Chapel Hill: University of North Carolina Press, 1941), 60; T. J. Woofter Jr. and Ellen Winston, *Seven Lean Years* (Chapel Hill: University of North Carolina Press, 1939), 11; William Amberson to Norman Thomas, March 4, 1934, William Ruthrauff Amberson Papers #3862, Southern Historical Collection, Louis Round Wilson Special Collections Library, University of North Carolina at Chapel Hill (hereafter SHC).

5. For African American laboring choices after emancipation, see Leon F. Litwack, *Trouble in Mind: Black Southerners in the Age of Jim Crow* (New York: Knopf, 1998).

6. William Amberson to Gertrude Orendorff, undated (sometime in 1934), William Ruthrauff Amberson Papers #3862, SHC.

7. Wright, *Old South, New South*, 98.

8. E. B. "Britt" McKinney to unknown, undated, Folder 1, Delta and Providence Cooperative Farms Papers #3474, SHC. McKinney's letter is undated. However, because McKinney mentions crops grown in 1935, it can safely be surmised that the letter was written around late 1935 or early 1936.

9. Ibid.

10. Ibid.

11. For the New Deal's influence on expanded notions of democracy and citizenship, see Patricia Sullivan, *Days of Hope: Race and Democracy in the New Deal Era* (Chapel Hill: University of North Carolina Press, 1996).

12. "Biographical Sketch," William R. Amberson Papers, Mississippi Valley Collection, McWherter Library, University of Memphis (hereafter, MVC); George Lichtheim, *A Short History of Socialism* (New York: Praeger, 1970), 239.

13. Jonathan Daniels, *A Southerner Discovers the South* (New York: Macmillan, 1938), 84; "Report on an Investigation of Short-Weighting and Similar Dishonest Practices by Merchants in the City of Memphis," William Ruthrauff Amberson Papers #3862, SHC; William Amberson to Norman Thomas, February 22, 1934, William Ruthrauff Amberson Papers #3862, SHC.

14. Donald H. Grubbs, *Cry from the Cotton: The Southern Tenant Farmers' Union and the New Deal* (Chapel Hill: University of North Carolina Press, 1971), 27–29; H. L. Mitchell, *Mean Things Happening in This Land: The Life and Times of H. L. Mitchell Co-founder of the Southern Tenant Farmers' Union* (Montclair: Allanheld, Osmun, 1979), 45–49; Jim Bissett, *Agrarian Socialism in America: Marx, Jefferson, and Jesus in the Oklahoma Countryside, 1904–1920* (Norman: University of Oklahoma Press, 1999); James D. Ross Jr., "'I Ain't Got No Name in This World': The Rise and Fall of the Southern Tenant Farmers' Union in Arkansas" (PhD diss., Auburn University, 2004), 43–45; H. L. Mitchell to William Amberson, November 2, 1934, William Amberson Papers, MVC.

15. For racial violence in early twentieth-century Arkansas, see Nan Elizabeth Woodruff, *American Congo: The African American Freedom Struggle in the Delta* (Cambridge, Mass.: Harvard University Press, 2003); Grif Stockley, *Ruled by Race: Black/White Relations in Arkansas from Slavery to the Present* (Fayetteville: University of Arkansas Press, 2009).

16. Grubbs, *Cry from the Cotton*, viii.

17. Sullivan, *Days of Hope*, 57; F. Twist to W. H. Kible, January 16, 1934, William Ruthrauff Amberson Papers #3862, SHC; Amberson to Norman Thomas, February 22, 1934, William Ruthrauff Amberson Papers #3862, SHC; Norman Thomas to William R. Amberson, February 26, 1934, William Ruthrauff Amberson Papers #3862, SHC.

18. Amberson, "New Deal for Share-Croppers," 187.

19. William Amberson to Sheriff Dubard, March 5, 1934, William Ruthrauff Amberson Papers #3862, SHC; William Amberson to Norman Thomas, April 8, 1934, William Ruthrauff Amberson Papers #3862, SHC.

20. Buck Jones to William Amberson, April 10, 1934, William Ruthrauff Amberson Papers #3862, SHC; Buck Jones to William Amberson, April 12, 1934, William Ruthrauff Amberson Papers #3862, SHC.

21. Jonathan Mitchell, "Cabins in the Cotton," *New Republic*, September 22, 1937, 175; Mitchell, *Mean Things*, 45–46.

22. Thomas, *Plight of the Share-Cropper*, 3, 9, 27.

23. Grubbs, *Cry from the Cotton*, 62–87.

24. Prentice Thomas to Roy Stryker, June 21, 1937, Roy Stryker Papers at the University of Louisville, Photographic Archives, Archives and Special Collections. For socialism development in the early twentieth-century South, see Philip S. Foner, *American Socialism and Black Americans: From the Age of Jackson to World War II* (Westport, Conn.: Greenwood, 1977); James R. Green, *Grass-Roots Socialism: Radical Movements in the Southwest, 1895–1943* (Baton Rouge: Louisiana State University Press, 1978).

25. John Curl, *For All the People: Uncovering the Hidden History of Cooperation, Cooperative Movements, and Communalism in America* (Oakland: PM Press, 2011), 284–295, 306; W. Fitzhugh Brundage, *A Socialist Utopia in the New South: The Ruskin Colonies in Tennessee and Georgia, 1894–1901* (Urbana: University of Illinois Press, 1996); 145–147, 162–163.

26. Paul K. Conkin, *Two Paths to Utopia: The Hutterites and the Llano Colony* (Lincoln: University of Nebraska Press, 1964), 122–125.

27. Foner, *American Socialism and Black Americans*, 128–138, 220–237. Only in the past thirty years have historians reflected on the long history of socialism in the United States. Some early observers of socialist thought confined the important developments to the European continent while ignoring any contributions from North America. When scholarship on American socialism finally blossomed, the vast majority of historians focused on the last decades of the nineteenth century and first three decades of the twentieth century as the alpha and omega of socialism in America. Similarly, many historians were often perplexed about how to address the role of African Americans within this story. Some ignored them altogether while others treated African Americans as they assumed socialists treated them: as no different from white workers. Philip S. Foner's *American Socialism and Black Americans* focused on the long history of socialism in America while casting the black workers as central to the development of socialist thought and exploring the myriad approaches socialist leaders undertook when addressing "the Negro question." Debates in Oklahoma over recruitment of black workers demonstrated just how perplexing the issue of racial equality was to socialists. Some state socialist organizers, mainly relocated northerners, demanded that the Socialist Party eschew Jim Crow customs, open membership to all workers regardless of race, and directly challenge social inequality. Native-born, white Oklahoma socialists disagreed and charged that socialism

did not automatically translate into social equality for whites and blacks. Despite infighting, the Socialist Party in Oklahoma campaigned to give the franchise to black voters in the 1910s. The result was ultimately a failure, but this support for black voting rights signaled that socialists could back workers in the South regardless of skin color.

28. Foner, *American Socialism and Black Americans*, 238–253, quoted in Mitchell, *Mean Things*, 48–49. For a succinct and revisionary discussion on the STFU's interracialism, see Jason Manthorne, "The View from the Cotton: Reconsidering the Southern Tenant Farmers' Union," *Agricultural History* 84 (Winter 2010): 20–45.

29. H. L. Mitchell to William Amberson, September 13, 1934, William Ruthrauff Amberson Papers #3862, SHC; H. L. Mitchell to William Amberson, November 27, 1934, William Ruthrauff Amberson Papers #3862, SHC.

30. William Amberson to Memphis *Commercial Appeal*, January 31, 1935, William Ruthrauff Amberson Papers #3862, SHC.

31. William A. Link, *The Paradox of Southern Progressivism, 1880–1930* (Chapel Hill: University of North Carolina Press, 1992), 248–267; Jacquelyn Dowd Hall, *Revolt against Chivalry: Jessie Daniel Ames and the Women's Campaign against Lynching*, rev. ed. (New York: Columbia University Press, 1993); Tracy Elaine K'Meyer, *Interracialism and Christian Community in the Postwar South: The Story of Koinonia Farm* (Charlottesville: University of Virginia Press, 1997), 18–19; Daniel Letwin, *The Challenge of Interracial Unionism: Alabama Coal Miners, 1878–1921* (Chapel Hill: University of North Carolina Press, 1998), 1–7.

32. Woodruff, *American Congo*, 91.

33. Timothy Miller, *The Quest for Utopia in Twentieth Century America*, vol. 1: *1900–1960* (New York: Syracuse University Press, 1998), 128–129; quoted in David E. Shi, *The Simple Life: Plain Living and High Thinking in American Culture* (New York: Oxford University Press, 1985), 227–228.

34. Paul Keith Conkin, *Tomorrow a New World: The New Deal Community Program* (Ithaca, N.Y.: Cornell University Press, 1959), 12; Curl, *For All the People*, 315–321.

35. Mitchell, *Mean Things*, 58.

36. Sam H. Franklin Jr., "Early Years of the Delta Cooperative Farm and the Providence Cooperative Farm" (unpublished), 6; Sam Franklin to A. E. Cox, October 30, 1971, A. Eugene Cox Collection, Special Collections Department, Mitchell Memorial Library, Mississippi State University (hereafter AEC).

37. Franklin, "Early Years," 7–9.

38. Brundage, *Socialist Utopia in the New South*, 3, 15; Curl, *For All the People* (Oakland: PM Press, 2011), v–xvi. For more on Poe and communitarian cooperatives, see Lawrence Goodwyn, *The Democratic Promise: The Populist Moment in America* (New York: Oxford University Press, 1976); Elizabeth Sanders, *Roots of Reform: Farmers, Workers, and the American State, 1877–1917* (Chicago: University of Chicago Press, 1999); Charles Postel, *The Populist Vision* (Oxford: Oxford University Press, 2007); Daniel T. Rodgers, *Atlantic Crossings: Social Politics in a Progressive Age* (Cambridge, Mass.: Belknap, 1998), 321–326.

39. Rodgers, *Atlantic Crossings*, 318–343, 452–472. Like Franklin would do later, Poe and Wisconsin politician Charles McCarthy traveled extensively in Europe and both were permanently influenced by the effects of agricultural cooperatives on the European countryside. Poe noticed the orderly state of the English landscape, marked by the lack of dilapidated tenant and sharecropper shacks found blotting the land in the American

South. McCarthy believed the agricultural cooperative practices of Irishman Horace Plunkett to be feasible in America. Plunkett, who started the Irish Agricultural Organisation Society in the 1890s, was inspired in turn by the cooperative rural reform efforts in Denmark. After the first workers' cooperatives were established in France and England by utopian socialists in the 1820s and 1830s, rural and urban cooperatives flourished across the European continent. Plunkett's globetrotting efforts to raise support for his agricultural reforms gained him many admirers, among them Poe, McCarthy, head of the U.S. Forest Service Gifford Pinchot, and future New Dealer Henry A. Wallace.

40. William Amberson to Lucille B. Milner, November 12, 1934, William Amberson Papers, MVC; Johnston Birchall, *Co-op: The People's Business* (Manchester: Manchester University Press, 1994), 34–64.

41. H. L. Mitchell to William Amberson, August 8, 1934, Folder 3, William Ruthrauff Amberson Papers #3862, SHC.

42. Franklin, "Early Years," 6; Sherwood Eddy, *Eighty Adventurous Years: An Autobiography* (New York: Harper, 1955), 207–208.

43. Thomas Alva Stubbins to Sam Franklin, March 16, 1936, Folder 2, Delta and Providence Cooperative Farms Papers #3474, SHC. For more on Kagawa's influence on Eddy and Franklin, see George B. Bikle Jr., *The New Jerusalem: Aspects of Utopianism in the Thought of Kagawa Toyohiko* (Tucson: University of Arizona Press, 1976); Kerry Smith, *A Time of Crisis: Japan, the Great Depression, and Rural Revitalization* (Cambridge, Mass.: Harvard University Press, 2001); Rick L. Nutt, *The Whole Gospel for the Whole World: Sherwood Eddy and the American Protestant Mission* (Macon, Ga.: Mercer University Press, 1997).

44. Franklin, "Early Years," 8–9; Sherwood Eddy, *A Pilgrimage of Ideas; or, The Reeducation of Sherwood Eddy* (New York: Farrar & Rinehart, 1934), 255–259.

45. Nutt, *Whole Gospel*, 166, 350.

46. For the American development of Social Christianity, see Paul T. Phillips, *A Kingdom on Earth: Anglo-American Social Christianity, 1880–1940* (University Park: Pennsylvania State University Press, 1996), xiv. Phillips stressed the transatlantic origins of Social Christianity, identifying British native John Frederick Denison Maurice as a key founder of the theology who, through his followers, would have a lasting impact on its development in America. See also James Dombrowski, *The Early Days of Christian Socialism in America* (New York: Octagon Books, 1966). An important development of nineteenth-century Social Christianity was the focus on the salvation of the group—the social organism—while shifting emphasis away from interpretations of an individual's relationship with the Holy. This ecumenical shift paved the way for Christian activists to devote their time to addressing the needs of whole populations. Theologians pointed to the "inherently" liberal, egalitarian teachings of Jesus Christ and drew much of their philosophies and practices from the growing social science movement. Social Christians and social scientists alike shunned a millennialist approach to life, advocating instead for a perfection of society—the Kingdom of Heaven on Earth. Social Christianity, as a philosophy and as a practice, put a great deal of emphasis on good works "done on earth as it is in Heaven." Dombrowski, *Early Days*, 16. See also Liston Pope, *Millhands and Preachers* (New Haven, Conn.: Yale University Press, 1942).

47. Phillips, *Kingdom on Earth*, 26.

48. David P. Cline, "Revolution and Reconciliation: The Student Interracial Ministry, Liberal Protestantism, and the Civil Rights Movement, 1960–1970" (PhD diss., University

of North Carolina at Chapel Hill, 2010), 34; Gary Dorrien, *Social Ethics in the Making: Interpreting an American Tradition* (West Sussex: Wiley-Blackwell, 2009), 235; David L. Chappell, "Niebuhrisms and Myrdaleries: The Intellectual Roots of the Civil Rights Movement Reconsidered," in *The Role of Ideas in the Civil Rights South*, ed. Ted Ownby (Jackson: University Press of Mississippi, 2002), 3–18.

49. Phillips, *Kingdom on Earth*, 254; Dorrien, *Social Ethics in the Making*, 237; Chappell, "Niebuhrisms and Myrdaleries," 3–18.

50. Dorrien, *Social Ethics in the Making*, 237; Fred C. Smith, *Trouble in Goshen: Plain Folk, Roosevelt, Jesus, and Marx in the Great Depression South* (Jackson: University Press of Mississippi, 2014), 115–117.

51. Sherwood Eddy, *Religion and Social Justice* (New York: George H. Doran Company, 1927), 5; Alfred Noyes, Zona Gale, Leo Tolstoi, Bruce A. Curry, Harry Emerson Fosdick, Ernest Fremont Tittle, Reinhold Niebuhr, Charles W. Gilkey, Halford E. Luccock, George A. Coe, and Sherwood Eddy, *Dynamic Religion: A Personal Experience* (New York: Eddy and Page, 1930), 41.

52. Ralph E. Luker, *The Social Gospel in Black and White: American Racial Reform, 1885–1912* (Chapel Hill: University of North Carolina Press, 1991); Paul Harvey, *Freedom's Coming: Religious Culture and the Shaping of the South from the Civil War through the Civil Rights Era* (Chapel Hill: University of North Carolina Press, 2005), 97–99, 101–105; Randy J. Sparks, *Religion in Mississippi* (Jackson: University Press of Mississippi for the Mississippi Historical Society, 2001); Noyes et al., *Dynamic Religion*, 43, quoted in Donald M. Royer, "A Comparative Study of Three Experiments in Rural 'Community' Reconstruction in the Southeast" (MA thesis, University of North Carolina at Chapel Hill, 1943), 48.

53. Nutt, *Whole Gospel*, 275; Franklin, "Early Years," 9.

54. Sherwood Eddy to unaddressed, April 2, 1936, Folder 3, Delta and Providence Cooperative Farms Papers #3474, SHC;

55. James D. Ross Jr., "'I Ain't Got No Home in This World': The Rise and Fall of the Southern Tenant Farmers' Union in Arkansas" (PhD diss., Auburn University, 2004), 22–23; Woodruff, *American Congo*, 75–109; Stockley, *Ruled by Race*, 157–179; Mary G. Rolinson, *Grassroots Garveyism: The Universal Negro Improvement Association in the Rural South, 1920–1927* (Chapel Hill: University of North Carolina Press, 2007), 186–187.

56. Sherwood Eddy, *A Door of Opportunity; or, An American Adventure in Cooperation with Sharecroppers* (New York: Eddy and Page, 1937), 31, Rare Book Collection, Louis Round Wilson Special Collections Library, University of North Carolina at Chapel Hill; Woodruff, *American Congo*, 74–100; Mitchell, *Mean Things*, 131; Franklin, "Early Years," 10.

57. Sherwood Eddy, "Some Basic Principles of the Delta Cooperative Farm," Delta Cooperative Farm Records, MVC; Sherwood Eddy to unaddressed, April 2, 1936, Folder 3, Delta and Providence Cooperative Farms Papers #3474, SHC.

58. William Amberson to Gene Cox, January 17, 1973, AEC.

59. Emily S. Bingham and Thomas A. Underwood, eds., *The Southern Agrarians and the New Deal: Essays after "I'll Take My Stand"* (Charlottesville: University Press of Virginia, 2001), 167n.

60. Mitchell, *Mean Things*, 127; Daniels, *Southerner Discovers the South* , 87.

61. William R. Amberson, "Forty Acres and a Mule," *Nation*, March 6, 1937, 264–266.

62. Mitchell, *Mean Things*, 127; Daniels, *Southerner Discovers the South* , 87; Jess

Gilbert and Steve Brown, "Alternative Land Reform Proposals in the 1930s: The Nashville Agrarians and the Southern Tenant Farmers' Union," *Agricultural History* 55 (October 1981): 361–363; Amberson, "Forty Acres and a Mule"; Conkin, *Tomorrow a New World*, 210.

Chapter 2. From the Frying Pan into the Fire

1. Sam H. Franklin Jr., "Early Years of the Delta Cooperative Farm and the Providence Cooperative Farm" (unpublished), 14; Delta & Providence—Former Residents, House Box #1, A. Eugene Cox Collection, Special Collections Department, Mitchell Memorial Library, Mississippi State University (hereafter AEC).

2. Hortense Powdermaker, *After Freedom: A Cultural Study in the Deep South* (New York: Atheneum, 1969), 3.

3. Delta Cooperative Farm Records, Mississippi Valley Collection, McWherter Library, University of Memphis; Lindsey Hail to Edna Voss, December 29, 1936, Folder 20, Delta and Providence Cooperative Farms Papers #3474, Southern Historical Collection, Louis Round Wilson Special Collections Library, University of North Carolina at Chapel Hill (hereafter SHC).

4. William R. Amberson to Thad Snow, August 12, 1937, AEC; William Amberson to Sam Franklin, quoted in Franklin, "Early Years," 11–12.

5. Sam Franklin to William Amberson, February 13, 1936, William Ruthrauff Amberson Papers #3862, SHC; Sam Franklin to Sherwood Eddy, March 27–28, 1936, Folder 2, Delta and Providence Cooperative Farms Papers #3474, SHC; Miscellaneous, Box VII, AEC.

6. Jonathan Daniels, *Southerner Discovers the South* (New York: Macmillan, 1938), 151; *Sewanee Review*, October–December 1934, 389.

7. Sherwood Eddy to Sam Franklin, April 14, 1936, Folder 3, Delta and Providence Cooperative Farms Papers #3474, SHC.

8. William R. Amberson to Alice Barrows, April 17, 1936, AEC; Delta & Providence—Former Residents, House Box #1, AEC; Sam Franklin to William Alexander Percy, December 17, 1936, Folder 20, Delta and Providence Cooperative Farms Papers #3474, SHC.

9. Sam Franklin to H. L. Mitchell, May 15, 1936, Folder 5, Delta and Providence Cooperative Farms Papers #3474, SHC; William Amberson to Helen F. Dudley, April 14, 1936, Folder 3, Delta and Providence Cooperative Farms Papers #3474, SHC; Franklin, "Early Years," 11; H. L. Mitchell, *Mean Things Happening in This Land: The Life and Times of H. L. Mitchell Co-founder of the Southern Tenant Farmers' Union* (Montclair: Allanheld, Osmun, 1979), 45; Delta & Providence—Former Residents, House Box #1, AEC; Sidney Baldwin, *Poverty and Politics: The Rise and Decline of the Farm Security Administration* (Chapel Hill: University of North Carolina Press, 1968), 85–125.

10. Franklin, "Early Years," 15; Untitled, Delta Cooperative Farm Papers, Mississippi Valley Collection, McWherter Library, University of Memphis (hereafter, MVC).

11. Delta & Providence—Former Residents, House Box #1, AEC.

12. William R. Amberson to Laurent Frantz, March 19, 1936, Box VII, AEC; Franklin, "Early Years," 14–16; "Southern Tenant Farmers' Union Calendar of Events, June–October 1936, William Amberson Papers, MVC.

13. "Southern Tenant Farmers' Union Calendar of Events," June–October 1936, William Amberson Papers, MVC; Michael K. Honey, *Sharecropper's Troubadour: John L.*

Handcox, the Southern Tenant Farmers' Union, and the African American Song Tradition (New York: Palgrave Macmillan, 2013), 72–73.

14. Delta & Providence—Former Residents, House Box #1, AEC.

15. Mitchell, *Mean Things*, 130–131, 133; Donald H. Grubbs, *Cry from the Cotton: The Southern Tenant Farmers' Union and the New Deal* (Chapel Hill: University of North Carolina Press, 1971), 88–90; Nan Elizabeth Woodruff, *American Congo: The African American Freedom Struggle in the Delta* (Cambridge, Mass.: Harvard University Press, 2003); Mark Fannin, *Labor's Promised Land: Radical Visions of Gender, Race, and Religion in the South* (Knoxville: University of Tennessee Press, 2003), 113; Franklin, "Early Years," 14; "Mississippi Delta Colonists Seeking Independence in New Type Community," undated newspaper clipping, Delta Cooperative Farm, Vertical File, Mississippi Department of Archives and History (hereafter MDAH); Delta Cooperative Farm—History, House Box #1, AEC.

16. "Mississippi Delta Colonists Seeking Independence in New Type Community," undated newspaper clipping, Delta Cooperative Farm, Vertical File, MDAH.

17. Sherwood Eddy to Homer Cummings, May 21, 1936, Southern Tenant Farmers' Union Papers, microfilm, Davis Library, University of North Carolina at Chapel Hill (hereafter STFU); Grubbs, *Cry from the Cotton*, 90–91, 117–118; Grif Stockley, *Ruled by Race: Black/White Relations in Arkansas from Slavery to the Present* (Fayetteville: University of Arkansas Press, 2009), 222–223; "Arkansas Officer Accused as Slaver," *New York Times*, September 25, 1936, 1; "Arkansas Officer Convicted by Jury on Slavery Charge," *New York Times*, November 26, 1936, 1.

18. "True Arkansas Hospitality," *Time*, June 29, 1936, 19.

19. Grubbs, *Cry from the Cotton*, 109–114; Mitchell, *Mean Things*, 86–90.

20. "The Story of Delta Cooperative Farm in Pictures" Photographs Box, AEC; Honey, *Sharecropper's Troubadour*, 125.

21. Harvey Barton to H. L. Mitchell, April 29, 1936, Folder 3, Delta and Providence Cooperative Farms Papers #3474, SHC; Mrs. Jim Thunderberg to Sherwood Eddy, May 12, 1936, Folder 4, Delta and Providence Cooperative Farms Papers #3474, SHC; Dorothea Lange, "Plight of Resettlement Administration Rehabilitation clients on Dixie Plantation, Hillhouse, Mississippi," AEC; Sherwood Eddy to H. L. Mitchell, May 14, 1937, STFU.

22. Rose Terlin to Sam Franklin, May 15, 1936, Folder 5, Delta and Providence Cooperative Farms Papers #3474, SHC; Sam Franklin to Rose Terlin, May 15, 1936, Folder 5, Delta and Providence Cooperative Farms Papers #3474, SHC; *Co-Op Call*, vol. 3, no. 8, Delta & Providence—Program, House Box #1, AEC. This would not be the last time that conscientious students from around the country would come to Mississippi to take part in social movements. In 1964, over one thousand students participated in the Mississippi Summer Project, better known as Freedom Summer. Building on the inroads that local African American residents had already made, students aided activists in voting, health, and education initiatives. Two of the most active counties in the Mississippi Summer Project were Bolivar, the previous home of Delta Cooperative, and Holmes, the previous home of Providence Farm. For more on Freedom Summer and the Freedom Schools in Bolivar and Holmes counties, see Kenneth T. Andrews, *Freedom Is a Constant Struggle: The Mississippi Civil Rights Movement and Its Legacy* (Chicago: University of Chicago Press, 2004); Sue Sojourner with Cheryl Reitan, *Thunder of Freedom: Black Leadership and the Transformation of 1960s Mississippi* (Lexington: University Press of Kentucky,

2013); and Jon N. Hale, *The Freedom Schools: Student Activists in the Mississippi Civil Rights Movement* (New York: Columbia University Press, 2016).

23. Sam Franklin to Warren H. Irwin, April 10, 1937, Folder 31, Delta and Providence Cooperative Farms Papers #3474, SHC; *Co-Op Call*, vol. 3, no. 8, Delta & Providence—Program, House Box #1, AEC.

24. Rose Terlin to Sam Franklin, May 15, 1936, Folder 5, Delta and Providence Cooperative Farms Papers #3474, SHC; Sam Franklin to Rose Terlin, May 15, 1936, Folder 5, Delta and Providence Cooperative Farms Papers #3474, SHC; Sam Franklin to Rose Terlin, April 30, 1936, History—Farms (Delta & Prov.), House Box #1, AEC.

25. Rose Terlin to Dorothy O. Williams at Spellman, May 6, 1936, Folder 5, Delta and Providence Cooperative Farms Papers #3474, SHC; Sam Franklin to Rose Terlin, May 15, 1936, Folder 5, Delta and Providence Cooperative Farms Papers #3474, SHC; Dorothy Franklin to Rose Terlin, May 15, 1936, Folder 5, Delta and Providence Cooperative Farms Papers #3474, SHC; *Co-Op Call* 3, no. 8 (July 4, 1938), Delta and Providence Cooperative Farms Papers #3474, SHC; Work Camps—AFSC, House Box #1, AEC.

26. Brochure for Volunteer Work Camps from the American Friends Service Committee for the Summer 1937, Folder 27, Delta and Providence Farms Cooperative Papers #3474, SHC; M. L. Golden, "Students from Co-op Farm Visit Southern Advocate," *Southern Advocate*, July 22, 1939.

27. Wilmer Young to Sam Franklin, April 18, 1936, Folder 3, Delta and Providence Cooperative Farms Papers #3474, SHC; "Memo on Trip to Delta Cooperative Farm," American Friends Service Committee Archive, Special Collections, Haverford College; Wilmer and Mildred Young to unknown, December 1937, Wilmer and Mildred Young Papers, Manuscripts Department, South Caroliniana Library, University of South Carolina.

28. Untitled, House Box #1, AEC.

29. Franklin, "Early Years," 15; Dero A. Saunders to Sam Franklin, May 20, 1936, Folder 5, Delta and Providence Cooperative Farms Papers #3474, SHC; "Mississippi Delta Colonists Seeking Independence in New Type Community," undated newspaper clipping, Delta Cooperative Farm, Vertical File, MDAH; Constance Rumbough to Paul Vanderwood, April 11, 1964, Folder 1, Delta Cooperative Farm Papers #03892-z, SHC.

30. Olson Sidney, "Unit Backed in Activities by New Deal," *Washington Post*, August 7, 1938.

31. Franklin, "Early Years," 14–17; Sam Franklin to Sherwood Eddy, April 28, 1936, Folder 3, Delta and Providence Cooperative Farms Papers #3474, SHC.

32. Sam Franklin to Sherwood Eddy, May 7, 1936, Folder 4, Delta and Providence Cooperative Farms Papers #3474, SHC; "Mississippi Delta Colonists Seeking Independence in New Type Community," undated newspaper clipping, Delta Cooperative Farm, Vertical File, MDAH.

33. Arthur Raper to A. Eugene Cox, January 5, 1972, Jerry Dallas Delta Farm Cooperative Collection, M 109, Delta State University Archives, Cleveland, Miss. (hereafter JDC); Sam Franklin to Jerry Dallas, October 22, 1986, JDC.

34. Sherwood Eddy, *A Door of Opportunity; or, An American Adventure in Cooperation with Sharecroppers* (New York: Eddy and Page, 1937), Rare Book Collection, Louis Round Wilson Special Collections Library, University of North Carolina at Chapel Hill, 2; Jerry W. Dallas, "The Delta and Providence Farms: A Mississippi Experiment in Cooperative Farming and Racial Cooperation, 1936–1956," *Mississippi Quarterly* 3 (Summer

1987): 295; Lindsey Hail to Edna Voss, December 29, 1936, Folder 20, Delta and Providence Cooperative Farms Papers #3474, SHC.

35. Sherwood Eddy to Sam Franklin, April 14, 1936, Folder 3, Delta and Providence Cooperative Farms Papers #3474, SHC.

36. Delta & Providence—Former Residents, House Box #1, AEC; Delta & Providence—Program, House Box #1, AEC.

37. Eddy, *Door of Opportunity*; "The Story of Delta Cooperative Farm in Pictures" Photographs Box, AEC; "Mississippi Delta Colonists Seeking Independence in New Type Community," undated newspaper clipping, Delta Cooperative Farm, Vertical File, MDAH.

38. William Amberson, "To Rescue the South," *Christian Register*, March 18, 1937, 23; "Mississippi Delta Colonists Seeking Independence in New Type Community," undated newspaper clipping, Delta Cooperative Farm, Vertical File, MDAH; T. J. Woofter Jr. and Ellen Winston, *Seven Lean Years* (Chapel Hill: University of North Carolina Press, 1939), 163–164.

39. Constance Rumbough to Paul Vanderwood, April 11, 1964, Delta Cooperative Farm Papers #3892-z, SHC.

40. "Some Basic Principles of the Delta Cooperative Farm," Delta Cooperative Farm Papers, MVC.

41. "Mississippi Delta Colonists Seeking Independence in New Type Community," undated newspaper clipping, Delta Cooperative Farm, Vertical File, MDAH; Amberson, "To Rescue the South," 23; "Record of Charters," Delta Cooperative Farm Papers, MVC.

42. Jonathan Mitchell, "Cabins in the Cotton," *New Republic*, September 22, 1937, 175; "Sherwood Eddy Luncheon, Chamber of Commerce," George Sherwood Eddy Papers, Special Collections, Yale Divinity School (hereafter GSE); "Sherwood Eddy Fund, Contribution Account," GSE.

43. Sherwood Eddy to Sam Franklin, April 19, 1936, Folder 3, Delta and Providence Cooperative Farms Papers #3474, SHC; Sam Franklin to Rev. James Myers, April 22, 1936, Folder 3, Delta and Providence Cooperative Farms Papers #3474, SHC.

44. "*THE DELTA COOPERATIVE FARM*: First Report of Progress" (Hillhouse, Miss., April 19, 1936), Folder 3, Delta and Providence Cooperative Farms Papers, SHC; Amberson, "To Rescue the South," 23; "Delta Cooperative Farm Review," Delta Cooperative Farm Papers, MVC.

45. "First Report of Progress," Delta and Providence Cooperative Farms Papers #3474, SHC.

46. "Mechanical Cotton Picker Almost But Not Quite Does Job," *Bolivar County Democrat*, September 10, 1936; William R. Amberson to Laurent Frantz, March 19, 1936, Box VII, AEC.

47. H. L. Mitchell to Bennie Fleming, April 29, 1936, STFU; "Delta Cooperative Farm Guest Book," Oversize Box, AEC.

48. Howard Kester to Sam Franklin, undated, 1975 Addendum, AEC; Sam Franklin to Howard Kester, September 14, 1938, STFU; Frank McCallister to Dorothy May Fischer, March 25, 1939, in the Delta Cooperative Farm Papers, MVC; "Local Secretary's Report," February 18, 1938, STFU Box, AEC; Erik S. Gellman and Jarod H. Roll, "Owen Whitfield and the Gospel of the Working Class in New Deal America, 1936–1946," *Journal of Southern History* 73 (May 2006): 304; Woodruff, *American Congo*, 166; Robert H. Craig,

Religion and Radical Politics: An Alternative Christian Tradition in the United States (Philadelphia: Temple University Press, 1992), 158–159.

49. "First Report of Progress," Delta and Providence Cooperative Farms Papers #3474, SHC.

50. "The Story of Delta Cooperative Farm in Pictures" Photographs Box, AEC; "Mississippi Delta Colonists Seeking Independence in New Type Community," undated newspaper clipping, Delta Cooperative Farm, Vertical File, MDAH.

51. Charles S. Johnson, *Shadow of the Plantation*, 5th ed. (Chicago: University of Chicago Press, 1969), 3.

52. Ibid.

53. "First Report of Progress," Delta and Providence Cooperative Farms Papers #3474, SHC.

54. "Mississippi Delta Colonists Seeking Independence in New Type Community," undated newspaper clipping, Delta Cooperative Farm, Vertical File, MDAH; Sam Franklin to Thomas Alva Stubbins, May 7, 1936, Folder 4, Delta and Providence Cooperative Farms Papers #3474, SHC; "Some Basic Principles of the Delta Cooperative Farm," Delta Cooperative Farm Papers, MVC.

55. Sam Franklin to Rev. James Myers, April 22, 1936, Folder 3, Delta and Providence Cooperative Farms Papers #3474, SHC; Sam Franklin to Jerry Dallas, October 22, 1986, JDC.

56. Frank McCallister to Dorothy May Fischer, March 25, 1939, Delta Cooperative Farm Papers, MVC; Sam Franklin to Howard Kester, September 14, 1938, STFU.

57. Franklin, "Early Years," 15.

58. Constance Rumbough to Paul Vanderwood, April 11, 1964, Folder 1, Delta Cooperative Farm Papers #3892-z, SHC; William Amberson to Charles S. Johnson, December 1936, Folder 2-g STFU, Box VII, AEC.

59. Daniels, *Southerner Discovers the South*, 150–151; Glenda Elizabeth Gilmore, *Defying Dixie: The Radical Roots of Civil Rights, 1919–1950* (New York: Norton, 2008), 222; Charles Eagles, *Jonathan Daniels and Race Relations: The Evolution of a Southern Liberal* (Knoxville: University of Tennessee Press, 1982); Jennifer Ritterhouse, *Discovering the South: One Man's Travels through a Changing America in the 1930s* (Chapel Hill: University of North Carolina Press, 2017).

60. William Amberson to Sam Franklin, December 21, 1936, AEC.

61. "REPORT on Delta Cooperative Farm," Delta Cooperative Farm Papers, MVC; Risa L. Goluboff, *The Lost Promise of Civil Rights* (Cambridge, Mass.: Harvard University Press, 2007), 52. For the complicated interactions between white and black southerners and how Jim Crow was performed, see Stephen A. Berrey, *The Jim Crow Routine: Everyday Performances of Race, Civil Rights, and Segregation in Mississippi* (Chapel Hill: University of North Carolina Press, 2015).

62. Sam H. Franklin to Sherwood Eddy, April 22, 1936, Folder 3, Delta and Providence Cooperative Farms Papers #3474, SHC; Daniels, *Southerner Discovers the South*, 149–151; Bradner J. Moore to William R. Amberson, May 1, 1936, Folder 4, Delta and Providence Cooperative Farms Papers #3474, SHC; Sam Franklin to John S. Radosta, May 7, 1936, Folder 4, Delta and Providence Cooperative Farms Papers #3474, SHC.

63. Norma Nelle Bullard to Sherwood Eddy, May 9, 1936, Folder 4, Delta and Providence Cooperative Farms Papers #3474, SHC; Robin D. G. Kelley, "'We Are Not What

We Seem': Rethinking Black Working-Class Opposition in the Jim Crow South," *Journal of American History* 80, 1 (June 1993): 83.

64. Arthur Raper to A. Eugene Cox, January 5, 1972, JDC; For community-based African American activism in the South, see Steven Hahn, *A Nation under Our Feet: Black Political Struggles in the Rural South, from Slavery to the Great Migration* (Cambridge, Mass.: Belknap, 2003); Robin D. G. Kelley, *Hammer and Hoe: Alabama Communists during the Great Depression* (Chapel Hill: University of North Carolina Press, 1990); Charles M. Payne, *I've Got the Light of Freedom: The Organizing Tradition and the Mississippi Freedom Struggle* (Berkeley: University of California Press, 1995); Mary G. Rolinson, *Grassroots Garveyism: The Universal Negro Improvement Association in the Rural South, 1920–1927* (Chapel Hill: University of North Carolina Press, 2007).

65. Quoted in Donald M. Royer, "A Comparative Study of Three Experiments in Rural 'Community' Reconstruction in the Southeast" (MA thesis, University of North Carolina at Chapel Hill, 1943), 62; "Officials Review '39 Work at Delta Cooperative," *Atlanta Daily World*, December 24, 1939.

66. Quoted in Alison Collis Greene, *No Depression in Heaven: The Great Depression, the New Deal, and the Transformation of Religion in the Delta* (New York: Oxford University Press, 2016), 61–63, 176. Greene also points out that the popularity of premillennialism rose during the 1930s as a way for rural southerners to explain and contend with the seemingly apocalyptic Great Depression.

67. For more on southern Democrats' fight against the New Deal, see Patricia Sullivan, *Days of Hope: Race and Democracy in the New Deal Era* (Chapel Hill: University of North Carolina Press, 1996), 221–247.

68. Quoted in Jerry W. Dallas, "The Delta and Providence Farms: A Mississippi Experiment in Cooperative Farming and Racial Cooperation, 1936–1956," *Mississippi Quarterly* 4 (1987): 283–308; John Robinson, "Many Activities of Sharecroppers Threaten Southern Social Order," *Chicago Defender*, August 13, 1938, 10.

69. Sheldon Avery, *Up from Washington: William Pickens and the Negro Struggle for Equality, 1900–1954* (Newark: University of Delaware Press, 1989).

70. Eddy, *Door of Opportunity*, 33. Mississippi Code 1103 of 1930 stated: "RACES— social equality. Marriage between—advocacy of punished. —Any person, firm, or corporation who shall be guilty of printing or circulating printed, typewritten or written matter urging or presenting for public acceptance or general information, arguments or suggestions in favor of social equality or of intermarriage between whites and negroes, shall be guilty of a misdemeanor and subject to a fine not exceeding five hundred dollars or imprisonment not exceeding six months or both fine and imprisonment in the discretion of the court."

71. Eddy, *Door of Opportunity*, 33.

72. Sherwood Eddy to Sam Franklin, April 7, 1936, Folder 3, Delta and Providence Cooperative Farms Papers #3474, SHC; F. S. Harmon to Sherwood Eddy, April 7, 1936, Folder 3, Delta and Providence Cooperative Farms Papers #3474, SHC.

73. For more on the Scottsboro case, see James E. Goodman, *Stories of Scottsboro* (New York: Vintage, 1995); Sherwood Eddy to Bishop Will Scarlett, April 3, 1936, Folder 3, Delta and Providence Cooperative Farms Papers #3474, SHC; Bishop Will Scarlett to Sherwood Eddy, April 9, 1936, Folder 3, Delta and Providence Cooperative Farms Papers #3474, SHC.

74. Howard Kester to Lee Hays, October 3, 1936, Folder 15, Delta and Providence Cooperative Farms Papers #3474, SHC.

75. William Amberson to Sam Franklin, July 14, 1936, AEC; Dorothy Fischer to Bishop William Scarlett, December 7, 1936, Folder 19, Delta and Providence Cooperative Farms Papers, #3474, SHC.

76. Sam Franklin to unaddressed, May 7, 1936, Folder 4, in the Delta and Cooperative Farms Papers #3474, SHC.

77. William Pickens, "Cooperative Farm Fine Experiment," *New Journal and Guide*, March 12, 1938; Daniels, *Southerner Discovers the South*, 159.

78. Sam Franklin to Sherwood Eddy, April 22, 1936, Folder 3, Delta and Providence Cooperative Farms Papers #3474, SHC.

79. Delta made a profit of $8,562.47 in 1936. Profits dramatically declined each year until 1942, when the farm made a profit of only $839.59. See Audits from Delta Cooperative Farm, Delta Cooperative Farm Papers, MVC; Daniels, *Southerner Discovers the South*, 149, 154.

80. Dorothy Franklin to Florence G. Tyler, January 20, 1937, Folder 23, Delta and Providence Cooperative Farms Papers #3474, SHC.

Chapter 3. The Limits of Interracialism and the Failure of Delta Cooperative Farm

1. Sam Franklin to Robert F. Strong, February 6, 1937, Folder 24, Delta and Providence Cooperative Farms Papers #3474, Southern Historical Collection, Louis Round Wilson Special Collections Library, University of North Carolina at Chapel Hill (hereafter SHC); Jonathan Mitchell, "Cabins in the Cotton," *New Republic*, September 22, 1937, 175–177; William Amberson to Vincent C. Widney, May 6, 1936, Folder 5, Delta and Providence Cooperative Farms Papers #3474, SHC; Gene Dattel, *Cotton and Race in the Making of America: The Human Costs of Economic Power* (Chicago: Ivan R. Dee, 2009), 343–344. The 1936 annual income for Delta Cooperative families equals approximately $9,917.61 to $16,529.25 in 2010 U.S. dollars.

2. Jonathan Daniels, *A Southerner Discovers the South* (New York: Macmillan, 1938), 154–155; William Amberson to Gene Cox, December 6, 1968, A. Eugene Cox Collection, Special Collections Department, Mitchell Memorial Library, Mississippi State University (hereafter AEC).

3. Marguerite E. Bicknell to Dorothy Franklin, October 14, 1936, Folder 19, Delta and Providence Cooperative Farms Papers #3474, SHC.

4. David Welky, *The Thousand-Year Flood: The Ohio-Mississippi Disaster of 1937* (Chicago: University of Chicago Press, 2011), 180–199; Sam Franklin to Barbara Parker, February 5, 1937, Folder 24, Delta and Providence Cooperative Farms Papers #3474, SHC.

5. Sam Franklin to Reinhold Niebuhr, February 11, 1937, Folder 25, Delta and Providence Cooperative Farms Papers #3474, SHC; "Minutes of the Cooperative Meeting," February 28, 1937, Folder 26, Delta and Providence Cooperative Farms Papers, #3474, SHC.

6. Dorothy Franklin to Edna Voss, November 23, 1936, Folder 19, Delta and Providence Cooperative Farms Papers #3474, SHC; Sam Franklin to Dear Friends, November 24, 1936, Folder 20, Delta and Providence Cooperative Farms Papers #3474, SHC.

7. Sam Franklin to Sherwood Eddy, April 22, 1936, Folder 3, Delta and Providence Cooperative Farms Papers #3474, SHC; Sam Franklin to Clare L. Pieno, February 19, 1937,

Folder 25 , Delta and Providence Cooperative Farms Papers #3474, SHC; Sam Franklin to Gertrude Orendorff, December 15, 1936, Folder 19, Delta and Providence Cooperative Farms Papers #3474, SHC.

8. Sam Franklin to Trustees, Cooperative Farms, December 12, 1936, Folder 20, Delta and Providence Cooperative Farms Papers #3474, SHC.

9. James L. Leloudis, *Schooling the New South: Pedagogy, Self, and Society in North Carolina, 1880–1920* (Chapel Hill: University of North Carolina Press, 1996), 213–214. Sam Franklin to Edwin R. Embree, January 21, 1937 Folder 23, Delta and Providence Cooperative Farms Papers #3474, SHC; Edwin R. Embree to Sam Franklin, January 27, 1937, Folder 23, Delta and Providence Cooperative Farms Papers #3474, SHC.

10. Untitled, House Box #1, AEC; "Mississippi Delta Colonists Seeking Independence in New Type Community, undated newspaper clipping, Delta Cooperative Farm, Vertical File, Mississippi Department of Archives and History (hereafter MDAH); Mitchell, "Cabins in the Cotton," 175.

11. Constance Rumbough to Paul J. Vanderwood, April 11, 1964, Folder 1, Delta Cooperative Farm Papers #3892-z, SHC.

12. *Co-Op Call*, May 6, 1938, Delta and Providence Cooperative Farms Papers #3474, SHC; *Co-Op Call*, August 25, 1938, Delta and Providence Cooperative Farms Papers #3474, SHC; *Chicago Defender*, August 13, 1938; "Summer Camps to Be Held," *Southern Advocate*, June 4, 1938; M. L. Golden, "Students from Co-op Visit Southern Advocate," *Southern Advocate*, July 22, 1939; *Co-Op Call*, July 4, 1938, Delta and Providence Cooperative Farms Papers #3474, SHC; William Amberson to Vincent C. Widney, May 6, 1936, Folder 5, Delta and Providence Cooperative Farms Papers #3474, SHC.

13. "Delta Cooperative Farm Guestbook," Oversize Box, AEC.

14. "N.A.A.C.P. Watchdog of a Race," *Chicago Defender*, July 1, 1939, 13; "N.A.A.C.P. to Consider Farm Tenants' Problems," *Chicago Defender*, June 10, 1939, 6; Colonel Lawrence Westbrook to William Amberson, March 22, 1937, Folder 18, William Ruthrauff Amberson Papers #3862, SHC.

15. "Jerry Dallas notes from interview with Coxes," Jerry Dallas Delta Farm Cooperative Collection, M 109, Delta State University Archives, Cleveland, Miss. (hereafter JDC); Sam H. Franklin Jr., "Early Years of the Delta Cooperative Farm and the Providence Cooperative Farm" (unpublished), 17–18; Daniels, *Southerner Discovers the South*, 152; "Biographical Data," AEC.

16. *Co-Op Call*, August 25, 1938, Delta and Providence Cooperative Farms Papers #3474, SHC.

17. *Co-Op Call*, April 10, 1937, Folder 30, Delta and Providence Cooperative Farms Papers #3474, SHC.

18. Marguerite E. Bicknell to Amherst Committee for Cooperative Aid, September 14, 1936, Folder 19, Delta and Providence Cooperative Farms Papers #3474, SHC.

19. Edna Voss to Dorothy Franklin, November 18, 1936, Folder 19, Delta and Providence Cooperative Farms Papers #3474, SHC.

20. Franklin, "Early Years," 38–39.

21. Sam Franklin to Gilbert W. Beebe, August 5, 1936, Folder 20, Delta and Providence Cooperative Farms Papers #3474, SHC; Sam Franklin to Clarence J. Gamble, December 17, 1936, Folder 20, Delta and Providence Cooperative Farms Papers #3474, SHC.

22. Thomas J. Ward, *Black Physicians in the Jim Crow South* (Fayetteville: University of Arkansas Press, 2003), 239–249.

23. Ibid.; Chalmers Archer Jr., *Growing Up Black in Rural Mississippi: Memories of a Family, Heritage of a Place* (New York: Walker and Company, 1992), 92.

24. Susan L. Smith, *Sick and Tired of Being Sick and Tired: Black Women's Health Activism in America, 1890–1950* (Philadelphia: University of Pennsylvania Press, 1995), 149; Ward, *Black Physicians*, 239–249; Carole R. McCann, *Birth Control Politics in the United States, 1916–1945* (Ithaca, N.Y.: Cornell University Press, 1994), 173.

25. Archer, *Growing Up Black*, 88; Willis D. Weatherford and Charles S. Johnson, *Race Relations: Adjustment of Whites and Negroes in the United States* (New York: Negro Universities Press, 1934), 368; Ward, *Black Physicians*, 121–123; Untitled, House Box #1, AEC; Blaine Treadway to Sam Franklin, October 25, 1936, Folder 16, Delta and Providence Cooperative Farms Papers #3474, SHC.

26. Sam Franklin to Reinhold Niebuhr, March 26, 1937, Folder 28, Delta and Providence Cooperative Farms Papers #3474, SHC; Sam Franklin to Sherwood Eddy, August 14, 1936, Folder 11, Delta and Providence Cooperative Farms Papers #3474, SHC; Franklin, "Early Years," 44.

27. Quoted in Donald M. Royer, "A Comparative Study of Three Experiments in Rural 'Community' Reconstruction in the Southeast" (MA thesis, University of North Carolina at Chapel Hill, 1943), 61.

28. Weatherford and Johnson, *Race Relations*, 3; Hortense Powdermaker, *After Freedom: A Cultural Study in the Deep South* (New York: Atheneum, 1969), 23.

29. Charles S. Johnson, *Growing Up in the Black Belt: Negro Youth in the Rural South* (Washington, D.C.: American Council on Education, 1941), 276–280.

30. "History of Bolivar County, Mississippi" (Jackson: Daughters of the American Revolution, 1948), 261–264; *The Brown American*, December 1936, 22; Bradner J. Moore to William Amberson, May 1, 1936, Folder 4, Delta and Providence Cooperative Farms Papers #3474, SHC.

31. William R. Amberson to Sam Schneider, September 7, 1937, Box VII, AEC; William R. Amberson to Clarence Senior, November 16, 1935, Folder 13a, William Ruthrauff Amberson Papers #3862, SHC.

32. George Lichtheim, *A Short History of Socialism* (New York: Praeger, 1970).

33. William Amberson to Sam Franklin, February 11, 1937, AEC; William R. Amberson to Francis A. Henson, May 6, 1936, Box VII, AEC.

34. Untitled, Box VII, AEC.

35. William Amberson to Gene Cox, January 17, 1973, AEC.

36. Franklin, "Early Years," 59–74.

37. Ibid., 59–74.

38. W. F. White to H. L. Mitchell, December 2, 1941, AEC; Sherwood Eddy, *A Door of Opportunity; or, An American Adventure in Cooperation with Sharecroppers* (New York: Eddy and Page, 1937), 46, Rare Book Collection, Louis Round Wilson Special Collections Library, University of North Carolina at Chapel Hill; Franklin, "Early Years," 49–63; "Dr. Eddy Advises U.S. to First Practice Democracy," *Chicago Defender*, February 1, 1941, 4.

39. Eddy, *Door of Opportunity*.

40. Arthur Raper to A. Eugene Cox, January 5, 1972, JDC; "Recommendations regarding Tenancy Legislation Submitted to the Special Committee on Farm Tenancy by the Southern Policy Association," December 14, 1936, Delta and Providence Cooperative Farms Papers #3474, SHC.

41. Reinhold Niebuhr to Sam Franklin, May 22, 1936, Folder 5, Delta and Providence Cooperative Farms Papers #3474, SHC.

42. J. R. Butler to Howard Kester, January 21, 1939, Southern Tenant Farmers' Union Papers, microfilm, Davis Library, University of North Carolina at Chapel Hill (hereafter STFU); Unsigned to J. R. Butler, May 27, 1937, STFU; Franklin, "Early Years," 48–49; Untitled, House Box #1, AEC.

43. "Report of the Committee Investigating Delta and Providence Farms," 1940, STFU.

44. Ibid.

45. A. James McDonald to Blaine Treadway, September 14, 1940, Folder 22, William Ruthrauff Amberson Papers #3862, SHC; A. James "Mac" McDonald to William Amberson, April 20, 1939, Folder 20, William Ruthrauff Amberson Papers #3862, SHC; William Amberson to J. H. Moody, September 29, 1940, Folder 22, William Ruthrauff Amberson Papers, SHC; Robert F. Martin, *Howard Kester and the Struggle for Social Justice in the South, 1904–1977* (Charlottesville: University Press of Virginia, 1991), 103–104.

46. H. L. Mitchell to J. R. Butler, May 14, 1940, STFU; "A Statement to the Board of Trustees Cooperative Farms, inc," William Amberson Papers, Mississippi Valley Collection, McWherter Library, University of Memphis (hereafter, MVC); William Amberson to J. H. Moody, September 29, 1940, Folder 22, William Ruthrauff Amberson Papers #3862, SHC.

47. J. P. Warbasse to William Amberson, May 2, 1939, William Ruthrauff Amberson Papers #3862, SHC; "Editorial," *Christian Century*, June 14, 1939; William Amberson to A. James McDonald, December 24, 1940, Folder 22, William Ruthrauff Amberson Papers #3862, SHC.

48. Olson Sidney, "Unit Back in Activities by the New Deal," *Washington Post*, August 7, 1938; J. R. Butler to Norman Thomas, June 23, 1941, STFU; William Amberson to A. James McDonald, November 2, 1940, William Ruthrauff Amberson Papers #3862, SHC; A. James McDonald to William Amberson, December 1, 1940, William Ruthrauff Amberson Papers #3862, SHC; Art Landes to H. L. Mitchell, August 3, 1941, STFU; Art Landes to H. L. Mitchell, February 12, 1942, STFU.

49. Miscellaneous handwritten notes from Jerry Dallas, JDC; "Delta Cooperative Farm Review," Delta Cooperative Farm Papers, MVC; Blaine Treadway to William Amberson, January 9, 1939, William Ruthrauff Amberson Papers #3862, SHC.

50. Arthur Raper to A. Eugene Cox, January 5, 1972, JDC; William Amberson to Gene Cox, January 17, 1973, House Box #1, AEC.

51. Wilmer and Mildred Young to unaddressed, December 1937, in the Wilmer and Mildred Young Papers, Manuscripts Department, South Caroliniana Library, University of South Carolina.

Chapter 4. The Concrete Needs of the Thousands among Us

1. Howard Kester to Sam Franklin, undated, Folder 155, Delta and Providence Cooperative Farms Papers #3473, Southern Historical Collection, Louis Round Wilson Special Collections Library, University of North Carolina at Chapel Hill (hereafter SHC).

2. Sam Franklin to Sherwood Eddy, March 30, 1943, Folder 155, Delta and Providence Cooperative Farms Papers #3473, SHC.

3. Pete Daniel, "Going among Strangers: Southern Reactions to World War II," *Journal of American History* 77 (December 1990): 886–911; Glenda Elizabeth Gilmore, *Defying Dixie: The Radical Roots of Civil Rights, 1919–1950* (New York: Norton, 2008),

346–399; Bryant Simon, "Introduction to the 1997 Edition," in Howard W. Odum, *Race and Rumors of Race: The American South in the Early Forties* (Baltimore: Johns Hopkins University Press, 1997), vii–xxxii.

4. Julie M. Weise, *Corazon de Dixie: Mexicanos in the U.S. South since 1910* (Chapel Hill: University of North Carolina Press, 2015), 80–81; Jason Morgan Ward, "'Nazis Hoe Cotton': Planters, POWs, and the Future of Farm Labor in the Deep South," *Agricultural History* 81, no. 4 (Fall 2007): 471–492; Ward, *Defending White Democracy: The Making of a Segregationist Movement and the Remaking of Racial Politics, 1936–1965* (Chapel Hill: University of North Carolina Press, 2011), 38–66; Neil R. McMillan, ed., *Remaking Dixie: The Impact of World War II on the American South* (Jackson: University Press of Mississippi, 1997); Kevin M. Kruse and Stephen Tuck, eds., *Fog of War: The Second World War and the Civil Rights Movement* (New York: Oxford University Press, 2011); James C. Cobb, *The South and America since World War II* (New York: Oxford University Press, 2011), 1–21.

5. Charles S. Johnson, "The Present Status of Race Relations in the South," *Social Forces* 23 (October 1943): 30; Cobb, *South and America*, 1–5.

6. Simon, "Introduction." For postwar racial tensions, see Odum, *Race and Rumors of Race*; Charles S. Johnson, *To Stem This Tide: Survey of Racial Tension Areas in the United States* (Boston: Pilgrim Press, 1943); Ward, *Defending White Democracy*, 81; Ward, *Hanging Bridge: Racial Violence and America's Civil Rights Century* (New York: Oxford University Press, 2016), 94–95, 137.

7. Charles S. Johnson, *Into the Main Stream: A Survey of Best Practices in Race Relations in the South* (Chapel Hill: University of North Carolina Press, 1947), 3; Elizabeth Borgwardt, *A New Deal for the World: America's Vision for Human Rights* (Cambridge, Mass.: Belknap, 2005).

8. Sam Franklin, unaddressed, undated, Folder 155, Delta and Providence Cooperative Farms Papers #3474, SHC.

9. Eric Foner, *Nothing But Freedom: Emancipation and Its Legacy* (Baton Rouge: Louisiana State University Press, 1983); Janet Sharp Hermann, *The Pursuit of a Dream* (New York: Oxford University Press, 1981), 219–245; Booker T. Washington, *Up from Slavery: An Autobiography* (New York: Doubleday, Page, 1901); Thomas J. Sugrue, *Sweet Land of Liberty: The Forgotten Struggle for Civil Rights in the North* (New York: Random House, 2008), 10.

10. Kimberley Johnson, *Reforming Jim Crow: Southern Politics and State in the Age of Brown* (New York: Oxford University Press, 2010), 213.

11. Koss Kimberlin to William Amberson, February 1, 1940, Folder 21, William Ruthrauff Amberson Papers #3474, SHC.

12. Charles S. Johnson, *Statistical Atlas of Southern Counties: Listing and Analysis of Socio-Economic Indices of 1104 Southern Counties* (Chapel Hill: University of North Carolina Press, 1941), 162, 165; Historical Census Browser, University of Virginia, Geospatial and Statistical Data Center; Chalmers Archer Jr., *Growing Up Black in Rural Mississippi: Memories of a Family, Heritage of a Place* (New York: Walker and Company, 1992), 134–135.

13. Sam H. Franklin Jr., "Early Years of the Delta Cooperative Farm and the Providence Cooperative Farm" (unpublished), 71.

14. Historical Census Browser, University of Virginia, Geospatial and Statistical Data Center.

15. Franklin, "Early Years," 75; Sam Franklin to Harry C. Herman, March 4, 1943, Folder 155, Delta and Providence Cooperative Farms Papers #3474, SHC.

16. Franklin, "Early Years," 72.

17. Ibid., 74; Sam Franklin to Miriam Walker, January 8, 1943, Folder 153, Delta and Providence Cooperative Farms Papers #3474, SHC.

18. Franklin, "Early Years," 74.

19. Sam Franklin to Ralph W. Cessna, January 11, 1943, Folder 153, Delta and Providence Cooperative Farms Papers #3474, SHC; Sam Franklin to the Fellowship of Socialist Christians, January 23, 1943, Folder 153, Delta and Providence Cooperative Farms Papers #3474, SHC.

20. "Dr. Jones Is State's First Woman Dentist," *Negro Star*, September 3, 1948.

21. "The Kappa Alpha Health Clinic Reopened," *Chicago Defender*, August 22, 1942, 18.

22. Franklin, "Early Years," 61.

23. Ibid., 61–62.

24. Ida L. Jackson to Sam Franklin, May 6, 1943, Folder 157, Delta and Providence Cooperative Farms Papers #3474, SHC.

25. Historical Census Browser, University of Virginia, Geospatial and Statistical Data Center; Miscellaneous, Folder 157, Delta and Providence Cooperative Farms Papers #3474, SHC.

26. Wilmer and Mildred Young to undisclosed recipients, February 1938, in the Wilmer and Mildred Young Papers Manuscripts Department, South Caroliniana Library, University of South Carolina.

27. Sam Franklin to Arthur Raper, January 11, 1943, Folder 153, Delta and Providence Cooperative Farms Papers #3474, SHC.

28. Franklin, "Early Years," 69.

29. Ibid., 69–70; Sam Franklin to Frances Denton, April 17, 1943, Folder 155, Delta and Providence Cooperative Farms Papers #3474, SHC.

30. Franklin, "Early Years," 76.

31. Sam Franklin to John R. Fain, February 12, 1943, Folder 154, Delta and Providence Cooperative Farms Papers #3474, SHC.

32. Although hospitals were required by law to have separate waiting rooms, country clinics often circumvented regulations because rural Jim Crow laws were often less stringent. Still, some of Minter's white patients preferred to wait in their cars instead of share the integrated waiting room with blacks.

33. Sam Franklin to Ralph W. Cessna, January 11, 1943, Folder 153, Delta and Providence Cooperative Farms Papers #3474, SHC.

34. Ibid.

35. Clarence Wigfall to Sam Franklin, April 7, 1943, Folder 156, Delta and Providence Cooperative Farms Papers #3474, SHC.

36. Ibid.

37. C. Dena Bulgaris to A. E. Cox, March 4, 1971, 1975 Addendum, Box 1, A. Eugene Cox Collection, Special Collections Department, Mitchell Memorial Library, Mississippi State University (hereafter AEC).

38. Sam Franklin to Sherwood Eddy, March 30, 1940, quoted in note from Eugene Cox, March 20, 1968, 1975 Addendum, Box 1, AEC.

39. Franklin, "Early Years," 64.

40. Sam Franklin to John R. Fain, February 12, 1943, Folder 154, Delta and Providence

Cooperative Farms Papers #3474, SHC; Sam Franklin to Sherwood Eddy, March 8, 1943, Folder 155, Delta and Providence Cooperative Farms Papers #3474, SHC.

41. Sam Franklin to Sherwood Eddy, March 8, 1943, Folder 155, Delta and Providence Cooperative Farms Papers #3474, SHC.

42. Ibid.

43. Ida L. Jackson to Sam Franklin, May 6, 1943, Folder 157, Delta and Providence Cooperative Farms Papers #3474, SHC.

44. Gene Cox to Sherwood Eddy, May 25, 1952, Folder 163, Delta and Providence Cooperative Farms Papers #3473, SHC.

45. Sherwood Eddy to Sam Franklin, February 23, 1943, Folder 154, Delta and Providence Cooperative Farms Papers #3474, SHC; Sam Franklin to Arthur Raper, May 8, 1943, Folder 156, Delta and Providence Cooperative Farms Papers #3474, SHC.

46. Dorothy Franklin to Garnet Van Buskirk, May 20, 1943, Folder 157, Delta and Providence Cooperative Farms Papers #3474, SHC; Harold Stanley Jacoby, *Tule Lake: From Relocation to Segregation* (Grass Valley, Calif.: Comstock Bonanza Press, 1996), 70–79.

47. Karl Lilliquist, "Farming in the Desert: Agriculture in the World War II–Era Japanese-American Relocation Centers," *Agricultural History* 84, no. 1 (Winter 2010): 74–80; Jason Morgan Ward, "'No Jap Crow': Japanese Americans Encounter the World War II South," *Journal of Southern History* 73, no. 1 (February 2007): 75–104.

48. Miscellaneous, Folder 157, Delta and Providence Cooperative Farms Papers #3474, SHC.

49. Ida L. Jackson to Gene Cox, August 10, 1943, Folder 157, Delta and Providence Cooperative Farms Papers #3474, SHC; "Health Clinic Is Called Off by AKA Sorors," *Chicago Defender*, September 4, 1943, 16.

50. Ralph Cessna to Sam Franklin, February 26, 1943, Folder 154, Delta and Providence Cooperative Farms Papers #3474, SHC; Charles S. Johnson to Sam Franklin, March 29, 1943, Folder 155, Delta and Providence Cooperative Farms Papers #3474, SHC.

51. Kieran W. Taylor, "I Done Made My Mind Up: The Legacy of the Providence Cooperative Farm" (MA thesis, University of Mississippi, 1998).

52. Eugene Cox to Sherwood Eddy, December 18, 1943, Folder 157, Delta and Providence Cooperative Farms Papers #3474, SHC.

53. Taylor, "I Done Made My Mind Up."

54. Franklin, "Early Years," 70; Eugene Cox to Sherwood Eddy, December 18, 1943, Folder 157, Delta and Providence Cooperative Farms Papers #3474, SHC.

55. Sherwood Eddy to Fellow Director of Cooperative Farms, inc, April 27, 1945, Delta and Providence Cooperative Farms Papers #3474, SHC.

56. Eugene Cox to Sherwood Eddy, December 18, 1943, Folder 157, Delta and Providence Cooperative Farms Papers #3474, SHC.

57. Eugene Cox to Dennis Hart, February 26, 1944, Folder 158, Delta and Providence Cooperative Farms Papers #3474, SHC; Eugene Cox to Sherwood Eddy, December 18, 1943, Folder 157, Delta and Providence Cooperative Farms Papers #3474, SHC.

58. Sherwood Eddy to Eugene Cox, May 10, 1945, Delta and Providence Cooperative Farms Papers #3474, SHC.

59. Sherwood Eddy to Fellow Director Cooperative Farms, inc, April 27, 1945, Delta and Providence Cooperative Farms Papers #3474, SHC.

60. Taylor, "I Done Made My Mind Up," 36–37; Demitri B. Shimkin, Edith M. Shim-

kin, and Dennis A. Frate, eds., *The Extended Family in Black Societies* (Chicago: Mouton, 1978), 159.

61. Quoted in Taylor, "I Done Made My Mind Up," 4, 38, 72.

62. "Holmes County Scholastic Years Session 1947–1948," Delta and Providence Cooperative Farms Papers #3474, SHC; Eugene Cox to L. N. D. Wells, September 25, 1947, Delta and Providence Cooperative Farms Papers #3474, SHC; Charles C. Bolton, "Mississippi's School Equalization Program, 1945–1954: 'A Last Gasp to Try to Maintain a Segregated Educational System,'" *Journal of Southern History* 66, no. 4 (November 2000): 781–814.

63. Sherwood Eddy to Directors, April 27, 1945, Delta and Providence Cooperative Farms Papers #3474, SHC; Taylor, "I Done Made My Mind Up," 40.

64. "Camp Springs" Pamphlet, Folder 163, Delta and Providence Cooperative Farms Papers #3474, SHC.

65. Sam Franklin to Sherwood Eddy, February 19, 1943, Folder 154, Delta and Providence Cooperative Farms Papers #3474, SHC; J. Carroll Moody and Gilbert C. Fite, *The Credit Union Movement: Origins and Development, 1850–1980* (Dubuque, Iowa: Kendall/Hunt, 1984), 94.

66. S. H. Myers to A. E. Cox, March 18, 1949, Box IV-A, AEC.

67. Sherwood Eddy to Eugene Cox, December 11, 1945, Folder 159, Delta and Providence Cooperative Farms Papers #3474, SHC.

68. Franklin, "Early Years," 81.

69. Cobb, *South and America*, 8–16; Ward, *Defending White Democracy*, 66–120.

70. Eugene Cox to Sherwood Eddy, November 20, 1947, Folder 160, Delta and Providence Cooperative Farms Papers #3474, SHC.

71. Eugene Cox to Sherwood Eddy, May 8, 1947, Folder 160, Delta and Providence Cooperative Farms Papers #3474, SHC.

72. "Conference of Sherwood Eddy, A.E. Cox, and David Minter," Folder 160, Delta and Providence Cooperative Farms Papers #3474, SHC.

73. Sam Franklin to Sherwood Eddy, February 19, 1943, Folder 154, Delta and Providence Cooperative Farms Papers #3474, SHC.

Chapter 5. Preventing Another Emmett Till

1. "Weather Observation," *Lexington Advertiser*, September 29, 1955, 1.

2. Hazel Brannon Smith, "Through Hazel Eyes," *Lexington Advertiser*, May 6, 1954, 1.

3. Thomas J. Sugrue, *Sweet Land of Liberty: The Forgotten Struggle for Civil Rights in the North* (New York: Random House, 2008), 106–111; Chris Myers Asch, *The Senator and the Sharecropper: The Freedom Struggles of James O. Eastland and Fannie Lou Hamer* (Chapel Hill: University of North Carolina Press, 2008), 104–112; George Lewis, *The White South and the Red Menace: Segregationists, Anticommunism, and Massive Resistance, 1945–1965* (Gainesville: University Press of Florida, 2004), 16; Jeff Woods, *Black Struggle, Red Scare: Segregation and Anti-communism in the South, 1948–1968* (Baton Rouge: Louisiana State University Press, 2004), 43; Yasuhiro Katagiri, *Black Freedom, White Resistance, and Red Menace: Civil Rights and Anticommunism in the Jim Crow South* (Baton Rouge: Louisiana State University Press, 2014).

4. "Eastland Discusses His 12-Year Stewardship in Senate to Holmes County," *Lexington Advertiser*, August 5, 1954, 1; "Holmes County Goes for Eastland 1745–382 in Primary Tuesday," *Lexington Advertiser*, August 26, 1954, 1; "Problems Facing South Today More

Serious Than the Civil War Conflict, Says Brady," *Lexington Advertiser*, March 24, 1955, 1; Asch, *Senator and the Sharecropper*, 113–119; Mary L. Dudziak, *Cold War Civil Rights: Race and the Image of American Democracy* (Princeton, N.J.: Princeton University Press, 2000), 12.

5. For detailed historical analysis of white violence toward blacks in twentieth-century Mississippi, see Danielle L. McGuire, *At the Dark End of the Street: Black Women, Rape and Resistance: A New History of the Civil Rights Movement from Rosa Parks to the Rise of Black Power* (New York: Knopf, 2010); J. Todd Moye, *Let the People Decide: Black Freedom and White Resistance Movements in Sunflower County Mississippi, 1945–1986* (Chapel Hill: University of North Carolina Press, 2004); John Dittmer, *Local People: The Struggle for Civil Rights in Mississippi* (Urbana: University of Illinois Press, 1995); Charles M. Payne, *I've Got the Light of Freedom: The Organizing Tradition and the Mississippi Freedom Struggle* (Berkeley: University of California Press, 1995); Neil R. McMillen, *Dark Journey: Black Mississippians in the Age of Jim Crow* (Urbana: University of Illinois Press, 1989).

6. C. R. Hamlin, "Tchula News," *Lexington Advertiser*, July 14, 1949, 7; C. R. Hamlin, "Tchula News," *Lexington Advertiser*, October 8, 1953, 7; C. R. Hamlin, "Tchula News," *Lexington Advertiser*, April 28, 1955, 6. For how activities at Providence helped spur area African Americans to push for civil rights, see Providence Cooperative Farm, Special Research Projects, Southern Oral History Program, #4007, Southern Historical Collection, Louis Round Wilson Special Collections Library, University of North Carolina at Chapel Hill (hereafter SHC).

7. Gene Cox to Sherwood and Louise Eddy, August 8, 1954, Folder 164, Delta and Providence Cooperative Farms Papers #3474, SHC.

8. John Rust to A. Eugene Cox, undated, House Box #2, A. Eugene Cox Collection, Special Collections Department, Mitchell Memorial Library, Mississippi State University (hereafter AEC).

9. "Holmes Designated Disaster Area," *Lexington Advertiser*, September 23, 1954, 1; "Weevil Infestation Reported in Holmes," *Lexington Advertiser*, June 23, 1949, 6; Phillip Rushing, *Empty Sleeves* (Grand Rapids: Zondervan, 1984), 95.

10. Gene Cox to the Trustees of Cooperative Foundation, inc, December 1950, Folder 163, Delta and Providence Cooperative Farms Papers #3474, SHC.

11. Gene Cox to the Trustees of Cooperative Foundation, inc, December 1950, Folder 163, Delta and Providence Cooperative Farms Papers #3474, SHC.

12. "Camp Springs" Pamphlet, Folder 163, Delta and Providence Cooperative Farms Papers #3474, SHC; Gene Cox to Sherwood and Louise Eddy, August 8, 1954, Folder 164, Delta and Providence Cooperative Farms Papers #3474, SHC.

13. Paul Burton, "'Old Man Mose' Sells Out, He'll Move to New York," *Clarion-Ledger*, September 26, 1955, 1; Gene Cox to Sherwood Eddy, May 25, 1952, Folder 163, Delta and Providence Cooperative Farms Papers #3474, SHC.

14. "Notes on Special Meeting Held in the Tchula Consolidated Community School," House Box #2, AEC; Murray Kempton, "Intruder," *New York Post*, November 17, 1955.

15. Kempton, "Intruder."

16. "Send U.S. Troops to Mississippi," *Pittsburgh Courier*, December 10, 1955.

17. Allie Povall, *The Time of Eddie Noel* (Concord, N.C.: Comfort, 2010), 16–22.

18. For an analysis of how Mississippians and the press reacted to the Noel incidents, see Stephen A. Berrey, *The Jim Crow Routine: Everyday Performances of Race, Civil Rights,*

and Segregation in Mississippi (Chapel Hill: University of North Carolina Press, 2015), 93–101; Povall, *Time of Eddie Noel*, 23–134.

19. Povall, *Time of Eddie Noel*.

20. Ibid., 86–110.

21. James Graham Cook, *The Segregationists* (New York: Appleton-Century-Crofts, 1962), 40.

22. Cook, *Segregationists*, 35; "Notes on Special Meeting Held in the Tchula Consolidated Community School," House Box #2, AEC; Gene Cox to Sherwood Eddy, October 6, 1954, Folder 164, Delta and Providence Cooperative Farms Papers #3474, SHC.

23. "Two Shootings Mar Holidays," *Lexington Advertiser*, July 8, 1954, 1; "Sheriff Wins Verdict," *Lexington Advertiser*, October 14, 1954, 1. The three law officers with Sheriff Byrd were Tchula Constable Bob Gillespie, Tchula Deputy-Jailer Coyier Farmer, and State Highway Patrolman J. A. Love. The men were riding in Love's patrol car.

24. "Sheriff Wins Verdict."

25. Cook, *Segregationists*, 37–39; Hazel Brannon Smith, "The Law Should Be for All," *Lexington Advertiser*, July 15, 1954, 1; Hazel Brannon Smith, "Through Hazel Eyes," *Lexington Advertiser*, July 22, 1954, 1.

26. Eugene Cox to J. Edgar Hoover, October 1, 1954, House Box #1, AEC; Cook, *Segregationists*, 39.

27. "Sheriff Wins Verdict," *Lexington Advertiser*, October 14, 1954, 1.

28. "Presbyterian Church Bulletin," House Box #1, AEC; "Tchula Presbyterians Make Statement On Belief And Policy," *Lexington Advertiser*, September 16, 1954, 1; "Tchula News," *Lexington Advertiser*, March 24, 1949, 2.

29. See Joseph Crespino, *In Search of Another Country: Mississippi and the Conservative Counterrevolution* (Princeton, N.J.: Princeton University Press, 2007), 63–70; Jane Dailey, "Sex, Segregation, and the Sacred after Brown," *Journal of American History* 91 (June 2004): 119–144; and Carolyn Renee Dupont, *Mississippi Praying: Southern White Evangelicals and the Civil Rights Movement, 1945–1975* (New York: New York University Press, 2015).

30. Jeanne and Mary Alice Shields to David Minter, April 3, 1955, House Box #1, AEC; Sam H. Franklin Jr., "Early Years of the Delta Cooperative Farm and the Providence Cooperative Farm" (unpublished), 85; "Peace on Earth Good Will toward Men," House Box #2, AEC.

31. Robert Rodgers Korstad, *Civil Rights Unionism: Tobacco Workers and the Struggle for Democracy in the Mid-Twentieth-Century South* (Chapel Hill: University of North Carolina Press, 2003), 340; Franklin, "Early Years," 48.

32. Gene Cox to Clark Bouwman, September 15, 1954, 1975 Addendum, Box 1, AEC.

33. "Holmes County Voters Approve Abolition Amendment on Tuesday 2,393–70," *Lexington Advertiser*, December 23, 1954, 1; "Holmes County School Progress Cited," *Lexington Advertiser*, January 13, 1955, 1.

34. Dittmer, *Local People*, 55–57.

35. "Notes on Special Meeting Held in the Tchula Consolidated Community School," House Box #2, AEC; William Lee Miller, "Trial by Tape Recorder," *Reporter*, December 15, 1955, 27–32; Cook, *Segregationists*, 40; Jeff Wiltse, *Contested Waters: A Social History of Swimming Pools in America* (Chapel Hill: University of North Carolina Press, 2007), 121–180.

36. "Notes on Special Meeting Held in the Tchula Consolidated Community School," House Box #2, AEC; Cook, *Segregationists*, 37; Franklin, "Early Years," 86.

37. "Notes on Special Meeting Held in the Tchula Consolidated Community School," House Box #2, AEC.

38. Edwin White to "White American Society," January 18, 1954, Box 9, Earnest Sevier Cox Papers, Duke University; David T. Beito, *Black Maverick: T.R.M. Howard's Fight for Civil Rights and Economic Power* (Urbana: University of Illinois Press, 2009), 104; "Peace on Earth Good Will toward Men," House Box #2, AEC; "Representative Edwin White Writes on Mississippi's People and Her School Situation," *Lexington Advertiser*, August 5, 1954, 1; "Representative Edwin White in Favor of Mississippi's Proposed School Amendment," *Lexington Advertiser*, November 18, 1954, 1.

39. "Love Is Candidate for Representative," *Lexington Advertiser*, June 9, 1955, 1; "Barrett IS Candidate for Re-election as County Attorney," *Lexington Advertiser*, June 16, 1955, 1; Tommy Guion, "All Gubernatorial Candidates Pledge to Maintain Southern Way of Life for Good of Both Races at Madison County Rally," *Lexington Advertiser*, June 16, 1955, 2; "Public Funds Asked for Citizens Councils," *Lexington Advertiser*, March 15, 1956, 1.

40. "Notes on Special Meeting Held in the Tchula Consolidated Community School," House Box #2, AEC; Miller, "Trial by Tape Recorder," 27–32; Franklin, "Early Years," 86–89.

41. Franklin, "Early Years"; Hazel Brannon Smith, "You Can't Fool God," *Lexington Advertiser*, November 17, 1955; James Desmond, "New Klan Burns Economic Cross," *Pittsburgh Courier*, December 24, 1955.

42. Franklin, "Early Years."

43. Eugene Cox to H. L. Mitchell, September 30, 1955, House Box #2, AEC; C. R. Hamlin, "Tchula News," *Lexington Advertiser*, March 3, 1949, 7; C. R. Hamlin, "Tchula News," *Lexington Advertiser*, April 14, 1949, 7; C. R. Hamlin, "Tchula News," *Lexington Advertiser*, September 9, 1954, 7; quoted in Will D. Campbell, *Providence* (Atlanta: Longstreet Press, 1992), 14–15.

44. "Asked to Leave the County," *Presbyterian Outlook*, October 17, 1955, 2–4.

45. Ibid.; Tom Scarbrough, "A. E. Cox, 933 Chambliss Road, Whitehaven, Tennessee," July 8, 1960, SCR ID# 2-54-1-39-5-1-1, Sovereignty Commission Online, MDAH, http://www.mdah.ms.gov/arrec/digital_archives/sovcom/result.php?image=images/png/cd02/013456.png&otherstuff=2|54|1|39|5|1|1|13203|; Kempton, "Intruder," *New York Post*. For more on miscegenation in the South, see Martha Hodes, *White Women, Black Men: Illicit Sex in the Nineteenth-Century South* (New Haven, Conn.: Yale University Press, 1997); Peggy Pascoe, *What Comes Naturally: Miscegenation Law and the Making of Race in America* (New York: Oxford University Press, 2009).

46. "Notes on Special Meeting Held in the Tchula Consolidated Community School," House Box #2, AEC; "Peace on Earth Good Will toward Men," House Box #2, AEC; "Letters That Had Been . . . Kept Closed until 1992," House Box #2, AEC; Lindsey Cox to Mrs. Hamlin, October 1955, Box #24, AEC.

47. "Notes on Special Meeting Held in the Tchula Consolidated Community School," House Box #2, AEC.

48. Eugene Cox to H. L. Mitchell, September 30, 1955, House Box #2, AEC; Lindsey H. Cox to Mrs. Hamlin, October 1955, House Box #2, AEC; Eugene Cox to Sherwood

Eddy, October 6, 1954, Folder 164, Delta and Providence Cooperative Farms Papers #3474, SHC.

49. "Notes on Special Meeting Held in the Tchula Consolidated Community School," Home Box #2, AEC; A. James McDonald to Gene Cox, June 24, 1956, Box #25A, AEC.

50. "Delta-Providence Guestbook," House Box #6, AEC; Franklin, "Early Years," 90.

51. "Letters That Had Been . . . Kept Closed until 1992," House Box #2, AEC; "Peace on Earth Good Will toward Men," House Box #2, AEC.

52. Crespino, *In Search of Another Country*, 19–26; "Notes on Special Meeting Held in the Tchula Consolidated Community School," Home Box #2, AEC; Handwritten note by A. E. Cox, 1955, Box #24, AEC.

53. Campbell, *Providence*, 21–24.

54. Eugene Cox to Sherwood Eddy, December 20, 1955, House Box #1, AEC; C. R. Hamlin, "Tchula News," *Lexington Advertiser*, November 17, 1955, 6; Eugene Cox to Fay Bennett, March 7, 1956, House Box #2, AEC.

55. "Peace on Earth Good Will toward Men," House Box #2, AEC; Mrs. Seth Wheatley (Elizabeth) to Sue Minter, 1955, House Box #4, AEC; Eugene Cox to Fay Bennett, March 7, 1956, House Box #2, AEC.

56. Cook, *Segregationists*, 42; "Notes on Special Meeting Held in the Tchula Consolidated Community School," Home Box #2, AEC; Neil R. McMillen, *The Citizens' Council: Organized Resistance to the Second Reconstruction, 1954–64* (Urbana: University of Illinois Press, 1971), 209.

57. "Notes on Special Meeting Held in the Tchula Consolidated Community School," Home Box #2, AEC.

58. Quoted in Campbell, *Providence*, 10.

59. Kieran W. Taylor, "I Done Made My Mind Up: The Legacy of the Providence Cooperative Farm" (MA thesis, University of Mississippi, 1998).

60. A. J. Snell to Gene Cox, July 17, 1956, Folder 164, Delta and Providence Cooperative Farms Papers #3474, SHC; CUNA Miscellaneous, Box IV-A, AEC.

61. "Peace on Earth Good Will toward Men," House Box #2, AEC; "*Members*—Delta Cooperative Farm, Rochdale, Mississippi," Folder 2, Delta Cooperative Farm Papers #3892-z, SHC; "Providence Cooperative Federal Credit Union" Miscellaneous, Box IV-A, AEC.

62. Gene Cox to Sherwood & Louise Eddy, May 26, 1956, House Box #1, AEC.

63. Gene Cox to undisclosed, April 1957, AEC; the Coxes to undisclosed recipients, April 1957, House Box #2, AEC.

Epilogue

1. Gene Cox to undisclosed, April 1957, A. Eugene Cox Collection, Special Collections Department, Mitchell Memorial Library, Mississippi State University (hereafter AEC); "Dr. David R. Minter Honored," *Lexington Advertiser*, June 12, 1969, 1.

2. Elenor M. Padillo to Mr. A. E. Cox, January 1972, Box #18, AEC; Eva Booker to Dr. Minter, February 19, 1972, Box #18, AEC.

3. The Coxes to undisclosed recipients, April 1957, House Box #2, AEC; Robert E. Luckett, *Joe T. Patterson and the White South's Dilemma: Evolving Resistance to Black Advancement* (Jackson: University Press of Mississippi, 2015), 73; To Mr. & Mrs. Cox from Viola Billington, 1966, Box #28, AEC.

4. Yasuhiro Katagiri, *The Mississippi State Sovereignty Commission: Civil Rights and*

States' Rights (Jackson: University Press of Mississippi, 2001), 69; Jenny Irons, *Reconstituting Whiteness: The Mississippi State Sovereignty Commission* (Nashville: Vanderbilt University Press, 2010), 100–105.

5. Tom Scarbrough, "Marshall County (President E. A. Smith, Rust College)," June 4, 1964, SCR ID# 2-20-1-76-2-1-1, Sovereignty Commission Online, MDAH, http://www.mdah.ms.gov/arrec/digital_archives/sovcom/result.php?image=images/png/cd01/003667.png&otherstuff=2|20|1|76|2|1|1|3559|.

6. Jamie G. Houston to Gene Cox, February 1, 1957, Box #13, AEC; to Mrs. Wallis Schutt, November 29, 1972, House Box #1, AEC; Will Campbell to Gene Cox, December 21, 1972, Jerry Dallas Delta Farm Cooperative Collection, M 109, Delta State University Archives, Cleveland, Miss.

7. Fannye Booker to Mr. and Mrs. Cox, August 24, 1989, House Box #2, AEC; Sam H. Franklin Jr., "Early Years of the Delta Cooperative Farm and the Providence Cooperative Farm" (unpublished), 91; David Beard, "Museum Holds Stuff of Everyday Stuff Once Used by Mississippi Blacks," *Los Angeles Times*, March 8, 1987; Crystal R. Sanders, *A Chance for Change: Head Start and Mississippi's Black Freedom Struggle* (Chapel Hill: University of North Carolina Press, 2015), 78–89.

8. Sue Sojourner with Cheryl Reitan, *Thunder of Freedom: Black Leadership and the Transformation of 1960s Mississippi* (Lexington: University Press of Kentucky, 2013), 202, 235, 265, 266, quoted on 265.

9. "*Confidential*," Delta & Providence Farms, House Box #2, AEC; Tom Scarbrough, "A. E. Cox, 933 Chambliss Road, Whitehaven, Tennessee," July 8, 1960, SCR ID# 2-54-1-39-5-1-1, Sovereignty Commission Online, MDAH, http://mdah.state.ms.us/arrec/digital_archives/sovcom/index.php; "Reward Is Offered in Tchula School Fire," January 8, 1970; "Tension Smolders over School Fire," January 5, 1970.

10. Sam Franklin to Mildred and Wilmer Young, undated, House Box #2, AEC.

11. H. L. Mitchell to Gene Cox, February 14, 1971, House Box #1, AEC.

12. William Amberson to H. L. Mitchell, December 24, 1970, House Box #1, AEC; H. L. Mitchell to Gene Cox, undated, House Box #1, AEC; H. L. Mitchell to Gene Cox, December 31, 1970, House Box #1, AEC; William Amberson to Gene Cox, January 26, 1973, House Box #1, AEC.

13. Will D. Campbell to Sue Minter, February 15, 1991, House Box #2, AEC.

14. Sam Franklin to Lindsey Cox, December 29, 1992, House Box #9, AEC; Michael Kelley, "Mourners Say Farewell to Cox, Fierce Fighter for Racial Harmony," *Commercial Appeal*, December 23, 1992; quoted in Yasuhiro Katagiri, *Black Freedom, White Resistance, and Red Menace: Civil Rights and Anticommunism in the Jim Crow South* (Baton Rouge: Louisiana State University Press, 2014), 256.

15. Mac O'Neal, "Fannye Thomas Booker," *Find a Grave*, March 29, 2013, https://www.findagrave.com/cgi-bin/fg.cgi?page=gr&GRid=107522318, accessed January 9, 2017.

16. Sherwood Eddy, *Eighty Adventurous Years: An Autobiography* (New York: Harper, 1955), 157–158; Jonathan Mitchell, "Cabins in the Cotton," *New Republic*, September 22, 1937, 175–178.

17. "Fellowship of Reconciliation" Brochure, October 1936, Folder 12, Delta and Providence Cooperative Farms Papers, #3474, Southern Historical Collection, Louis Round Wilson Special Collections Library, University of North Carolina at Chapel Hill.

18. Tracy Elaine K'Meyer, *Interracialism and Christian Community in the Postwar South: The Story of Koinonia Farm* (Charlottesville: University of Virginia Press, 1997); John Curl, *For All the People: Uncovering the Hidden History of Cooperation, Cooperative Movements, and Communalism in America* (Oakland: PM Press, 2011), 344.

19. Victor Witter Turner, *Dramas, Fields, and Metaphors: Symbolic Action in Human Society* (Ithaca, N.Y.: Cornel University Press, 1974), 232.

20. Ibid.

21. Mrs. Karl M. (Esther Lou) Moody to Lindsey and Gene Cox, April 7, 1966, House Box #1, AEC.

INDEX

Agricultural Adjustment Act, 17, 30, 73
Agricultural Adjustment Administration, 2,
     16–18, 21, 23–26, 32, 47
alfalfa, 59, 61
Alpha Kappa Alpha Sorority, Inc., 119–120, 125,
     133; Dorothy Ferebee and, 89, 90; health
     clinics, 89–91, 114–116, 118, 166, 172; Ida L.
     Jackson and, 115, 119–120, 123, 125
Amberson, William Ruthrauff, 18–20, 29, 85;
     criticism of New Deal, 64; origins of Delta
     Cooperative Farm and, 2, 3, 20–26, 32–35,
     41–43, 45–47; threats of violence and, 28–29,
     40, 76; trustee of Delta Cooperative Farm,
     48, 80–81, 101–103, 111. *See also* Amberson
     Commission
Amberson Commission, 17–18, 21, 47, 170
American Dilemma, An (Myrdal), 86
American Friends Service Committee (AFSC),
     57
American Socialist Party. *See* Socialist Party of
     America
Anderson, Marian, 86, 88
anticommunism, 14, 61, 66, 111, 139–140, 151,
     156; Joseph McCarthy and, 138–139; Senate
     Internal Security Subcommittee (SISS) and,
     139
Arkansas: Dyess Colony, 31, 81; founding of
     Delta Cooperative Farm and, 44, 46, 49–51,
     54, 59, 74, 104, 144, 169; labor activism and,
     27; sharecropping and, 9, 17, 19, 21, 23–24,
     25–26, 33, 35, 39–41; socialism and, 18, 23,
     27–30; use of Japanese American internees
     for labor, 124; white supremacy and, 40,
     52–54
Arkansas Delta, 23, 39, 144
Associated Negro Press (ANP), 74, 77
Ayers, Edward, 7

Badger, Anthony, 7
Baker, Ben, 83
Bankhead-Jones Act, 42
Barrett, Pat, 116, 145, 148, 152–157, 159–160

Barton, Harvey, 54
Berrey, Stephen, 7, 178n13
Bilbo, Theodore G., 133
Billington, Annie Belle, 91
Billington, Jim, 71, 110, 116, 117, 163
Billington, Viola, 116, 163, 166–167
Binns, Dorothy. *See* Treadway, Dorothy Binns
black self-help, 10; Delta Farm and, 87;
     development of, 109–110; education and,
     129–130, 143; since 1956, 15, 174; shift from
     interracial cooperation to, 14, 113, 135–136
Bogue, Jeffery "T. J.," 156, 158, 166
Bolivar County, Miss.: agriculture and, 64;
     education and, 84; health care in, 89; race
     relations and, 77, 93, 99, 111; site of Delta
     Cooperative Farm, 41, 46, 65
Booker, Eva, 166
Booker, Fannye Thomas: death of, 171;
     interracial sex, accusations of, 157;
     leadership of, 15, 129–131, 134, 141, 143,
     151, 163, 164, 165; politics and, 168–169;
     Providence Cooperative Federal Credit
     Union and, 132, 162; Providence Cooperative
     store and, 127, 143, 162, 169
Booker, William Shank, 129, 162
Booker-Thomas Museum, 168
Borsodi, Ralph, 30–31
Brady, Tom, 140
British Rochdale Equitable Pioneers Society. *See*
     Rochdale Equitable Pioneers Society
Brown v. Board of Education of Topeka, 14, 138,
     147, 148, 150, 152–154
Brundage, W. Fitzhugh, 10
Bryant, Roy, 144, 152
Byrd, Richard, 145–153, 155, 157

Calloway, Marsh, 153, 155–156
Campbell, Will, 160, 168, 171
Camp Springs, 143
Carlton, Isaiah, 148–149
Carter, Hodding, 159
Cessna, Ralph, 126

Checkver, Sam, 120–121
Christian missionaries, 1, 13, 22, 52, 72–73, 78, 94. *See also* Eddy, George Sherwood; Franklin, Sam H.
Christian Realism. *See* Christian Socialism
Christian Socialism, 2, 5, 6, 9, 13, 21–22, 38–39, 46, 172–173
Church of the Brethren, 134
Citizens' Council: founding of, 15, 140, 147–148; Providence Farm and threats from, 10, 137, 145, 148, 153–155, 158, 161, 162, 164, 167
civil rights activism, 5–6, 40–41, 72–73, 129, 165–174. *See also* black self-help
civil rights movement: backlash to, 14, 138, 140, 148; ideology and, 9; origins of, 111, 179n23; Providence Farm and, 129, 164; significance of Mississippi for, 3
Clark, Robert G., 168–169
Clarksdale, Miss., 45–46, 56, 92
Cleveland, Miss., 45, 166
"closed society," 5
Coahoma County, Miss., 93, 108
Cold War, 139. *See also* anticommunism
Coleman, James P., 159–160
Collapse of Cotton Tenancy, The (Johnson), 17
Commission on Interracial Cooperation (CIC), 8, 29, 60, 72
communism, 66. *See also* anticommunism
cooperative communalism: back-to-the-land movement and, 30–31; decline of, 174; definition of, 177n2; international and national movements for, 2, 5, 6, 48, 57, 141, 173; socialism and, 9, 14, 28, 45. *See also* Delta Cooperative Farm; Providence Farm
Cooperative Foundation, Inc., 63
cotton: Delta Cooperative Farm and, 61, 62–63, 65, 79–80, 82, 92, 97, 98, 107, 111, 141, 142–143; farming and production of, 11, 14, 16, 23, 39, 40, 42, 48, 59, 64, 96. *See also* plantation labor system
Cox, Allen Eugene "Gene," 86–87, 90, 96; activism after Providence, 164–166, 172; attempted expulsion of, 137–138, 145–146, 148–149, 151–161, 166, 169; death of, 171; departure of, from Delta Cooperative Farm to Providence, 104, 116; departure of, from Providence, 163–164; family life of, 141; interracial sex, accusations of, 157; leadership of, at Delta, 97, 101; leadership of, at Providence, 105, 123–124, 126–127, 128, 134, 135; marriage to Lindsey Hail, 88; Mississippi Sovereignty Commission and,

167–168, 169; personal papers of, 169–170; Providence Cooperative Federal Credit Union and, 131–132, 142, 162
Cox, Lindsey Hail: activism after Providence, 166–167; departure of, from Delta Cooperative Farm to Providence, 104, 116; departure of, from Providence, 163–164; family life of, 141, 160; First Presbyterian Church of Tchula and, 150–151; intimidation of, 156–159, 161; leadership of, 122, 135; role of, as nurse, 66, 88–90, 114, 118–119, 133, 141, 142, 166–167
Coxey, Jacob S., 86
Credit Union National Association (CUNA), 132, 142, 162
Crespino, Joseph, 3
Crittendon County, Ark., 51, 52–53
Cummings, Homer S., 40, 53
Curl, John, 6

Daniels, Jonathan, 47, 70–72, 78, 79–80
Day, Albert, 97, 99–100, 102
Delta Cooperative Farm: Board of Trustees of, 48, 59, 63, 82, 94, 98–99; children and, 21, 57, 67, 78, 81, 84–85; church services at, 4, 10, 69, 72–73; Cooperative Foundation, Inc., 63; cooperative store, 4, 34, 47, 58, 62; crops, 59, 61, 62; dairy, 4; decline and closing of, 10, 11, 14, 83–84, 91–92, 103–104; education, 61, 84–85; farming, 4, 10–11, 31, 59, 60, 78, 79–80, 105; fundraising and, 55, 63–65, 84–85; governance of, 58–59, 71–72, 82–83, 92, 94, 95–96, 99–103; housing, 59–60, 71, 82; interracial cooperation and, 4, 6, 8, 9, 20, 21, 67–71, 74–75, 85–86, 108; medical, 4, 57, 61, 87–91; naming of, 60–61; natural disasters and, 81–82; newsletter, 85; origins of, 12–13, 21–22, 34–35, 39–41, 43, 44–52, 61–62; post office, 61, 87; producers' cooperative, 62–63; Rochdale cooperative model and, 34, 39, 41, 60, 61, 62, 65, 87, 99, 117; saw mill, 59, 64; social life, 56, 58, 60, 61, 78, 87; Southern Tenant Farmers' Union and, 39, 49, 56, 66–67, 94, 99–100, 103–104; summer camp, 85, 111; Sunday school, 61, 69, 85; threats of violence against, 75–76, 77; volunteers at, 55–57, 78, 86
Delta FARM, 171–172
Delta Foundation, Inc., 134–135, 142, 163, 171
Delta Pine and Land Company, 25–26, 79, 151
Dibble, C. H., 50–51
Dibble Plantation, 50–51, 66

Dickard, Willie Ramon, 146
Dixiecrats, 133; James O. Eastland, 108, 133,
    139–140. *See also* massive resistance
Dombrowski, James, 36
Door of Opportunity (G. S. Eddy), 74–75

Earle, Ark., 49, 50, 53, 54
East, Alex, 28–29
East, Clay, 18, 23–28
Eastland, James O., 108, 133, 139–140
Eddy, George Sherwood, 22; anticommunism
    of, 66, 75; *Door of Opportunity*, 74–75;
    fundraising of, 55, 63–65, 80, 85, 90, 103,
    104; investigation of Paul D. Peacher and,
    52–53; leadership of, 80–81, 94–96, 99; New
    Deal and, 73; paternalism and, 67–68, 72;
    philanthropy and, 33, 34, 35, 36, 37, 38, 39;
    purchase of land for Delta Cooperative
    Farm, 41, 45, 46; shift toward socialism,
    37–38. *See also* Christian Socialism
Eddy, Louise Gates, 135, 160–161, 163
Elaine (Ark.) Massacre, 40
Ellenberg, George B., 11
Erwin, Barbara Jean, 124
Erwin, Hubert, 51
Erwin, Jess, 51, 128
Evers, Medgar, 161

farming, mechanization of, 2, 11, 13–14, 65, 98,
    107, 110
Farm Security Administration, 27, 42, 113, 128
Fellowship of Reconciliation, 38, 48, 174
Fellowship of Southern Churchmen, 106
Ferebee, Dorothy, 89, 90
First Presbyterian Church of Tchula, 150
Fleming, Bennie, 50–51, 64, 66, 69
Foose, Samuel J. "Bobo," 155
Franklin, Dorothy: arrival of, at Delta, 46;
    attitude toward African Americans, 82,
    87; evacuation of, 81; fundraising of, 80;
    leadership of, 121–122; missionary work of,
    32–33, 88; move of, to Providence, 97; visit
    of, to Providence, 159
Franklin, Sam H.: accusations against, 95–96,
    99–100, 170; association of, with Pat Barrett,
    148, 159; Cooperative Association and, 112,
    113–114; creamery and, 116–117; departure
    of, from Providence, 123–125, 132; education
    and, 84; leadership at Providence Farm,
    118–121, 135, missionary work of, 32–33, 34,
    35, 41, 88; paternalism and, 71–72, 82–83, 94;
    purchase of land for Providence Farm, 96;

recruitment for Delta, 44–45, 49–50; role
    of, as Delta's resident director, 46–48, 55–56,
    58–59, 75, 92, 100–101; role of, as Delta
    trustee, 63, 80–81; role of, as reverend, 57;
    threats of violence and, 51, 76; World War II
    and, 121–123
Freeman, Curtis, 144–147, 151, 152, 157, 165

Gamble, Clarence J., 88–89
Georgia, 27, 54, 55, 119, 142, 174
Granderson, Hattie, 127
Granderson, Robert, 112–113, 127, 162
Great Migration, 11, 107
Greene, Alison, 9
Griffin, D. A., 100–101

Halberstam, David, 159
Hamer, Fannie Lou, 169
Hamlin, Francoise N., 9
Handcox, John L., 54
Hayes, Lee, 76
Head Start programs, 15, 168
Henderson, Jim (father), 51, 57, 64, 71, 83, 116,
    128, 144
Henderson, Jim (son), 57, 116, 144, 165
Henderson, Mary Ellen, 144–145, 163
Henderson, Shirley Moody, 144, 163, 166
Hillhouse, Miss., 46, 52, 62, 171
Holmes County, Miss.: agriculture and, 111,
    142–143; civil rights activism during 1960s
    in, 164, 168–169; education and, 112, 129–130;
    health care and, 89, 112, 114–116, 118, 125;
    Mileston, 30, 128; site of Providence Farm,
    14, 83, 96–97, 104; white supremacy and, 15,
    107, 111, 137–140, 143–148, 151–164, 166–167;
    World War II and, 117
Hooker, Wilburn, 167
Hull, Cordell, 63–64
Hulsey, Nute, 44, 45, 163
Hunter, Missouri, 148–149
Hynds, J. F., 100–101

Illinois, 54
Indiana, 27, 55, 90, 113, 118, 163
International Harvester Company, 48, 98
Irwin, Warren H., 55

Jackson, Ida L., 115, 119–120, 123, 125
Jackson, Miss., 106, 121, 131, 141, 148, 150
Jamaica, 57
Japanese Americans, 124
Jefferson, Thomas, 2, 31, 33

Jim Crow: anticommunism and, 140, 151; churches and, 150; Commission on Interracial Cooperation (CIC) and, 8; different types of, 93, 119; miscegenation, accusations of, 75, 157; Mississippi Sovereignty Commission and, 157, 167–171; white supremacy and, 75, 107, 138–139, 145, 152–155, 157, 160, 161, 178n13. See also *Brown v. Board of Education of Topeka*; Citizens' Council; Eastland, James O.; Ku Klux Klan; massive resistance

John Rust Foundation, Inc., 142

Johnson, Charles Spurgeon: *The Collapse of Cotton Tenancy*, 17; Fisk University and, 17, 70, 98; leadership of, 2, 86, 98–99, 111, 126, 135; *Shadow of the Plantation*, 17; views on race, 67, 92, 108–109

Johnston, Oscar, 25, 26, 79, 151

Jones, Buck, 25–26

Jones, Tom, 91

Julius Rosenwald Foundation, 84

Kagawa, Toyohiko, 13, 35, 39

Kate B. Reynolds Hospital, 119

Kester, Howard, 86, 95, 100, 101, 106, 113, 159, 170; involvement with Delta Cooperative Farm, 22, 46, 47, 76, 101; Southern Tenant Farmers' Union and, 27, 39, 66, 69, 95, 100

Kimberlin, Koss, 110

Koinonia Farm, 174

Ku Klux Klan, 10, 164, 167, 173. See also Citizens' Council

labor unions: Christianity and, 9, 36–37; interracialism and, 28–29, 32, 43, 45, 49–50, 130, 173, 178n12; Toyohiko Kagawa and, 13, 35, 39; E. B. "Britt" McKinney and, 20–21, 27, 43; popularity of, 29; strikes, 32, 50, 54, 92, 108. See also Amberson, William Ruthrauff; anticommunism; Cox, Allen Eugene "Gene"; Eddy, George Sherwood; Fleming, Bennie; Franklin, Sam H.; Kester, Howard; League for Industrial Democracy; Mitchell, Harry Leland "H. L."; Southern Tenant Farmers' Union; Treadway, Blaine

Landes, Art, 58, 103–104

Landes, Margaret Lamont, 58, 104

Lange, Dorothea, 29, 86

law enforcement: Richard Byrd and, 145–153, 155, 157; corruption and, 147; hostility toward labor activism of, 27, 32, 51; Paul D.

Peacher and, 52–53; racial intimidation by, 23, 140, 146, 158, 160

League for Industrial Democracy (LID), 17, 18, 24–25

Lewis, Earl, 10

Liberation Theology, 6, 9, 39

Little, Lilly, 127

Litwack, Leon, 7

Lookout Mountain, Tenn., 41–43

Love, J. P., 153–157, 168–169

Luccock, Emory, 111, 135

Mason, Birvin, 57

Mason, Margaret McKee, 57

massive resistance, 3, 14, 138, 174, 175; J. P. Love and, 153–157, 168–169. See also Barrett, Pat; White, Edwin

Matanuska Colony, 31

McCarthy, Joseph, 138–139

McCarthyism, 139. See also anticommunism; Senate Internal Security Subcommittee (SISS)

McDonald, A. James, 95–96, 101, 103, 159

McKinney, E. B. "Britt," 20–21, 27, 43

Memphis, Tenn.: chapter of League for Industrial Democracy of, 18; Delta evacuees and, 81; geography of, 3, 45; Socialist Party of, 22, 94; Socialist Party of Tennessee and, 47, 95; Southern Tenant Farmers' Union in, 33; University of Tennessee Medical School in, 22; white supremacy and, 77. See also Amberson, William Ruthrauff; Treadway, Blaine

Memphis Socialist Party, 22

Merrill, Charles, 117–118

Merrill-Lynch & Co., 117

Milam, J. W., 144, 152

Mileston, 30, 128

Minter, David: activism after Providence, 164–166; attempted expulsion of, 137–138, 145–146, 148–150, 151–161, 166, 169; death of, 171; family life of, 141; final departure of, from Providence, 164; first departure of, from Providence, 118–120, 125; First Presbyterian Church of Tchula and, 150–151; investigations of, 15, 90; leadership of, 134–135; return of, to Providence, 133; role of, as community physician, 15, 90–91, 114, 115, 116, 161–163

Minter, Sue Wootten: family life of, 141; final departure of, from Providence, 164; first

departure of, from Providence, 118; First Presbyterian Church of Tchula and, 150–151; move of, to Providence, 116; return of, to Providence, 133; volunteering of, at Delta, 90
Mississippi Credit Union League, 132
Mississippi Delta, geography of, 3, 10–11, 45, 97
Mississippi Department of Archives and History (MDAH), 171
Mississippi Freedom Democratic Party (MFDP), 168–169
Mississippi Health Project. See Alpha Kappa Alpha Sorority, Inc.
Mississippi River, 23, 41, 45–46, 60, 81, 104
Mississippi Sovereignty Commission, 157, 167–171
Missouri, 17, 48, 54, 81
Mitchell, Harry Leland "H. L.," 23, 170; defense of Providence Farm by, 158; Dibble Plantation and, 50; organization of Southern Tenant Farmers' Union by, 18, 26–27; origins of Delta Cooperative Farm and, 22, 45; Rochdale model and, 34; STFU chapter at Delta Cooperative Farm and, 66, 99–100. See also Southern Tenant Farmers' Union
Moody, Esther Lou, 175
Moody, James H., 51, 57, 103, 144
Moody (Henderson), Shirley, 144, 163, 166
Morgan, Otto, Jr., 116, 124
Morgan, Otto C., 59, 61, 116
Mound Bayou, Miss., 57, 85, 89, 109, 114
Myrdal, Gunnar S., 86

Nashoba, 177–178n10
Nashville Agrarians, 30, 42, 47
National Association for the Advancement of Colored People (NAACP), 27, 69, 74, 139, 161, 169
National Industrial Recovery Act (NIRA), 7
National Sharecroppers Fund, 161
New Deal, 1, 7, 29, 107, 174; cooperative farms and, 2, 21, 23–24, 31, 34, 49, 86–87, 178n12; Dorothea Lange and, 29, 86; limitations of, 12–13, 16, 18, 32, 40, 64, 73–74, 93; National Industrial Recovery Act (NIRA), 7; socialism and, 28, 30; Henry A. Wallace and, 24, 26, 40; Lawrence Westbrook and, 85–86; Works Progress Administration (WPA), 63, 79, 86. See also Daniels, Jonathan; Eddy, George Sherwood; Resettlement Administration
New Harmony, Ind., 27

New Llano Cooperative Colony, 28, 96
Niebuhr, Reinhold: leadership of, 2, 13, 22, 48, 81, 92, 94, 101, 111, 135; missionary work of, 32–33, 36; Union Theological Seminary and, 37. See also Christian Socialism
Noel, Eddie, 146–147, 152, 154
Noel, Lu Ethel, 146
Nolden, Eliza, 54
Norcross, Hiram, 26
Norcross Plantation, 28–29

Odum, Howard W., 107–108; Race and Rumors of Race, 107
Oliver, Clarence, 83
Owen, Robert, 27, 61

Parkin, Ark., 50
paternalism, race relations and, 10, 13, 29, 67–68, 72–73, 82–83, 90, 92, 94, 101, 109, 173
Patterson, Frederick Douglass "F. D.," 111, 135
Patterson, Robert B., 140, 147–148
Peacher, Paul D., 52–53
peonage, 32, 52–53
Percy, William Alexander, 48, 49, 63
Phillip, Lee, 91
Phillips County, Ark., 23, 40
Pickens, William, 74, 77
plantation labor system: critiques of, 17, 22; Delta Pine and Land Company, 25–26, 79, 151; Dibble Plantation, 50–51, 66; economics of, 3, 4–5, 11–12, 18, 21, 42, 67, 108; eviction of tenants and sharecroppers, 2, 17, 21, 24; The Plight of the Sharecropper (N. Thomas), 16, 17, 26; similarities between Delta Cooperative Farm and, 61–62, 93; violence and, 51–54, 64; white supremacy and, 11, 40. See also farming, mechanization of; poverty; sharecropping
Plight of the Sharecropper, The (N. Thomas), 16, 17, 26
Poe, Clarence, 33
Pope, Liston, 36
Popular Front, 94–95
Populist movement, 6, 27, 33
Post, Marion, 86
poverty: Great Depression and, 29–30, 132; race and, 21, 114; sharecropping and, 4, 18–20, 21, 24, 26, 33, 40–41
Powdermaker, Hortense, 92–93
practical Christianity. See Christian Socialism
Preface to Peasantry (Raper), 17

Procter & Gamble, 88

Providence Farm: Board of Trustees, 99, 111, 134, 135; children and, 157–158, 158, 160, 163, 165; Cooperative Farms, Inc., 116–117, 128–129, 133, 134–135; creamery, 97, 110, 116–117; crops, 97, 141; dairy, 96, 97, 116–117, 121, 126; decline and closing of, 140–142, 162–164, 165, 175; differences from Delta, 140–141; drilling and, 128; education, 110, 113, 130–131, 141; Extension Farm, 126, 129; farming, 4, 97–98, 143; fundraising and, 109, 125, 126, 142; governance of, 123–124, 125, 129, 134, 135–136; health clinics and, 111, 114–116, 125, 133, 141, 163; mission of, 112; natural disasters and, 142; origins of, 83, 96–98, 103–104, 111; Providence Cooperative Association, 112, 126, 128, 129, 131, 132; Providence Cooperative Federal Credit Union, 1, 131–132, 142, 162–163; Providence Cooperative store, 97, 120–121, 126–127, 143, 158, 162; sawmill, 99; shift away from interracial cooperation of, 110, 135; Southern Tenant Farmers' Union and, 120; summer camps, 111, 131, 143; volunteers, 116, 117, 121; white supremacy and, 143–161; World War II and, 14, 111, 117–118, 120–123, 135

Quakers, 57, 58, 66, 90, 92, 122

Race and Rumors of Race (Odum), 107

Randle, Henry, 148–149

Raper, Arthur, 104; leadership of, 60, 86, 98–99, 100–101, 111, 124, 135; paternalism and, 72–73; *Preface to Peasantry*, 17; *Sharecroppers All*, 17

Reconstruction: agriculture and, 10, 18; black self-help and, 109; politics and, 6, 139, 169; Social Christianity and, 36

Red Cross, 81

Red Scare. *See* anticommunism

Reese, Jim, 53–54

Reese, Virgil, 52, 85

Resettlement Administration, 34; Dixie Plantation, 30, 64; Dyess Colony, 31, 81; limitations of, 32, 49, 50; Matanuska Colony, 31; Eleanor Roosevelt and, 73. *See also* New Deal

Rochdale Equitable Pioneers Society, 6; influence of, on Delta Cooperative Farm, 34, 39, 41, 60, 61, 62, 65, 87, 99, 117; influence of, on Providence Farm, 126

Roosevelt, Eleanor, 48, 63, 86

Roosevelt, Franklin, 23–24, 29, 70, 124. *See also* New Deal

Rumbough, Constance, 58, 70, 85

rural poor, 18, 23, 81, 173; activism of, 5, 9, 15, 21, 72; New Deal and, 2, 32; race relations and, 73, 109, 118

Ruskin Cooperative Colony, 27

Rust, John, 65, 98; John Rust Foundation, 142; Rust Brothers' Factory, 81, 96; trustee of Delta, 48, 100, 101, 111, 135

Rust, Mack, 39, 48, 65, 81, 96, 98

Rust Cotton Picker, 39, 48, 65, 96, 98

Saints Industrial School, 89, 113

Scarbrough, Tom, 167, 169

Scarlett, William, 48, 76, 91

Schultz, Mark, 5, 7

Scottsboro Boys, 75–76

segregation. *See* Jim Crow

Senate Internal Security Subcommittee (SISS), 139

Shadow of the Plantation (Johnson), 17

Sharecroppers All (Raper), 17

sharecropping: credit system, 4; mechanization of farming and, 11; poverty and, 4, 18–20, 21, 24, 26, 33, 40–41; predominance in South, 3, 14, 17; replacement for slavery, 3, 45; violence and, 19, 23, 53–54. *See also* plantation labor system

Silver, James W., 5

Smith, Evelyn, 56, 66

Smith, George, 58, 66, 69–70, 86, 92

Smith, Hazel Brannon, 138, 147, 149–150, 152, 155, 159–160

Smith, Leola, 58

Smith, Mary Alice, 58

Smith v. Allwright, 133

Social Gospel, 8, 16, 37–39, 41, 47–48, 174

Socialist Party of America: William Ruthrauff Amberson and, 21, 22; decline of, 94–95; efforts of, in South, 26, 27–28, 48, 69; Buck Jones and, 25; Reinhold Niebuhr and, 38. *See also* Thomas, Norman

Socialist Party of Tennessee, 47, 95

Southern Tenant Farmers' Union (STFU), 26–27, 30; William Ruthrauff Amberson and, 21, 39, 95; Delta Cooperative Farm and, 41, 43–45, 49, 51–52, 56, 66–67, 76, 94, 99–100, 103–104; Dibble Plantation and, 50–51; formation of, 7; Sam H. Franklin

and, 44–45; Jim Henderson (father) and, 144; integration and, 28–29; Howard Kester and, 27, 39, 69; E. B. McKinney and, 27; H. L. Mitchell and, 26, 33, 74, 97, 170; New Deal and, 32; Paul D. Peacher and, 53; Providence Farm and, 120; Evelyn Smith and, 56; George Smith and, 49, 86, 69–70, 86; support for cooperative methods of, 34, 42, 48; Blaine Treadway and, 47, 104; Owen Whitfield and, 27. *See also* violence
Soviet Union: international cooperatives and, 28; Red Scare and, 139
States' Rights Democratic Party (Dixiecrats), 133
Strong, Ernest, 83

Tate, Allen, 42–43
Tchula, Miss. *See* Holmes County, Miss.
Tennessee: Cox family's move to, 163–164, 166; Cordell Hull and, 63; League for Industrial Democracy and, 18; Lookout Mountain, 41–43; Nashoba, 177–178n10; Ruskin Cooperative Colony, 27; sharecropping in, 17, 54; Socialist Party of, 47, 95; University of Tennessee Medical School, 22. *See also* Amberson, William Ruthrauff; Eddy, George Sherwood; Franklin, Sam H.; Memphis, Tenn.
Terlin, Rose, 55, 56
Thomas, Norman: Delta Cooperative Farm and, 48; *The Plight of the Sharecropper*, 16, 17, 26; socialism of, 22–23, 38, 51, 86, 144; views on sharecropping, 16–18, 24
Thomas, Prentice, 27
Thunderberg, Mrs. Jim, 54–55
Till, Emmett, 138, 144, 145, 152, 156
Tougaloo College, 113, 163
Treadway, Blaine, 18, 20, 76; departure from Delta, 104, 114; leadership of, 47–48, 59, 62, 63, 91, 97, 99, 101; marriage to Dorothy Binns, 57; Southern Tenant Farmers' Union and, 47, 104
Treadway, Dorothy Binns: departure from Delta, 104, 114; leadership of, 114; marriage to Blaine Treadway, 57; role of, as nurse, 114
Truman, Ark., 54
Tule Lake Relocation Center, 124

Union Theological Seminary, 32, 36, 37, 38, 63
University of North Carolina, 17, 42
University of Tennessee Medical School, 22
U.S. Department of Agriculture, 17, 24, 25, 32
U.S. Fidelity and Guaranty Company, 162

Vance, Rupert B., 17
Vicksburg, Miss., 3, 45
violence: labor activism and, 29, 51, 53–54; Providence Farm and, 140, 156–160, 165; racial, 40, 138, 140, 174; sharecropping and, 19, 20, 23, 30, 51–54

Wallace, Henry A., 24, 26, 40
Warbasse, J. P., 102–103
Weems, Frank, 53–54
Weems, Vera, 53–54
Westbrook, Lawrence, 85–86
White, Edwin, 153–154, 155, 157, 160
White, Wilburn, 49, 51, 91, 98, 120
Whitfield, Owen, 27
Whitney, Monroe, 49, 50, 163
Wigfall, Clarence M., 119–120, 125
Wilkinson family, 64
Williams, Claude C., 54, 170
Williams, Eugene, 83
Wilson, Clarence, 83
Wilson, Warren, 63
Woofter, T. J., 19, 61–62
Wootten, Sue. *See* Minter, Sue Wootten
Works Progress Administration (WPA), 63, 79, 86
World War II: effects on race relations, 98, 107, 108–109, 110; Providence Farm and, 111, 117–118, 120–123, 135
Wright, Fielding, 133
Wright, Gavin, 19
Wright, Mose, 144

Yazoo River, 45, 97
Young, Mildred, 57, 92, 105
Young, Wilmer, 57, 66, 97
Young Men's Christian Association (YMCA), 2, 36, 37, 55, 109–110
Young Women's Christian Association (YWCA), 8; Rose Terlin, 55, 56

POLITICS AND CULTURE IN THE TWENTIETH-CENTURY SOUTH

A Common Thread: Labor, Politics, and Capital Mobility in the Textile Industry
BY BETH ENGLISH

"Everybody Was Black Down There": Race and Industrial Change in the Alabama Coalfields
BY ROBERT H. WOODRUM

Race, Reason, and Massive Resistance: The Diary of David J. Mays, 1954–1959
EDITED BY JAMES R. SWEENEY

The Unemployed People's Movement: Leftists, Liberals, and Labor in Georgia, 1929–1941
BY JAMES J. LORENCE

Liberalism, Black Power, and the Making of American Politics, 1965–1980
BY DEVIN FERGUS

Guten Tag, Y'all: Globalization and the South Carolina Piedmont, 1950–2000
BY MARKO MAUNULA

The Culture of Property: Race, Class, and Housing Landscapes in Atlanta, 1880–1950
BY LEEANN LANDS

Marching in Step: Masculinity, Citizenship, and The Citadel in Post–World War II America
BY ALEXANDER MACAULAY

Rabble Rousers: The American Far Right in the Civil Rights Era
BY CLIVE WEBB

Who Gets a Childhood: Race and Juvenile Justice in Twentieth-Century Texas
BY WILLIAM S. BUSH

Alabama Getaway: The Political Imaginary and the Heart of Dixie
BY ALLEN TULLOS

The Problem South: Region, Empire, and the New Liberal State, 1880–1930
BY NATALIE J. RING

The Nashville Way: Racial Etiquette and the Struggle for Social Justice in a Southern City
BY BENJAMIN HOUSTON

Cold War Dixie: Militarization and Modernization in the American South
BY KARI FREDERICKSON

Faith in Bikinis: Politics and Leisure in the Coastal South since the Civil War
BY ANTHONY J. STANONIS

*"We Who Believe in Freedom": Womanpower Unlimited
and the Black Freedom Struggle in Mississippi*
BY TIYI M. MORRIS

New Negro Politics in the Jim Crow South
BY CLAUDRENA N. HAROLD

Jim Crow Terminals: The Desegregation of American Airports
BY ANKE ORTLEPP

*Remaking the Rural South: Interracialism, Christian Socialism,
and Cooperative Farming in Jim Crow Mississippi*
BY ROBERT HUNT FERGUSON

CPSIA information can be obtained
at www.ICGtesting.com
Printed in the USA
LVOW08*1934020118

561536LV00007B/191/P